Language

in

Exile

Caribbean Archaeology and Ethnohistory

L. Antonio Curet, Series Editor

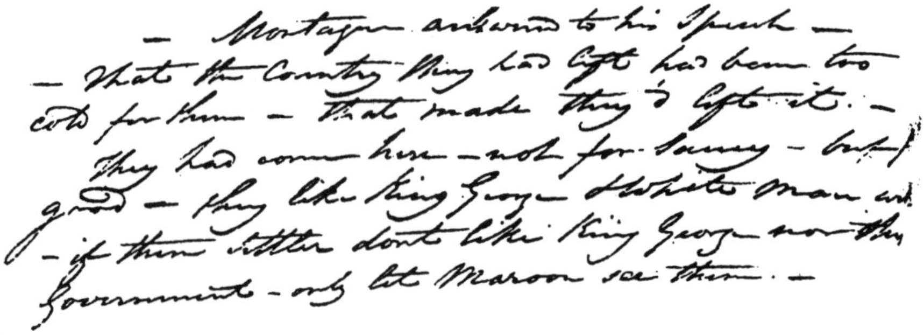

Plate 1. Extract from the diary of George Ross for October 1, 1800 (manuscript in Fourah Bay College Library, Freetown, Sierra Leone). The Maroon leader, Montagu, puts their case to the governor: "Montagu answered to his speech—That the country they had left had been too cold for them.—That made they'd left it.—

"They had come here not for sorry—but for good—they like King George & White man w[ays]—if them Settler dont like King George nor this Government—only let Maroon see them."

Language *in* Exile

Three Hundred Years of Jamaican Creole

Barbara Lalla
and
Jean D'Costa

The University of Alabama Press

Tuscaloosa

∞

The paper on which this book is printed meets the minimum requirements of American National Standard for Information Sciences-Permanence of Paper for Printed Library Materials, ANSI Z39.48-1984.

Library of Congress Cataloging-in-Publication Data

Lalla, Barbara, 1949–

Language in exile : three hundred years of Jamaican Creole / Barbara Lalla and Jean D'Costa.

p. cm.

Bibliography: p.

Includes index.

ISBN 0-8173-0447-9 (cloth : alk. paper)

ISBN 978-0-8173-5565-4 (pbk : alk. paper)

1. Creole dialects, English—Jamaica—History. 2. Creole dialects, English—Jamaica—Texts. I. D'Costa, Jean. II. Title. PM7874.J3L35 1990

427'.97292—dc19 88-34012

CIP

To the memory of
David DeCamp

Contents

8. The Eighteenth Century

9. The Early Nineteenth Century

Illustrations

Plates

Charts

Maps

Tables

Preface

Ten years ago, the writers of this book embarked on a search for the beginnings of Jamaican Creole, image of Jamaica's history, ally and enemy of Standard Jamaican English, and, mother tongue of Jamaica's majority, the enforcer of complex language behavior in every Jamaican. Some sources (such as the writings of the Baptist missionary James Mursell Phillippo) presented a detailed picture of Jamaican life and speech. Others that promised much yielded little: the Slave Court Records, which cover the last forty years of Jamaican slavery, contain only the metropolitan English of the court stenographers.

The nineteenth century turned out to be rich in other ways: the records made by magistrates, planters, missionaries, and visitors offered a range of stories, anecdotes, and songs. In contrast, the eighteenth century has left relatively little evidence of the speech of the time, and the earliest and most intriguing period of all, the seventeenth century, granted only enigmatic scraps of discourse and little description. Yet by piecing together historical, demographic, and linguistic data, we have been able to suggest a picture of what Jamaica's speech community must have been like in the formative years of the seventeenth and eighteenth centuries, when the great migrant waves from Africa and the British Isles brought the makers of Jamaican Creole to this island.

The reliability of individual writers and the integrity of their material have been established by studying their careers and performance as recorders of language varieties, by examining their motives and individual language backgrounds, and by noting the influence of literary conventions and even the occasional overlapping of material. (For example, Phillippo 1843: 247–48 reproduces Barclay 1826: 191, and the same incident is related by Rampini 1873.)

The data on which this book is based derive from works written in and about Jamaica from 1500 until the end of the nineteenth century. We have attempted to discuss such evidence against the backdrop of Jamaican social history, relying not only on contemporary writers such as Edward Long but also on the research and demographic interpretations of modern scholars, including Orlando Patterson, Edward Brathwaite, Michael Craton, and Barry Higman. We have set the findings of the historians in the context of current creole studies: Mervyn Alleyne's reconstruction of Afro-American creoles, Derek Bickerton's theories of creolization, and the fundamental work of F. G. Cassidy, David DeCamp, Robert LePage, and Beryl Bailey, who laid the foundations of Jamaican Creole studies. The work of younger scholars, such as Lawrence Carrington, Ian Hancock, Salikoko Mufwene, Pieter Mühlhäusler, Norma Niles, and John Rickford, has been of immense value.

Language in Exile discusses the external and internal language history of Jamaican Creole. Working against the background of Jamaican social history, it considers the nature and consequences of language contact, examines the sound system and related orthographical problems, comments on the difficulties of reconstruction and interpretation implicit in the data, and connects the varieties of the past to the known structure of modern Jamaican Creole.

Part One attempts to establish a historical and demographic context (Chapter 1) against which the data set out in Part Two should be considered. In Chapter 2 we assess the validity of the data and set out the methodological problems of dealing with written records of a language for which no recognized writing system existed. The main features of Jamaican Creole phonology, morphosyntax, and lexicon are set forth in Chapters 3 and 4. The question of how Jamaican Creole is connected to languages and dialects whose speakers took part in the settlement of plantation Jamaica is discussed in Chapters 5 and 6. In Part Two the texts appear in chronological order, subdivided by century and (within the nineteenth century) by the watershed of abolition.

Language in Exile offers the reader a body of evidence and analysis presented solely for its linguistic significance, although much of the data does shed light on other aspects of Jamaica's past. In the companion volume, *Voices in Exile: Jamaican Texts of the 18th and 19th Centuries*, the reader may gain an even wider view of the language and culture of this vanished Jamaica in the collection of songs, tales, sermons, and other material selected for that volume.

Without the assistance of many libraries, this work could not have come into being. The authors thank John Aarons and the staff of the National Library of Jamaica; Alvona Alleyne and the staff of the Library of the University of the West Indies at Mona, Jamaica, and at St. Augustine,

Trinidad; Joan Wolek and the staff of the Burke Library, Hamilton College, New York; the late Reverend Mr. Philip Hart and the staff of the Institute of Jamaica; Beverley Alleyne and the staff of the African-Caribbean Institute, Kingston, Jamaica.

We also acknowledge our gratitude to the following institutions: the British Library, London; the Bodleian Library, Oxford; Rhodes House Library, Oxford; the Library and Museum of the Royal Engineers, Chatham, Kent; the Library of Louisiana State University; the Library of the University of Sierra Leone; the Library of the United Theological College of the West Indies, Mona, Jamaica; the Burke Library of Hamilton College, Clinton, New York, and the Beinecke Collection housed there; and the National Archives of Jamaica and of Bermuda.

The work and encouragement of the folklorist, the late H. P. Jacobs, played an important role in the framing of this collection, as did the advice of Olive Lewin, musicologist and folk historian. Professor Keith Laurence kindly granted us access to the papers of the late Dr. Kemling Laurence. The skill of Mrs. Abena Enyonam Agbley-Odamtten enabled us to unlock the meaning of the cumina chant (Text 24); we are deeply indebted. Vincent Odamtten of the Department of English, Hamilton College, gave invaluable assistance with all of the African-based songs and chants, translating texts and interpreting the context and usage of the pieces. We are indebted to him for his poetic translation of Text 24, the cumina chant. Clinton Black, Jamaican historian and archivist, gave useful directions at the very inception of the enterprise. We are grateful for Professor F. G. Cassidy's encouragement and suggestions.

We are especially indebted to Mervyn Alleyne, Lawrence Carrington, Glenn Gilbert, Ian Robertson, and Don Winford, who read portions of the manuscript and discussed several aspects of the project with us, injecting helpful criticisms and encouragement as we prepared the final drafts. We also thank the historians Robert Paquette, Howard Johnson, and Monica Schuler for verifying historical details and answering anxious queries.

We thank the National Library of Jamaica for permission to reproduce the photograph of a nineteenth-century platter inscribed with a verse of creole poetry, "Me take me road da Canepiece," taken from the song "Quaco Sam." We thank Karoma Press for permission to use the phonological reconstructions of Mervyn Alleyne (1980). We thank Oxford University Press for permission to use Edward Brathwaite's map of Jamaica in 1790 as a base for Map 8 (Brathwaite 1978). We thank Johns Hopkins University Press for permission to use Monica Schuler's map of African indentured settlement (Schuler 1980). We thank Mrs. Ruth Moore for permission to use the cumina chant from the dissertation of her husband, the late Joseph Graessle Moore. We also thank the Australian National University for permission to reproduce Pieter Mühlhäusler's chart of language-acquisition processes.

Lastly, we express our gratitude to our institutions: without the support of research money, research assistance, and steady interest from colleagues at all levels, we would have found the task all but impossible.

Abbreviations

BE	Barbadian English
DJE	*Dictionary of Jamaican English*
EDD	*English Dialect Dictionary*
EModE	Early Modern English
GCCE	Guinea Coast Creole English
JC	Jamaican Creole
ME	Middle English
OE	Old English
OED	*Oxford English Dictionary*
RP	Received Pronunciation
SE	Standard English

Language
in
Exile

Part One
Early Jamaican Creole

Introduction

The questions most fascinating to creolists are those that ask exactly how and when such languages as Jamaican Creole or Cameroon Pidgin or Gullah came into existence. All too often, the questions must be asked in the absence of historical data adequate to determine either the precise timing of the process of creolization or the way in which the speakers of contributing languages shaped the unique language forms now classified as creoles.

The study of Jamaican Creole has benefited from pioneering research that laid the foundations not only for JC studies but for work in other Caribbean creoles (LePage and DeCamp 1960; Cassidy 1961; Cassidy and LePage 1980; and Bailey 1966). Creole linguistics today reaches into many branches of language theory and research, and significant recent studies have opened up new possibilities for answering how and when the new language was born. The work of Bickerton (1975, 1981) on the genesis and structure of creoles, of Rickford (1987) on nineteenth-century Guyanese Creole, of Niles (1980) on the connections between Barbadian English and the nonstandard, rural dialects of Early Modern English, as well as Mervyn Alleyne's comparative study (1980) of Afro-American creoles, has shed new light on the likely beginnings of JC and required new approaches to the data. For example, Niles's comparative study of Barbadian English and EModE dialects has a double significance for JC. First, Barbados provided a significant proportion of the first settlers of English colonial Jamaica. Second, the same kinds of poor whites (but not necessarily from the same areas) came to both islands in the seventeenth and eighteenth centuries. Further work on the varieties of EModE as well as the contribution of African languages other than the Kwa group is of utmost importance in view of the nature of the data collected here and the implications of linguistic and historical research now available.

The range and nature of linguistic studies that have expanded and shaped present approaches to creole languages are impossible to summarize here. Certain important historical and sociolinguistic aspects of Jamaican Creole have been raised by LePage and Tabouret-Keller (1985). The connections of JC to other Atlantic creoles are brought out by Hancock's work on Krio, Guinea Coast Creole English, and the seventeenth-century speech of sailors (1976, 1986a, 1986b, 1987). The question of trade languages involved in the slave trade arises in Dalby (1970/71) and leads to other matters of a more historical nature.

Survivals haunt the historian of events as well as the historian of languages. The work of Joseph G. Moore (1983), Maureen Warner Lewis (1979), and Kenneth Bilby (1983) on African survivals complements that of Barbara Kopytoff (1978) and Monica Schuler (1980). And the attempts by historians such as B. W. Higman, Michael Craton, Carey Robinson, and Philip E. Curtin to reconstruct the world of the slave plantation have important insights to offer to linguists.

The data in this volume provide brief insights into language contact at an early period, as well as into the social rules of language behavior in a stratified creole society. The documents surviving from the eighteenth and nineteenth centuries offer rich evidence for work on JC phonology but yield less for the study of syntax, revealing a grammatical system closely akin to that of twentieth-century JC.

Every text given here points to the crucial relationship of African languages and English dialects as the major sources of JC. The Angolan and Twi songs that the physician Sir Hans Sloane recorded in 1687–1689 emphasize Jamaican multilingualism of the period. Sloane reports no difficulty in treating (and, presumably, in questioning) his many patients on the plantations he visited, even though many of these people were Africans. Sloane knew a little of their ethnic origins and tried to describe their music, dance, child-rearing customs, and beliefs. Yet he offers no translation for the two songs. It remained for a twentieth-century Ghanaian to recognize the Kromanti song as a play song learned by very young children.

Behind each text some similar mystery may lie. Much more work must be done on the exact details of community structure, of patterns of habitation and fertility, immigration, ethnicity, and on the structure of languages and dialects that influenced the formation of JC.

While some questions can never be answered, they must nonetheless be raised. We cannot know for certain what languages were spoken by the Maroons, who form the link between Spanish Jamaica and English Jamaica. We can only guess at the role of Carib languages such as Taino and the trade language Baragouin in the sixteenth-century Caribbean.

In this volume we have tried to assess the language attitudes and linguistic skills of the early recorders of JC: the planters, travelers, magistrates, missionaries, and slave traders—all of whom nourished their own biases. We have used the data as a lens through which to see the vanished world of the slave and the Maroon, the creole whites and the "brown" people who lived in an uneasy middle ground between black and white.

Brought into being by historical accident, the brown creole symbolized for many in Jamaica the underlying fact of exile on which the society was founded: "You brown man hab no country—only de neger an de buckra hab country," says a black to a brown slave in the anonymous novel *Marly* (1828). At the same time, the Jamaican children of the exiles were the principal makers of the language native to them and to them alone. To all others a second language, JC remained unwritten by native speakers until the nineteenth century. It is the purpose of this book to try to clarify the efforts of those native and non-native recorders of Jamaican Creole, who, denying it the status of a language, were nevertheless constrained by its vigor to set it down in writing.

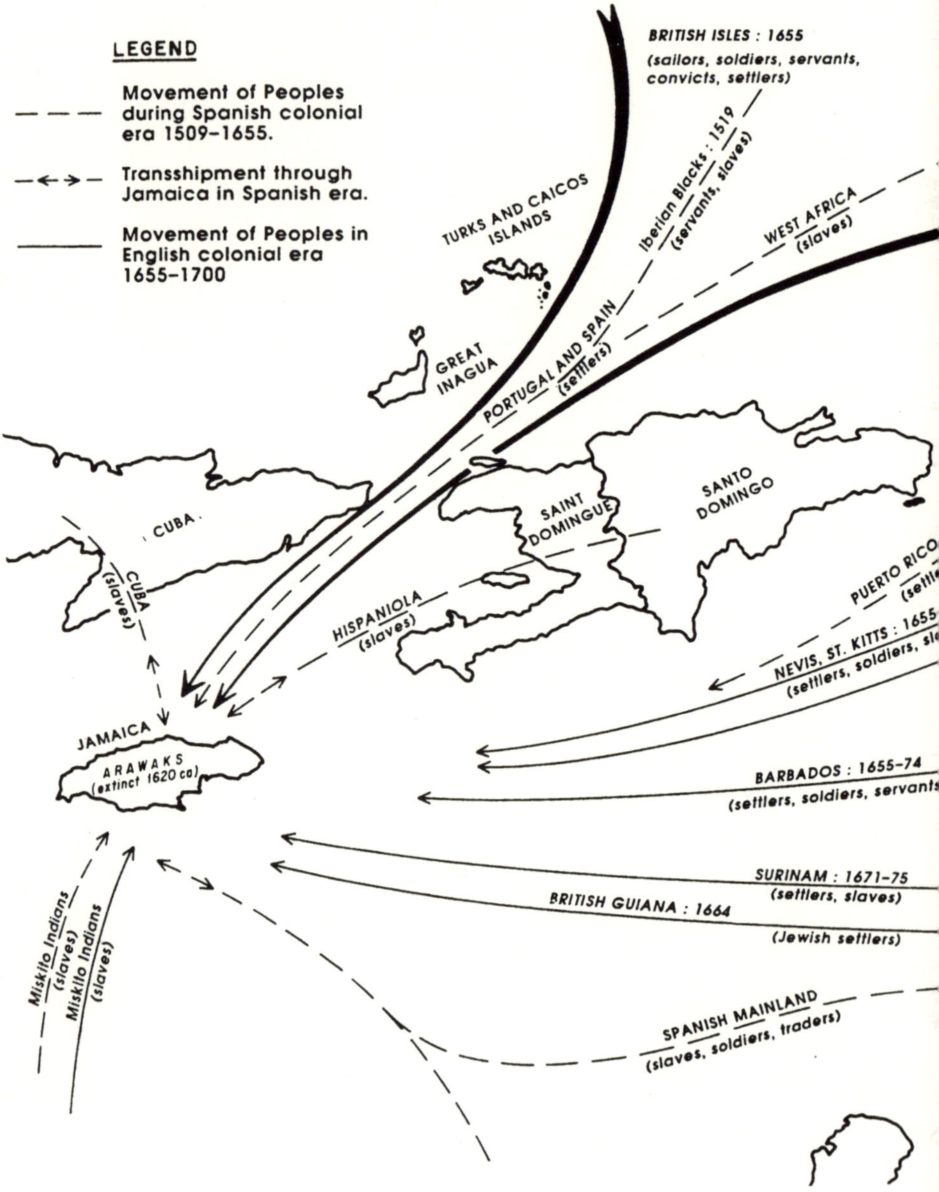

Map 1. Sources of Jamaican Population, 1500–1700

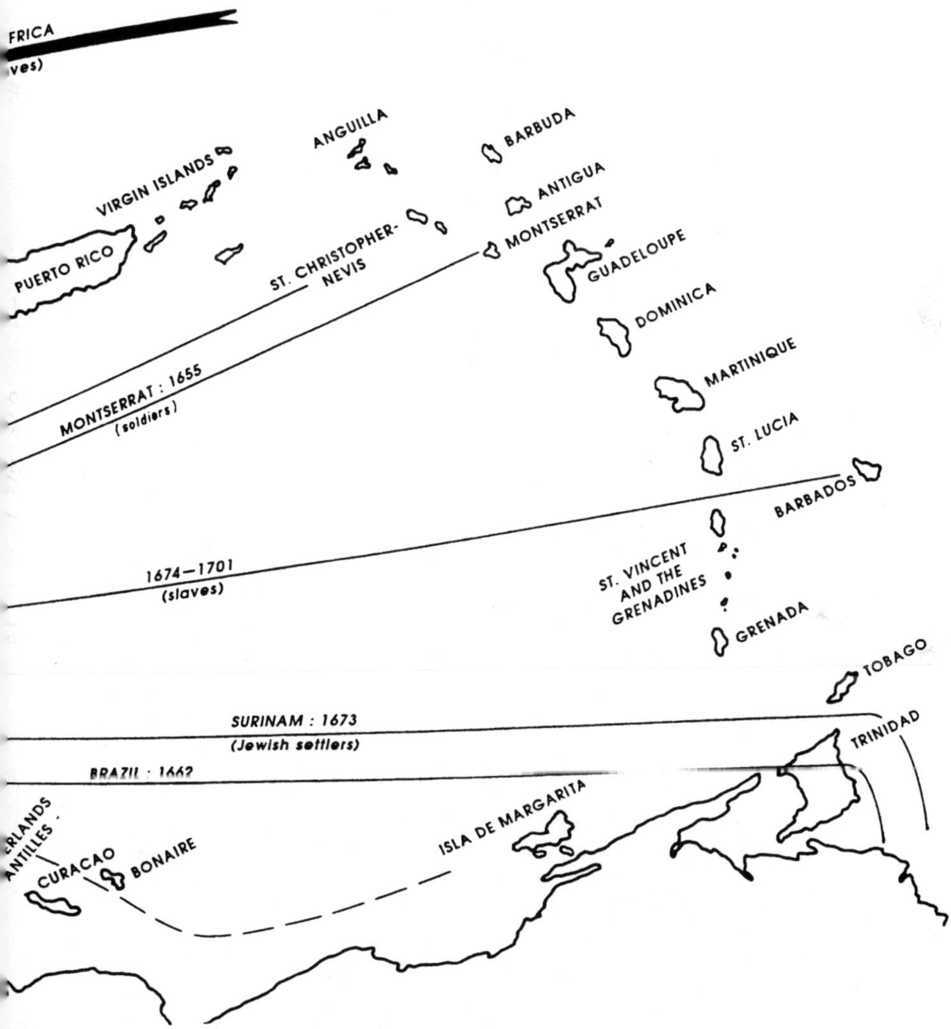

FRICA
ves)
VIRGIN ISLANDS
ANGUILLA
BARBUDA
ANTIGUA
PUERTO RICO
ST. CHRISTOPHER-NEVIS
MONTSERRAT
GUADELOUPE
DOMINICA
MARTINIQUE
MONTSERRAT : 1655
(soldiers)
ST. LUCIA
BARBADOS
1674—1701
(slaves)
ST. VINCENT AND THE GRENADINES
GRENADA
TOBAGO
SURINAM : 1673
(Jewish settlers)
TRINIDAD
BRAZIL : 1662
ERLANDS ANTILLES
CURACAO
BONAIRE
ISLA DE MARGARITA

1

The Colonial Crucible

> Lord, I have been washed from shore to shore, as a tree in the ocean. The branches of my fingers, the roots of my feet, could grip nothing; but now, God, they have found ground.
>
> Makak's last speech, Derek Walcott, *Dream on Monkey Mountain*

Language usage in today's Jamaica represents a history of contact among many different types of speakers drawn from many ethnic, linguistic, and social backgrounds. Save for the first known inhabitants—extinct by about 1620—all were exiles or the children of exiles. Map 1 sets out the sources of Jamaican population between 1500 and 1700, showing the times at which different groups arrived. Dominant among those immigrants who made up the community of speakers in early colonial Jamaica were speakers of West African languages and speakers of various dialects of Early Modern English. Although other groups have left their impress on language usage in Jamaica, none has played as notable a role as these two.

Among the African languages, the role of the Kwa group has been amply demonstrated; more research remains to be carried out on the contribution of the Manding and Kru languages to the Atlantic creoles in general[1] and Jamaican Creole in particular. The languages of the Congo region and other areas have yet to be assessed for their role in this colony of immigrants.

The exact influences brought in from the British Isles by sailors, soldiers, indentured servants, convicts, and settlers have also to be more fully studied in terms of immigration patterns. Early Modern English came to the Caribbean in the form of regional and nonstandard dialects, highly conservative for the most part. These seventeenth-century dialects of English (and of Scottish and Irish speech also) were taken to the islands first occupied by the British: St. Christopher and Nevis (1623), Barbados

(1625–1627), Montserrat (1632), and Jamaica (1655).[2] Speakers from these islands as well as lower-class whites from the British Isles provided the models for the English language in Jamaica.

Jamaica before the English Invasion of 1655

Most discussion regarding the growth of Jamaican Creole begins with the arrival of the English expeditionary forces to the south coast of Jamaica in 1655. The legacy of Jamaica's Arawak and Spanish past seems to reside merely in place names, but the Maroons—Africans who asserted their freedom from both Spanish and English domination after 1655—constitute a link to that world in which Amerindian, African, and Hispanic speakers lived for well over a century. In this broader sense, Spanish colonial life in Jamaica may be relevant to the conditions under which JC began to form. Sloane (1707–25: 1.xlvi) speaks of a small number of Africans and Amerindians who remained in Jamaica after the departure of the Spanish. This group included farmers and hunters who eventually passed on some of their knowledge of crops and forestry to the English and new Africans. Although no direct claim can be made for the formative influence of the languages used in Jamaica prior to the arrival of the English invaders in 1655, the question of Spanish and Arawak influence must still be raised despite obvious difficulties.

The original inhabitants of Jamaica were Arawaks, who had lived on the island for about seven centuries before the coming of Europeans. Columbus's arrival in 1494 opened the way for Spanish settlement, which began in 1509. Estimates of the Arawak population at this point vary widely, and its decline is not easily traced. The archaeologist Howard R. Randolph (1969: 34–35) suggests a figure of 600,000 for the year 1500 while Franklin Knight and Margaret Crahan (1979: 7) propose 20,000. Such are the uncertainties that attend efforts to reconstruct the early colonial life of Jamaica. More important than raw numbers are the settlement patterns of the Arawaks and their vulnerability to Spanish conquest.

Settled along the hills overlooking the coastal plains, the Arawaks became the first slave labor force of the Spanish (see Map 2). Within one hundred years very few survived. No distinctive Arawak culture remained in Jamaica after the sixteenth century, but Arawak influence on the emerging colonial culture suggests itself in loan words, place names, foodstuffs, and other material borrowings.

> In the unfamiliar environment of the Americas, both Europeans and [later] Africans must have borrowed freely in the uneven exchange neces-

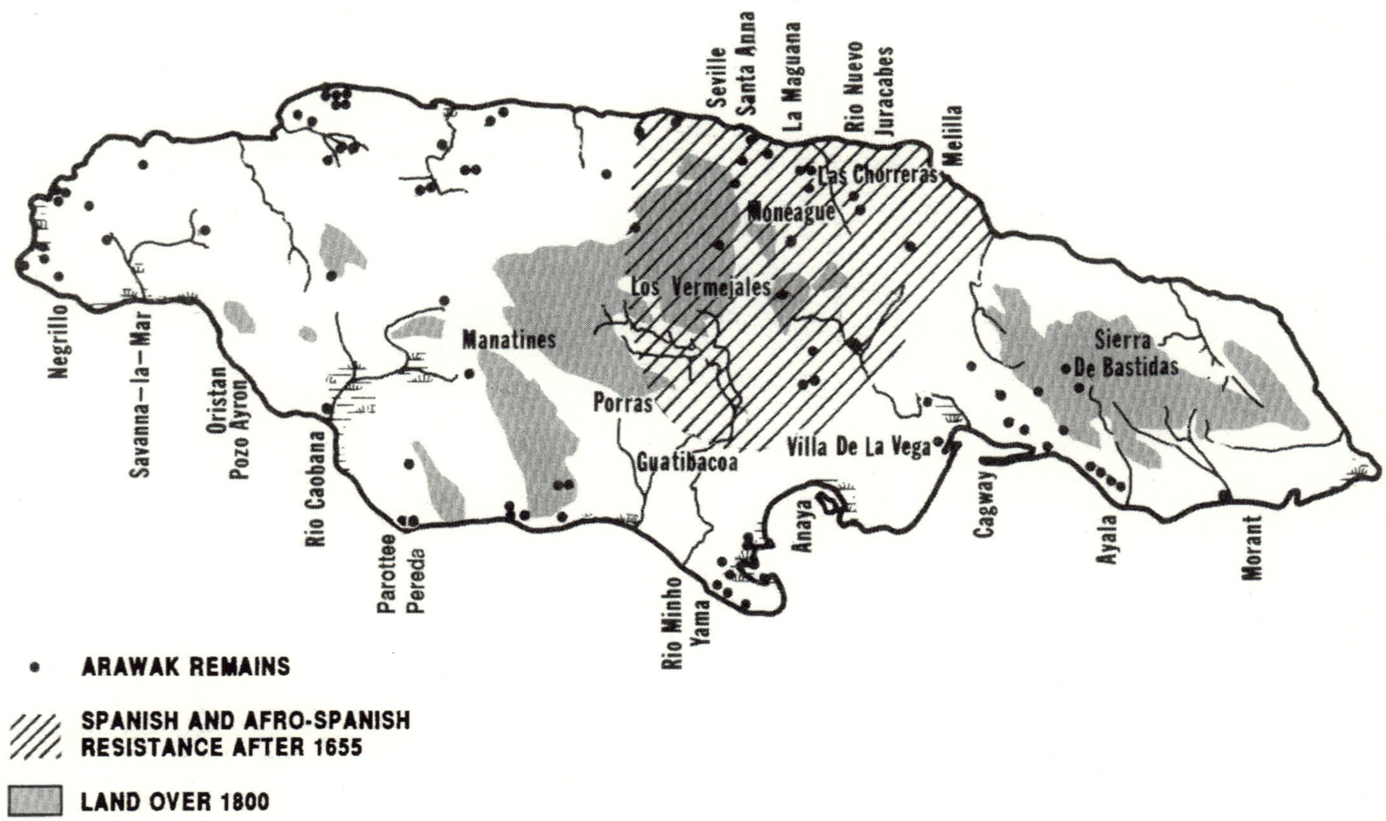

Map 2. Spanish and Arawak Locations in Jamaica, Sixteenth and Seventeenth Centuries

> sary for the survival of the fledgling colonies. We have evidence of the acceptance by the newly arrived of some aspects of the material culture of the Indians—their food crops, hammocks, utensils, and architectural styles. . . . Other aspects of the non-material culture were also accepted, although the evidence so far is scanty—as it was bound to be for less cultivated classes, especially the slaves. (Crahan and Knight 1979: 8)

Filtered through Spanish, the surviving Arawak terms include words for natural objects and events (*savannah, agouti, hurricane, cassava*); others (*batos,* "a ball game," and *goschies,* "a small hunting dog") have disappeared along with the culture in which they were rooted.

Spanish colonization introduced forced labor in mining, farming, building, and stock breeding. This first contact situation may have encouraged an endogenous pidgin or may have led to bilingualism among the first generation of mixed blood, but no clear evidence survives. No figures are available for the movement of people and the changes of population within sixteenth-century Jamaica, but a Spanish census of 1570 for the Spanish Antilles does give a picture of the population directly under Spanish control. For the entire region, the census claims 86,650 people "settled in twenty-four legally recognized towns" and plainly excludes rural populations of whatever ethnic group (Knight and Crahan 1979: 7–8). The percentile breakdown in Table 1 suggests a population structure for Jamaica, based on the assumption that this most stagnant of Spanish colonies resembled its siblings in a humble way.

By this time the total number of Amerindians accounted for in Cuba, Hispaniola, Jamaica, and other Spanish islands barely exceeded the conservative estimate quoted for Jamaica alone in 1500. The disastrous decline of the native Jamaican population became apparent by the end of the sixteenth century. "As early as 1520 an epidemic killed many of the [Arawaks] and slaves," Carey Robinson notes (1969: 12), but what proportion of the population died is unknown. In 1615 the abbot of Jamaica reported to the king of Spain that seventy-four Arawaks survived on the island (Robinson 1969: 14).

Table 1. Population of the Spanish Antilles in 1570

Spanish	8,500	(9%)
Indians	22,150	(26%)
Africans, Mestizos, Mulattoes	56,000	(65%)

Table 2. Importation of Slaves to Spanish America

Date	Number	Annual Average
1521–1550	15,000	500
1551–1595	36,000	810
1595–1640	19,000	444

Soon dissatisfied with Arawak labor, the Spanish began importing West African slaves to work the plantations and to herd cattle. The first blacks to come to Jamaica were creole Iberians who served as body servants and were culturally indistinct from their Spanish and Portuguese masters.[3] By 1550 the numbers of Africans had grown much higher as the native population declined. The figures in Table 2 show a rough estimate of the slave trade for Spanish-America in the sixteenth and seventeenth centuries. These figures represent totals for the Spanish Americas, not for Jamaica itself. The figures for 1521–1595 derive from Philip Curtin's classic study of the Atlantic slave trade. Those for 1595–1640 represent not necessarily a decrease in the trade but a new calculation for that period.[4]

During the sixteenth century, the Caribbean became the focus of intense European rivalry. As the trade in African slaves became part of this rivalry, with the Portuguese (well experienced in the African slave trade by then) serving as the principal carriers, language usage in the Caribbean must have begun its multiple transformations. Harry Hoetink (1979: 27) suggests that "language, as a vehicle of indispensable social communication, *must* have changed in chameleon fashion with every adaptation to a new territorial system. It is not unthinkable that within a Portuguese port a Portuguese *lingua franca,* on a Dutch ship a Dutch *pidgin,* and in a British colony an English-based language, were all learned successively within a few years."

Under Hispanic rule in Jamaica the Arawaks (Taino speakers) had contact with Spanish colonists, Portuguese Christians and Jews, Amerindians brought in as slaves from other parts of the Caribbean, and West Africans. New research may help to clarify the social and demographic history of the colony, but at present one must work from broad assumptions based on a few known factors: the economic stagnation of Jamaica between 1550 and 1655; mining, farming, ranching, and the exportation of foodstuffs to the mainland colonies; and the gradual abandonment of the first Spanish settlements on the north coast in favor of the southern savannahs. The crucial shift from Arawak majority to African majority must have occurred during the late sixteenth century. The change took place under conditions that would permit a wide range of language acquisition patterns.

Many Africans became hispanicized and were probably bilingual speakers of Spanish (Robinson 1969: 12–24). S. A. G. Taylor (1965: 63) notes that in 1655 when "Duarte de Acosta, who was held by the English as a hostage, sent his slave with a message to his brother Gaspar, Bernardino de Fuentes, the Alcalde, . . . had him garrotted as a spy. This caused much comment in both camps, for the man, who was from Angola, could read and write, he could recite long passages from the Scriptures, he knew the days of the movable feasts, and, above all, he was a good sugar boiler." Those Africans who became hunters and cowherds, field hands and subsistence farmers must have had a different kind of exposure to Spanish and Portuguese (the languages of the masters) from the exposure of those who worked as domestics and artisans. Their contact with Taino may also have been closer than that of urban slaves; Carey Robinson and others report intermarriages between Arawak women and African men, and the Spanish refer to mestizos, mulattoes, and half-castes in their descriptions of Jamaican affairs.

The Jamaican setting of small farms, scattered ranches, wide savannahs roamed by wild cattle, and mountain forests full of game, allowed for a freer contact between Arawak and African and between African and African than would be possible on the structured, closed plantation system of English colonial Jamaica later on. Moreover, Spanish influence may have weakened at times as the Spanish population itself declined. By the end of the sixteenth century, the most numerous ethnic group in the island was that comprising Africans and creoles of mixed blood. In 1596 there were only about 130 Spanish in Jamaica; by 1606 migrants from Puerto Rico increased the Spanish population. The estimated population in 1611 is given in Table 3 (Robinson 1969: 13–14).

The strongest evidence for cultural interchange between the Taino-speaking Arawaks and the Afro-Spanish culture lies in place names and terms for foodstuffs: Mammee Bay from Maima, the name of an Arawak

Table 3. Population of Jamaica, 1611

Ethnic Group	Number
Arawaks	74
Spanish	523 adults, 173 children
Blacks	558 slaves, 107 free
Foreigners	75

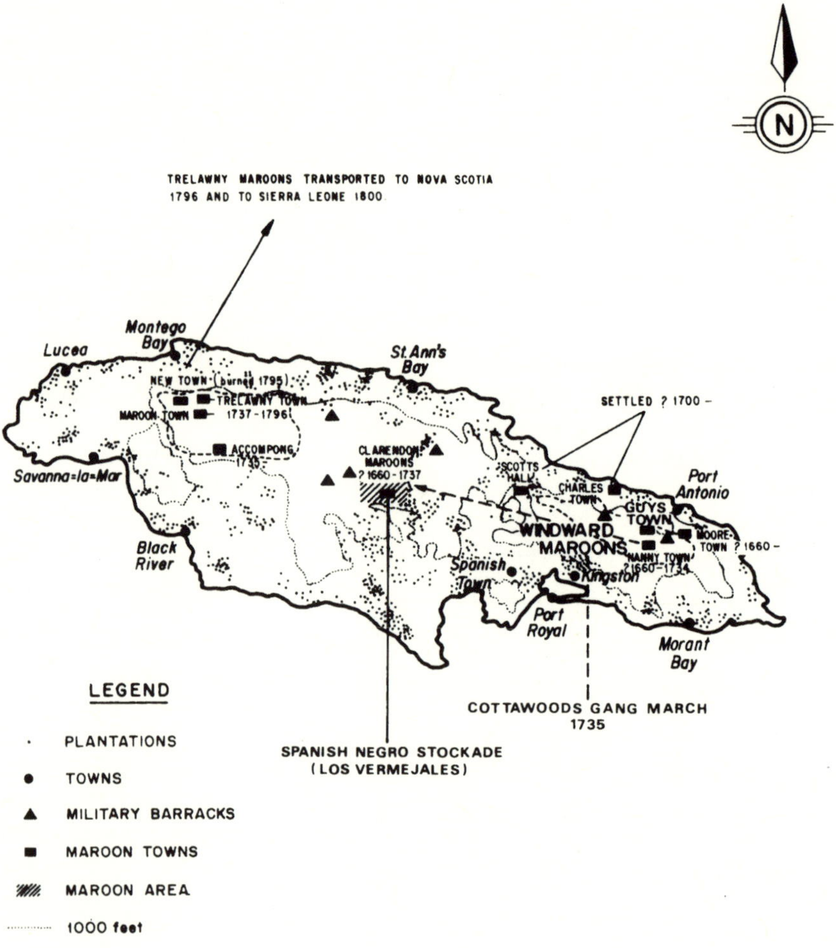

Map 3. Maroon Settlements, 1660–1800

village (LePage 1960: 3); the variant forms *cassava, cassada* (*OED*); *hicatee,* the freshwater turtle (*DJE*); and place names such as Liguanea in which Carib elements are present (i.e., *iguana,* a highly regarded food in sixteenth- and seventeenth-century Jamaica). The list is very short. Other terms now traced to Carib may in fact have entered Jamaican usage during this period, carried over into the English colony not only by the small numbers of Portuguese Jews and Spanish poor remaining behind in 1655 but also by the Maroons, who provided a link with both their own African traditions and the languages and customs of the peoples with whom they had mixed.

In 1655 the English attacked the weak Spanish colony in Jamaica. Its population amounted to about eight thousand, as estimated by the Spanish governor (LePage 1960: 6). The Spanish resistance—aided very largely by the blacks who fed, guided, and fought alongside the Spanish—came to an end in 1659. In 1660 the strongest of the black leaders, Juan Lubolo, changed sides in the struggle, an action which led to his own death but not to the end of Maroon resistance.

Between 1660 and 1700 the Maroon culture (see Map 3) took on the shape and role it would have for the coming two centuries. It merits attention as a likely vehicle for transmitting Arawak and Spanish culture to English colonial Jamaica.

The English first used Spanish-speaking interpreters and bilingual proclamations in their dealings with the Maroons, whose numbers grew steadily during the next decades, swelled by runaways from the English plantations. "The Spanish Maroons presumably spoke no English, and the escapees . . . no Spanish. The ethnic provenience of the Spanish Maroons is not known, but since some . . . [had been] imported from the Gold Coast, it may be assumed that Akan traditions were represented among them, and a common African language may have provided the first means of communication between Spanish and English Maroons" (Kopytoff 1978: 291–92). In the late eighteenth century Bryan Edwards claimed that the Maroons spoke a mixture of Spanish, English, and various African languages (Edwards 1796: xxvii, xxix), while R. C. Dallas (1803) records their speech as contemporary Jamaican Creole.

The question of Maroon language and its importance in JC substrata has been raised by Alleyne (1980: 308–9), noting Ken Bilby's discussion (1983) of the Akan elements in Maroon spirit possession language and probable connections with influences from Sierra Leone and Surinam (see Chapter 6). David Dalby's discussion of Ashanti elements in Maroon culture (1971) emphasizes the Cormantin element that has been attested by eighteenth-century observers.

The contribution of other African cultures must also be traced. The original African imports into Jamaica were brought, most probably, from those areas in Africa exploited by the Portuguese. Although the Akan element in Maroon culture remains indisputable,[5] James A. Rawley estimates that in the first half of the sixteenth century, a majority of slaves came from the area between Senegal and Sierra Leone. In the latter part of the century as many as half came from there, about a third came from Congo-Angola, and the remainder came from the Slave and Gold coasts (1981: 24–25). Most of the slaves were coastal peoples, the interior of Africa not yet having been involved in the Atlantic trade.

It is not possible to tell in what numbers Africans from these areas came into Jamaica under the Spanish or to gauge the relative influences of the languages brought by each ethnic group. However, their Hispanic and Arawak contacts, their raids on English settlements, their long-standing trade with the Jews of Jamaica (Long 1774: 1.124), and their survival in the mountains all suggest a cultural and linguistic heritage quite different from that of the new plantations.

Jamaica after the English Invasion, 1655–1700

On the eve of the English invasion, the European languages spoken in Jamaica were Spanish and Portuguese, the latter used mainly by the small community of Sephardic Jews (Schlesinger 1967: 46). Given the small population, its thin distribution over savannahs and hill country, its socioeconomic structure, and its ethnic complexity, one may postulate that a range of languages and intermediate varieties probably prevailed. Townsfolk, for example, would have been in regular contact with the two European languages, the speech of black and mixed creoles (who may have acquired some Taino and kept features of their African mother tongues), and the languages of newly arrived Africans. In the rural parts, one would probably have found, for example, Afro-Hispanic and Afro-Arawak farmhands and cow-hunters using a speech form in which Spanish, Taino, and one or more languages of Upper Guinea or of the Congo area played a part.

New influences of an even more complicating kind descended on the island with the coming of the English invaders (see Maps 1 and 4). By the end of the seventeenth century, Jamaica received soldiers recruited in London and elsewhere in England (1655–1657); others recruited in Barbados, Montserrat, and St. Kitts (1655); settlers from Nevis (1656); settlers from Barbados (1664); settlers from Surinam (1671–1675); and a few from Bermuda, New England, and Virginia. To these we must add Sephardic Jews from Brazil and Surinam (a small but steady stream

Map 4. English Regional Dialects and Ports of Exit for Indentured Labor

throughout the period); indentured servants shipping out from Bristol and bringing with them the dialects of Southwest England (LePage 1960: 12; Niles 1980); a number of midland and northern lower-class speakers; convicts from the large prisons in England; and perhaps a number of Romany speakers, Gypsies exiled by Cromwell (Hancock, personal communication). And of course, a mounting number of Africans.

It is difficult to ascertain when and how these disparate elements merged into something resembling a settled society. The transition from Spanish to English rule was costly in terms of human life, but the toll owed more to disease and hunger than to warfare. Between 1655 and 1659, most of the Spanish families withdrew to Cuba, leaving behind an unknown (but small) number of blacks, mulattoes, and Portuguese Jews. These last were promised favorable terms by the English. The blacks continued their resistance and withdrew into the first Maroon settlements, and a few stragglers in outlying *hatos* and farms survived to settle again under the English. The subtle nature of surviving Spanish influence in Jamaican Creole shows in the variant names for the tree *Sapota achras* and its fruit. Today, some regional and old-fashioned speakers use the term /niizberi/ (from Spanish *níspero*, the name for the tree). The common JC name /neizberi/ derives from *néspera*, the Spanish name for the fruit.

At the same time, the distinction may well derive from phonological rules of EModE (the Great Vowel Shift), which could have entered seventeenth-century Jamaica and created the variants while blurring the meaning of the Spanish originals.

As for the English colonial effort, its success between 1655 and 1661 can be judged from the statistics S. A. G. Taylor gives (1965: 206): of a rough total of 12,000 newcomers (English colonists, soldiers, and slaves), only 3,451 remained alive six years later. The tiny surviving population—mainly white—settled in the southern savannahs in the same areas previously occupied by the Spanish. Some colonists, such as those from Surinam, who settled the district of Surinam Quarters, formed communities that have maintained a distinctive heritage. In the next fifteen years, emigration from other parts of the Caribbean would enlarge the population. Barbados would serve as the principal supplier of white colonists of all classes as well as creole blacks and transshipped Africans.

Scholars have tended to hypothesize that Jamaican Creole took shape in the period 1660 to 1700. No seventeenth-century texts have been found to confirm or disprove this hypothesis, however, and regrettably, no descriptions of seventeenth-century Jamaican speech behavior have been uncovered.

In this period Jamaica maintained the highest ratio of whites to blacks it would ever have, about seven thousand whites to nine thousand blacks, rising to forty thousand blacks by 1693 (Table 4). Most of these whites spoke nonstandard forms of English that bore many features of sound, morphology, and syntax directly relevant to Jamaican Creole. Sir Hans Sloane (1707–25: 1.xlvi) describes the Jamaicans of the late 1680s: "The inhabitants of Jamaica are for the most part Europeans, some Creolians, born and bred in the Island Barbados, the Windward Islands, or Surinam, who are the Masters; and Indians, Negros, Mulatos, Alcatrazes, Mestises, Quarterons, &c. who are the Slaves."

Norma Niles (1980) proposes a seventeenth-century Barbadian lan-

Table 4. Population of Jamaica, 1661–1739 (Excluding Freedmen and Maroons)

	Whites	Blacks
1661	2,458 men 455 women 44 children	584
1662	4,123 men 645 women 408 children	552
1673	7,768	9,504
1675	5,500	9,000
1693–94	7,000	40,000
1703	—	45,000
1722	7,100	80,000
1730	7,658	74,525
1739	10,080	99,239

guage community in which dialect-speaking whites formed the majority and enabled Africans to acquire dialectal rather than creole English. If one accepts Niles's analysis (and it is highly persuasive), then one must consider that Jamaica between 1660 and 1690 resembled Barbados in many demographic and linguistic ways. Only when Africans begin to outnumber whites in a sudden and steep increase can one see that creolization rather than dialect mixing must have become the norm. One must also recall the very different physical features of Jamaica, and how the distribution of peoples would have affected language change.

Jamaica's population was distributed unevenly among the town of Port Royal, the capital Spanish Town, military forts, and the first struggling plantations. Many small farms existed, as in Spanish times. The nature of social organization and its effect on language usage cannot be readily assessed, but the household of one early settler, Cary Helyar, offers a model of what rural Jamaica must have been (Bennett 1964: 53–76).

The younger son of a West Country family, Helyar came to Jamaica and set up as a trader in slaves and ivory in 1664. In 1669 he started a modest plantation with six slaves, one white servant, and a white overseer. Helyar himself lived nearby with his mulatto mistress, the couple's two small sons, and the children's maternal grandmother (a free Brazilian black who had borne her daughter to a white Barbadian colonist). In 1669 Helyar cleared six acres for provision grounds and his first planting of cacao trees. In 1670 he bought six more blacks, carefully choosing his slaves for health and for experience of Jamaica. He next brought out a few tradesmen (one with a family) from the area of Bristol, England. For the next few years, the lonely little farm northwest of Spanish Town was home to twelve blacks and seven or eight whites. Although none of Helyar's Africans died and a single runaway came back, such settlements suffered a high rate of loss from death and *marronage*.

The influence of other population centers must not be undervalued, important as the plantation and the Maroon village have been. Jamaica in the latter seventeenth century was not only a place in which small groups of whites cultivated sugar, coffee, indigo, and other crops. The island also served as a center for shipping and buccaneering. Port Royal, Passage Fort, and after the earthquake of 1692, Kingston were the haunt of sailors and sea rovers of all descriptions whose usage is discussed in Chapter 4. In the towns, white dialects might have dominated to the extent that urban Africans could have acquired these forms of English.

We must also consider the possible influence of two trade languages—one African, the other English—which were spoken in those places from which enslaved Africans came in the latter seventeenth century. The first, Manding, is described by Dalby (1970/71: 285) as "a trade language and . . . the mother-tongue of a number of distinct ethnic groups stretching from Gambia in the west to Upper Volta and northern Ghana in the east, and from the Sahara in the north to the Atlantic coast in the south: its regional dialects throughout this area are known today under a variety of names, including Mandingo, Malinke, Bambara and Dyula." These areas and language groups are among the remnants of the Mali empire for which the north-south trade across the Sahara constituted wealth and power (Fage 1969: 13–46).

The trade language would have followed the internal trade routes leading up the great rivers and across the east-west caravan trails (see Map 5). Dalby notes that "in terms of vocabulary, there is great divergence among these languages, but—interestingly enough—there is frequently much less divergence in terms of their sound systems, grammatical systems and semantic systems." He suggests also that a behavioral aspect of West African bilinguality "will have been the ability to 'switch' from one set of vocabulary to another without any extensive switch in the overall linguistic system involved" (1970/71: 285).

Dalby's point in no way nullifies the question of mutual unintelligibility among the majority of transported Africans. This point is made by the Royal African Company surveyor, William Smith, who observed the trade in Gambia (1744: 28): "As for the Languages of Gambia, they are so many and so different, that the Natives on either Side the River [*sic*], cannot understand each other; which . . . is no small Happiness to the Euro-

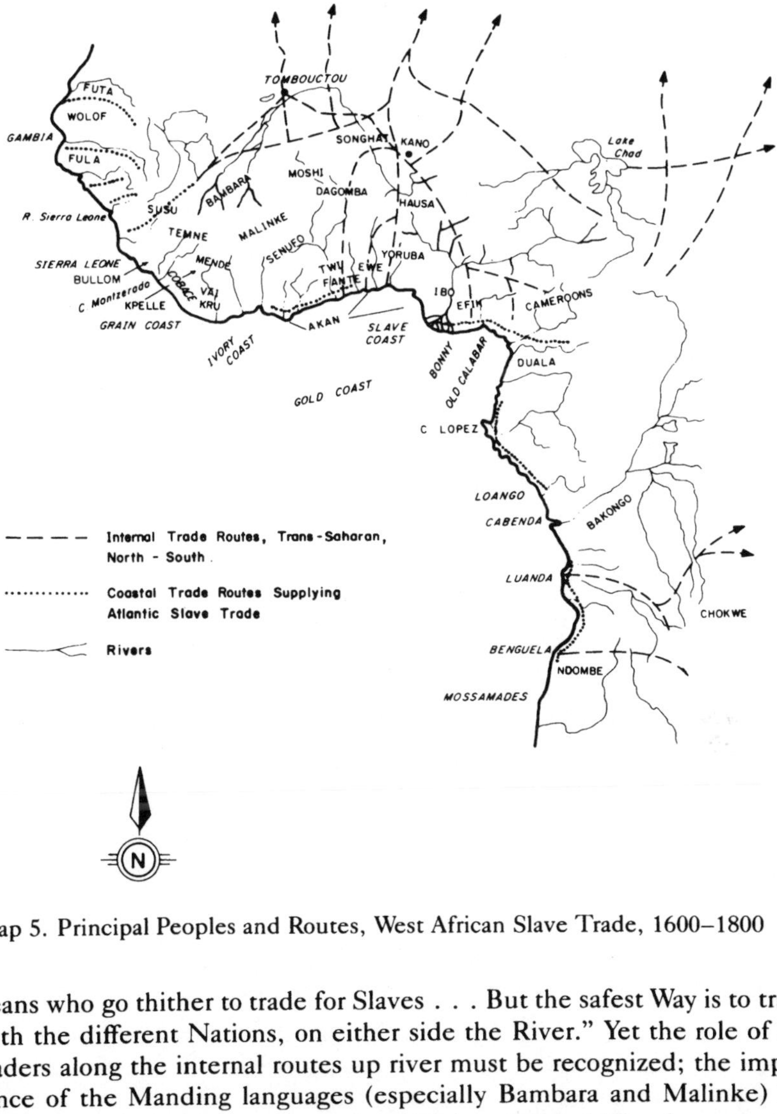

Map 5. Principal Peoples and Routes, West African Slave Trade, 1600–1800

peans who go thither to trade for Slaves . . . But the safest Way is to trade with the different Nations, on either side the River." Yet the role of the traders along the internal routes up river must be recognized; the importance of the Manding languages (especially Bambara and Malinke) has been pointed out by linguists such as Alleyne (1980: 147), who notes that this set of languages may have connections with the formation of the Atlantic creoles. An interesting aspect of the "widespread use of Manding as a lingua franca, is the extreme regularity of its grammatical structure, and the absence of a complex morphology" (Dalby 1970/71: 286). This trade language must have filtered down to the coast as slave trading shifted more and more (see Map 5) to the Atlantic seaboard.

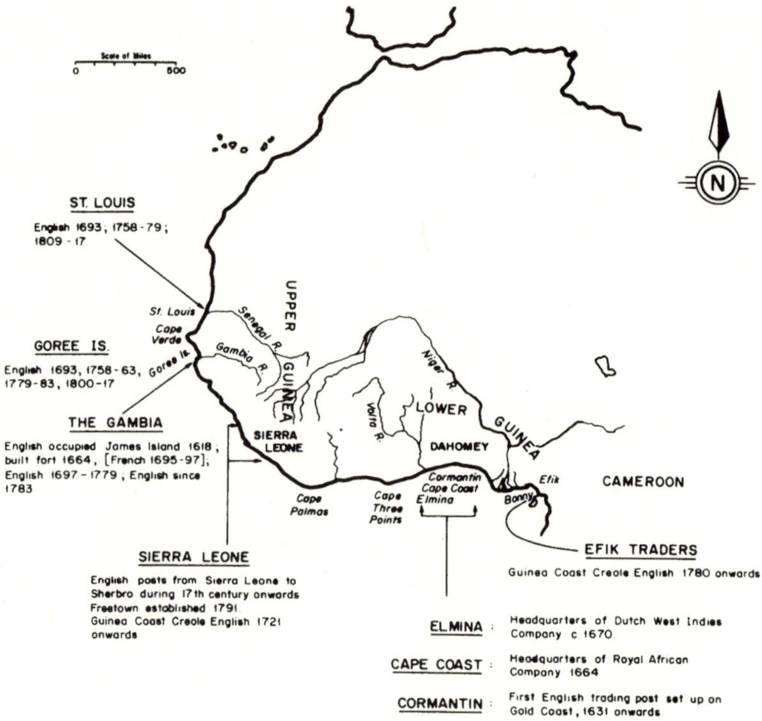

Map 6. English Trading Areas in West Africa, 1600–1800

The second trade language to consider is the English-based creole that probably developed first in the English trading posts of Upper Guinea in the seventeenth century (see Map 6). Guinea Coast Creole English may have arisen during the seventeenth and eighteenth centuries among the whites, mulattoes, and blacks living in the tiny English trading posts of the Gambia and, later on, of Cormantin and Cape Coast on the Gold Coast. The beginnings of this creole are hazy: the earliest English trade of any continuity and consequence seems to have started in 1618 with the Adventurers of London trading to "Gynney and Binney" (Davies 1970: 39–40), and the setting up of traders on James Island in that year.

Trade lagged during the middle years of the seventeenth century but probably never ceased altogether (see Map 6). In 1631 the English set up a small post at Cormantin, a short distance from the huge Portuguese fort at Elmina; in 1660–1663 the Royal Adventurers was formed, and the English fortified James Island (1664) and strengthened their base at the mouth of the Gambia River. In 1672 the Royal African Company was established.[6] While the growth and nature of Guinea Coast Creole English are difficult to assess, its range and probable influence must be considered significant (Alleyne 1980: 143–46; Hancock 1987).

During the last three decades of the seventeenth century the English trading posts multiplied along the coast of Upper Guinea and the Gold Coast, shipping Africans directly to "Barbados, Jamaica, Nevis, St Christopher's, Antigua" (Davies 1970: 45). The trading posts typically consisted of a few Englishmen, their black or mulatto women, and the *grumettoes,* African servants who hired themselves out to the whites (Smith 1744; Atkins 1736: 34–41). To these would be added a varying number of slaves and a varying number of white sailors in port who might stay for a few days or a few months, depending on circumstances.

The African element in the creole English of Upper Guinea would be drawn from the coastal languages: Mende, Fula, Vai, Bullom, Temne, and Kru (Map 5). GCCE might also have been influenced by the Manding trade language. Alleyne (1980: 146–47) notes the importance of Manding (especially Bambara and Malinke), as well as that of Portuguese Pidgin, which dated back to the fifteenth century and was represented by many speakers from Cape Verde in the northwest to Elmina on the Gold Coast. All three—GCCE, Portuguese Pidgin, and the Manding group—must have been involved in language making both on the Guinea Coast and in the Caribbean. William Smith, who visited the Gambia, Sierra Leone, and other parts of the West African coast in the 1720s, mentions Christian blacks and mulattoes who spoke English or Portuguese; he also speaks of local kings and traders who spoke some English and of whites who spoke local languages in their households as well as in their daily trading (1744: 22, 25, 65, 75, 93–94, 213).

The probable linguistic importance of such trading posts becomes clearer when one sets the official figures for the Royal African Company's deliveries of slaves to Jamaica against population estimates for the same period.[7] In addition to the slaves brought by freebooters of all nations, the Royal African Company brought 22,244 slaves to Jamaica between 1674 and 1688 (Davies 1970: 363), about half the total imported for the period (LePage 1960: 71). Although it is impossible to identify the ethnic origins of the slaves on existing evidence, the English trading posts shown on Map 6 do suggest the geographical range of the trade.

Jamaica during the Heyday of Sugar, 1700–1834

Beaten down by natural disasters such as the cacao blight of the 1680s and the great earthquake of 1692, drained by war and ill fortune, the white population of Jamaica went into severe decline at the end of the seventeenth century. Gone were the small settlements of soldiers-turned-planters. Cary Helyar's six-acre plot had grown into Bybrook estate, worked by 150 slaves or more (Bennett 1964: 76). Jamaican communities of the future would be modeled on the large plantations worked by thousands of Africans—mostly young men—who were imported in increasing numbers.

Based on estimates of Jamaica's population compiled by several scholars, Tables 4 and 5 show the growth of the slave population and the net importation of Africans (Patterson 1973: 95–96, 97) as well as the slow increase of the white population (LePage 1960: 91; Brathwaite 1978: 152; Roberts 1979: 33, 36; Higman 1984: 77) during the period 1694–1830.[8]

Between 1694 and 1739, Jamaica's white population grew very little. By 1762 it increased slightly and expanded more positively once more between 1768 and 1805. Between 1700 and 1739 the ratio of white to black shifted from about 1 : 4.5 to 1 : 12. The question of population figures for blacks remains almost as obscure as that for whites. The estimate of forty-five thousand blacks in 1703 must be understood against the lieutenant governor's remark that "I did compute by the rolls that the island had

Table 5. Population of Jamaica, 1739–1830 (Excluding Freedmen and Maroons)

Year	Number of Slaves	Net Importation	Whites
1739	99,239	20,341	10,080
1746	112,428	36,510	10,000
1754	130,000	43,295	12,000
1762	146,464	54,908	15,000
1768	166,914	41,472	17,949
1778	205,261	54,951	18,420
1787	210,894	73,754	25,000
1795	250,000	—	—
1800	300,939	—	—
1805	308,775	—	28,000
1810	346,399	—	27,889
1830	319,074	None	18,902

45,000 men but cannot find above half" (Roberts 1979: 36). For the whole period the ratio stands at about 1 : 10. These ratios suggest a world in which slave-to-slave communication had a larger place than was possible in the earlier years, when whites equaled or exceeded slaves in numbers. Moreover, both populations (black and white) kept their numbers not by natural increase but by replacements from outside.[9]

"By the middle of the eighteenth century 300 [white] children a year were leaving Jamaica for England" (Patterson 1973: 35).[10] Whites who became prosperous tended to send their children "home" to England to be educated. Many never returned, as Orlando Patterson's study of absentee ownership shows (1973: 35–36). In the place of these departing whites came others, usually penniless young men seeking employment as bookkeepers and petty managers. The white artisans, small farmers, tradesmen, and other poor who emigrated to Jamaica in the seventeenth century found themselves either rising into the proprietor class or competing with a growing pool of skilled workers made up of free blacks, browns (whose white fathers sometimes freed them and set them up in small businesses and trades), and slaves hired out as skilled artisans.

During the eighteenth century, creole whites took on the split identity that has marked them ever since. Many looked outside for cultural models and worldly approbation, but many others firmly identified themselves with Jamaica. "By 1700," writes Patterson, "local patriotism was so pronounced among the early settlers, and their children who became known as 'the creole party,' that on several occasions they attempted to exclude English-born persons from filling posts in the island and even went as far as declaring that they 'will not allow themselves to be called Englishmen' " (1973: 34). This conflict of identity—experienced in a different way by blacks—appears in such works as *Lady Nugent's Journal* (written in 1801–1805) and the anonymous novel *Marly* (1828). In the latter, the Singleton family consists of a defiantly pro-Jamaican aunt and niece and an anglicized nephew ashamed of his relatives' creole speech and manners.

It is very difficult to point to a moment or even to a period by which the language forms now known as Jamaican Creole and Standard Jamaican English must have emerged. One clue may be the strong Jamaican identity among white creoles in 1700. Another may lie in John Atkins's description of Jamaican society when, after visiting Upper Guinea, he came to Jamaica in 1721–1722 (1736: 244–45): "The Creoles (those born here) which are properly the Natives of the Island, . . . are a spurious Race; the first Change by a Black and White, they call a Mulatto; the second a Mustee, and the third a Castee. . . . They are half Negrish in their Manners, proceeding from the promiscuous and confined Conversation with their Relations, the Servants at the Plantations, and have a Language especially Pleasant, a kind of Gypsy Gibberish, that runs smoothest in swearing."

Atkins had previously commented briefly on the languages used on the Guinea Coast (described in more detail by another contemporary visitor, William Smith). The anonymous author of *The Importance of Jamaica . . .* (1740) quotes examples of slave speech that display obvious JC features. Such fragments of JC and GCCE recorded early in the eighteenth century show clearly related features of lexicon and phonotaxis. The social structure of the West African trading posts corresponds in many ways to that of Caribbean plantations, save that the latter might be said to have had a more stable population. In both settings the few held control over the many. In Jamaica the control was exerted not merely by whites but by blacks whose role corresponded to that of the hired servants of West Africa, the *grumettoes*. The black soldiers, drivers, craftsmen, sugar boilers, and upper servants in the Caribbean slave hierarchy formed a group that mediated and dispensed authority and influence upward to the whites and downward to the black majority (see Chapter 5).

The situation, however, is far more complicated than might be implied by hierarchical roles and population figures. The black majority comprised people of varying ethnic background grouped without regard for native language for the purposes of labor.[11] Even in the seventeenth and early eighteenth centuries, certain ethnic groups emerged as leaders in the many slave rebellions (Patterson 1973: 265–76). Cormantin leaders fomented rebellion; Cormantin obeah men and women kept alive the now-secret religions of the slaves; Cormantin runaways (Akan and most probably Ashanti) fled to the Maroon settlements. These were still partly Hispanic even in 1702 (Patterson 1973: 269), and the Akan runaways, skilled warriors in their homelands, began to dominate the growing Maroon culture (Kopytoff 1978: 295).

The Maroons had maintained a steady resistance to the English colonists all throughout the seventeenth and early eighteenth centuries. They intermarried with plantation slaves, traded at slave markets, and settled in many different places within the mountains (see Map 3), raiding white settlements and evading both the English soldiery and the "Black Shot," black soldiers used as trackers and hunters.

The Maroon treaties of 1739, however, changed the relationship of this group to Jamaican slavery. Thereafter Maroons helped hunt down runaways in return for tracts of land and self-government within their settlements. Archaeological findings at Nanny Town, a major center of resistance until 1734 (Bonner 1974: 46–51; Kopytoff 1978: 298) suggest years of trading and raiding in which the Maroons must have acquired some English as well as other African ethnic influences.

The role of the Akan languages must be tested against that of other languages in the context of social structures in the early colonial period. Michael Craton (1978: 53) speaks of Worthy Park estate in the seventeenth century as possibly including "lively Senegambians" and "some Amerindians or mestizos, seized from the Miskito Coast of Honduras or inherited from the Spanish." Other Miskito Indians were brought in as slave trackers and Maroon hunters, and all of them worked in contact with soldiers, servants, and white convicts from every part of the British Isles.

The strong Akan element in JC history is also supported by the planters' continuing preference for people from the Gold Coast. Even the violent rebellions led by Cormantins in the 1760s could not wholly shift that preference.[12] What is more, between 1795 and 1808 the British government secretly sought and purchased 13,400 men from that area to serve in the West India Regiment (Rawley 1981: 169). It is small wonder that in 1801 when Lady Nugent accompanied her husband, the governor of Jamaica, on a review of the West India Regiment, she reported that the soldiers seemed unable to understand what she said to them (Nugent 1966: 103), although the "blackies" everywhere else understood her very well.

Throughout the period 1700 to 1834, the question of internal and external security concerned Jamaica's ruling class. If, on the one hand, the life of the plantation appears closed, it is clear from accounts of running away, hunting Maroons and runaways, and planning and suppressing revolts that covert movement in and out of the plantations was constant. By the early nineteenth century, the pattern of running away for a period of weeks or months had become a standard feature of slave life. Although the Maroon treaties of 1739 deterred further *marronage,* absenteeism did not cease. Occasional absences might be pardoned if the slave asked a neighboring landowner to intercede on his behalf (Lewis 1834: 115). Persistent running away was punished by severe flogging or confinement to the workhouse at hard labor or transportation to the deadly camps of Honduras.

Worse punishment attended those slaves found guilty of practicing African religions or mystical rituals. Like the organizers of revolt, the religious leaders tended to be African rather than creole. The connection between religion and resistance becomes clear in the study of African survivals (Moore 1983; Kopytoff 1978; Schuler 1979; and Bilby 1983).

A significant aspect of cultural transmission lies in the gradual shift from African majority to creole majority, although numbers alone do not confer dominance. The figures for 1693–1694 in Table 4 show that the first great increase to forty thousand slaves was achieved by importation, but a black creole consciousness arose in rivalry to African identity and expressed itself in the condescension of black creoles toward the "saltwater" Africans.

By the mid–eighteenth century creoles and Africans each made up

Table 6. Population of Jamaica, 1810–1830

	Whites	Freedmen	Slaves	Total
1810	27,889 6.9%	29,912 7.4%	346,399 85.7%	404,200
1830	18,902 5.0%	40,074 10.6%	319,074 84.4%	378,050

about half of the total slave population, and by the end of the century Africans made up only about one-quarter (Patterson 1973: 275). This slowly growing creole population became the link between the original homelands of the exiles and the Jamaican society of the future, a society in which things creole took precedence over the African past (Craton 1978: 55). With the ending of the British slave trade in 1809–1810, contact with Africa diminished, but it did not cease altogether until later in the nineteenth century. B. W. Higman's population estimates for 1810 and 1830 show not only the decline of the slave population after the slave trade ended but also the expansion of an important group, the freed blacks and people of color (Higman 1984: 77; see Table 6). These figures suggest the decline of direct African influence in the nineteenth century and the movement toward a creole society that accepted Jamaica as its home.

During the eighteenth and early nineteenth centuries, speakers other than those of African origin continued to exert some influence on the language forms of Jamaica. It is difficult to trace how the speech of the eighteenth-century British immigrants affected that of white creoles of different classes, but for the slaves, the incoming dialects of Britain (see Map 4) must have reinforced features already present from the seventeenth century. Convict labor, political prisoners (some of them Scots), other Scots seeking work as bookkeepers on the plantations,[13] indentured servants (many of whom were Irish Catholics), as well as tradespeople from the hinterland of Bristol and, later, Liverpool (the two main ports of exit for the triangular trade), kept up the numbers of white men in Jamaica. Among these immigrants, however, were very few white women. The gender imbalance in both white and black populations has important implications for matters of identity, upward mobility, value systems, and cultural transmission.[14]

The growth of the Jamaican economy and the spread of population can be appreciated by comparing Maps 7 and 8, which show Jamaica in 1670 and at the end of the eighteenth century. Keep in mind that both black and white populations failed to increase naturally. Yet even though the

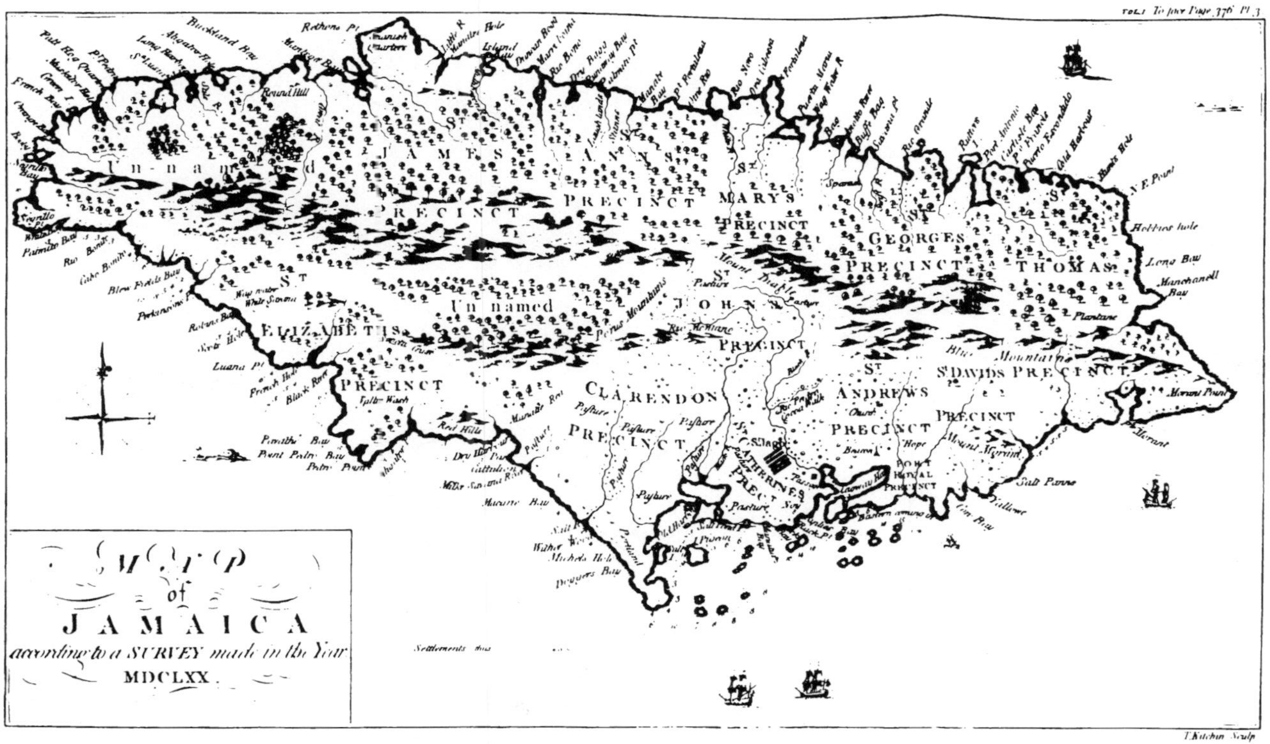

Map 7. Jamaica in 1670 (Long 1774: 1.376)

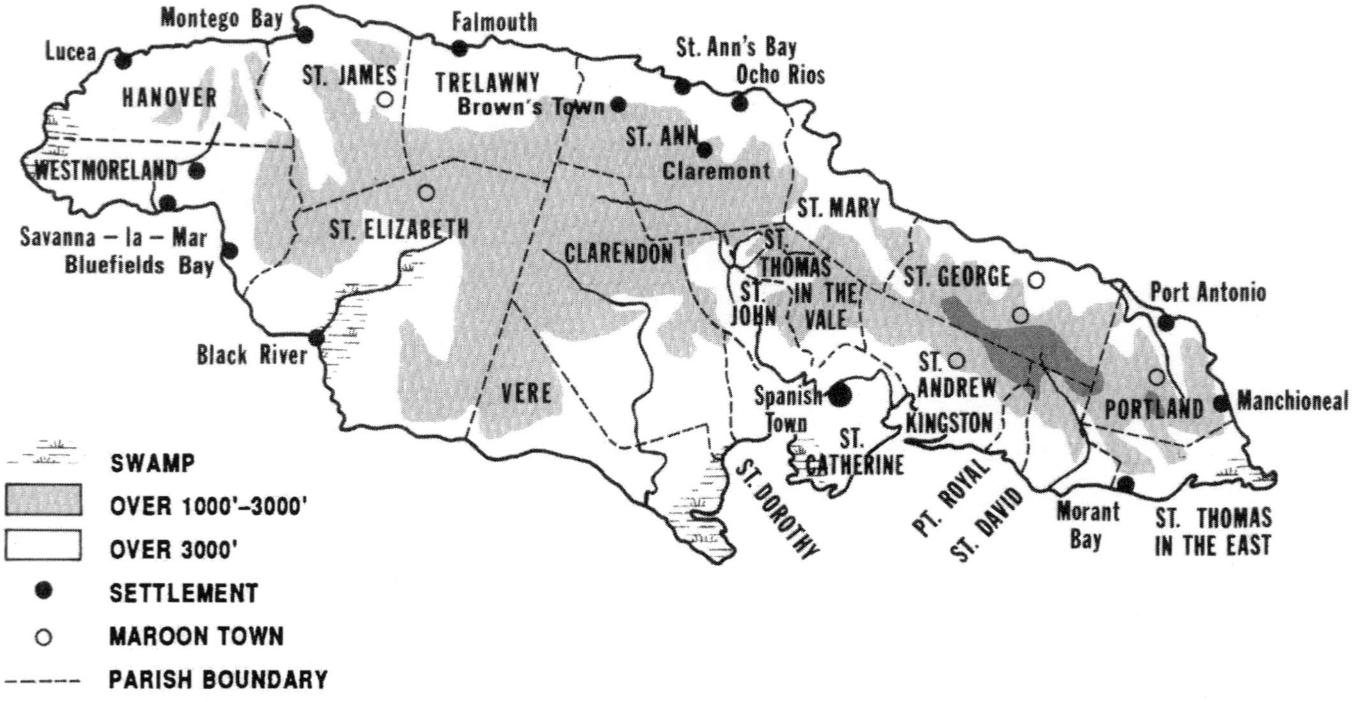

Map 8. Jamaica at the End of the Eighteenth Century (after Brathwaite 1978: xii)

white population remained small, its influence on the speech forms of the community was strong. Living in daily contact with slaves, the speakers of regional English, Hiberno-English and the Celtic languages of Ireland, Scotland, and Cornwall (Cornish was extinct by the end of the eighteenth century), provided the models of English for Africans and creoles alike. Long notes that the "natives of Scotland and Ireland seem to thrive here much better than the European English." He had heard of one hundred Campbells resident in Jamaica, "all claiming alliance with the Duke of Argyle" (Long 1774: 2, 286), and the Scots' support of one another—noted in many commentaries on Jamaica—reaches a kind of climax in *Marly* (1828: 9), when the hero hears of a Mr. Campbell who hires only Gaelic-speaking Highlanders. "The very negroes . . . so well understand his predilection for the language of his clan, that when they see a walking buckra seeking employment . . . , they accost him with the question, 'Can you talk Gaelic? for, if you can't, massa no employ you.' "

Quite a different matter was the role and status of white missionaries, whose activities infuriated the planters during the abolitionist movement (ca. 1770–1838). This period roughly parallels that in which texts of Jamaican Creole first become numerous, the increase in written records being notable after 1800. In part this upsurge of writings by visitors and residents marks a change in European attitudes. Sir Walter Scott and others who used regional dialect in their novels gained immense popularity; the brothers Grimm laid the foundations of the modern study of folklore with their collection of folktales (1812–1822); and the Romantic movement encouraged a humanistic interest in non-European peoples. In Britain a growing philanthropic movement supported the Baptists, Moravians, and Methodists in places such as Jamaica, while the abolitionist movement was to earn William Wilberforce a place in black folklore greater than that of Admiral Nelson, the other white hero of the age.

The missionary influence on Jamaican speech appears in the sermons, prayers, and depositions recorded by missionaries such as the Reverend Mr. Phillippo (Text 14) and in those preserved for ridicule by visitors such as Cynric Williams (Text 10). Unlike the established Church of England, the missionary churches worked closely with the slaves and the free blacks and browns. The first Baptist church in Kingston was started by an American black who came to Jamaica in 1783 with a royalist family. Baptized and ordained in Savannah, Georgia, the Reverend Mr. George Liele "built the first Baptist chapel in Jamaica and commanded a wide following among the slaves" (Senior 1983: 16). Another free American black, Moses Baker (a convert of Liele's), was the first to give Christian religious instruction to slaves on the north side of the island. He too had come to Jamaica with royalists.

Baker's mission at Adelphi in the parish of St. James (the hinterland of Montego Bay) began at the invitation of the new owner of the estate, a Quaker named Winn, who had discovered Baptists among a group of slaves newly purchased in Kingston. Between 1787 and 1791 Baker founded two churches in the area. By 1814 appeals to Britain for missionary help brought out white missionaries, and the influence of the Baptists was to grow to such strength that planters regarded the greatest slave uprising of all as "the Baptist rebellion" of 1831. What is more important, the religious movements in Jamaica during the last eighty years of slavery (ca. 1760–1838) drew strongly on both African and European traditions to form such new cults as myalism. The Sam Sharpe rebellion of 1831 (as it is now known, after the slave, a Baptist deacon, who helped inspire it), emphasized the importance of religion in the lives of the slaves (Schuler 1980: 33–36) and led inevitably to the persecution of missionaries and nonconformist churches.

The 1831 rebellion shows a shift in the roles of creoles and Africans. The rebellions of the previous two centuries had been planned by Africans and aimed at securing an escape from slave society; that of 1831, however, was organized by creoles, "especially those who had achieved some degree of status within slave society and saw the possibilities of complete liberty. As argued by Schuler, 'If anything, a "creolization" of slave protest had taken place, and the slaves seemed anxious to find a better place for themselves *within* the traditional plantation society' " (Higman 1976: 227).

The missionary effort in Jamaica brought slaves into contact with speakers of middle-class varieties of British English, many coming from the north and midlands. Such speakers provided models for free blacks and browns seeking social advancement through church and school. The rapid growth of Afro-Christian (including revivalist) sects in Jamaica illustrates the reach of the movement. Biblical language and prayer-book language thereafter became branches of diction for high speech and formal utterance: "Dea belubb'd, we gather together dis face congregation, because it horrible among all men not to take delight in hand for wantonness, lust, and appetite, like brute mule, dat hab no understanding" (Williams 1826: 104–6).

Jamaican language usage drew on the speech of various new immigrant groups in this period also. In the last decade of the eighteenth century and the first of the nineteenth, many French refugees (some with their slaves and servants) came to Jamaica to escape from the uprising on Hispaniola. The external security of Jamaica had become a critical matter during the Napoleonic Wars, and considerable contact was kept up between the two islands. From this period derive such family names as

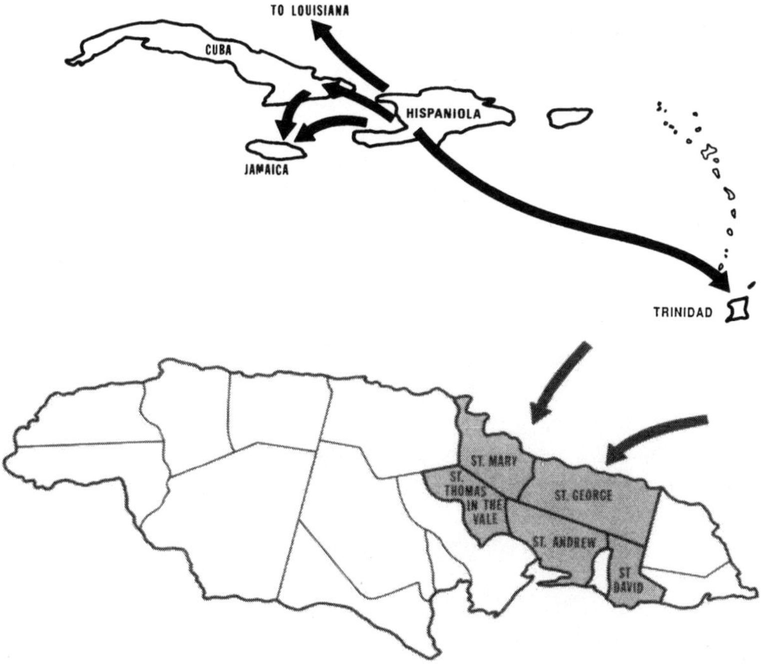

Map 9. French-Haitian Influx at the End of the Eighteenth Century (after Bryan 1973)

Gabay, Malabre, and de Montagnac and some French-Jamaican terms: a few older Jamaicans still refer to breadfruit as *fruit à pain*. The refugees may also have included speakers of Ewe, the language of Haitian *vodun* (Alleyne, personal communication). The settlement pattern of these refugees, which appears on Map 9, partly overlaps that of the African indentured labor that came to Jamaica between 1840 and 1865.

Jamaica after 1834

With the ending of the slave trade in 1809–1810, Jamaica became increasingly creolized and distanced from the African past, but African tradition was rekindled here and there by the coming of the indentured African labor. At the time of emancipation, Africans accounted for about a quarter or less of the black population; women outnumbered men among the Africans but not among the creoles. With the deaths of Africans naturally outstripping creole births, the slave population had declined in the second and third decades of the century but began to show small signs of natural increase by 1838 (Higman 1976: 61–68). Mortality remained high, according to B. W. Higman: "Between 1829 and 1832 in Jamaica . . . 26,700 slaves died, while only 1,362 were manumitted, and 446 ran away" (1984: 379).

The many bitter questions over compensation to planters, treatment of freed slaves, and the effect of emancipation on the economy of the island cannot be dealt with here. Clearly, the breakup of slavery had a critical effect on the social attitudes of all classes and ethnic groups. The testimony of the apprentice James Williams (Text 16) hints at a new pride and sense of selfhood on the part of former slaves. Other texts from writers such as Richard Robert Madden and Phillippo affirm such a change. The implications for language behavior constitute a fascinating challenge to the linguist.

Full emancipation in 1838, therefore, set the scene for profound social and economic change in the island. Very few Africans were repatriated, and in some ways, everything seemed to remain the same: the island was still a monoculture devoted to sugar production, and the large plantations, with their workers' barracks and field gangs under busha's eye, survived. Studies of nineteenth-century Jamaica by Philip Curtin, Monica Schuler, B. W. Higman, Douglas Hall, and others offer data that might help to chart the possible trends of language development in this period, especially with regard to the internal movement of population and the formation of new communities and new patterns of family and fertility. The figures in Table 7 (Hall 1969: 265) contrast with those for the earlier nineteenth century in the trend they suggest toward natural increase.

Immigration now played little or no part in Jamaica's population structure, and the forces for language change must have reflected the internal social, ethnic, demographic, and psychological changes of a country coming to terms with a new order. At the most obvious level, certain linguistic influences must have declined and others increased. With the ending of the wars against the French, Jamaica ceased to garrison large numbers of troops or to provision many warships as it had during the twenty-five years of war. Soldiers' and sailors' talk, once commonplace in the country, became less and less familiar, surviving as phrases and half-forgotten expressions from a closed past. White servants brought in from the British Isles had ceased to be a feature of everyday life. Their places had largely

Table 7. Population of Jamaica, 1844

Blacks	361,657
Browns (coloreds)	68,259
Whites	ca. 38,000

been taken by the growing group of upper-working-class brown and black people.

From this period, also, the motives for interisland trade declined steadily. The transshipment of human cargo between the islands had officially ended, and with it much of the traffic between the islands ended too. Multilingualism declined, to be remembered dimly in the early twentieth century as an oddity of the ancestral past. Although Jamaica later supplied workers to Panama for the building of the canal; to settlements in Costa Rica; and to the sugar plantations of Cuba in the early twentieth century, the island received fewer immigrants from other parts of the Caribbean. It gradually became more Jamaican and less Caribbean in the late nineteenth century.

Even so, a few minor influences in this period are worth noting, largely for their effect on regional speech forms in different parts of Jamaica. People from Sierra Leone and Central Africa—as well as recaptives from the ships of slave-trading nations—came to Jamaica in response to the planters' demand for field labor (Schuler 1980: 68–69). Their numbers were small (about eight thousand in all between 1840 and 1864), but their influence (especially that of the Yoruba) was great in the areas where they settled, and can be traced today.

As Schuler (1980) and Joseph Graessle Moore (1983) have shown, St. Thomas-in-the-East is the focus of active African religious tradition in Jamaica, and Schuler demonstrates the influence of the midcentury African immigrants very effectively. Map 10 shows that the African indentured immigrants settled mainly in St. Thomas, with a few in the west of the island. The eastern settlements correspond roughly with those of the refugees from Hispaniola of half a century earlier, and it is significant that a religious chant in Ewe (Text 24) has been found there, inasmuch as Ewe is the language of *vodun*.

The translators of the chant, Vincent Odamtten and Abena Enyonam Agbley-Odamtten, point to archaic Ewe features in the text; Moore (1983) notes that the users of the chant define themselves as part African and part Maroon (see Text 24). The term *Nago* occurs in Westmoreland and St. Thomas as the name given to certain ethnic groups of African indentured workers and might well have included people of Ewe origin from Central

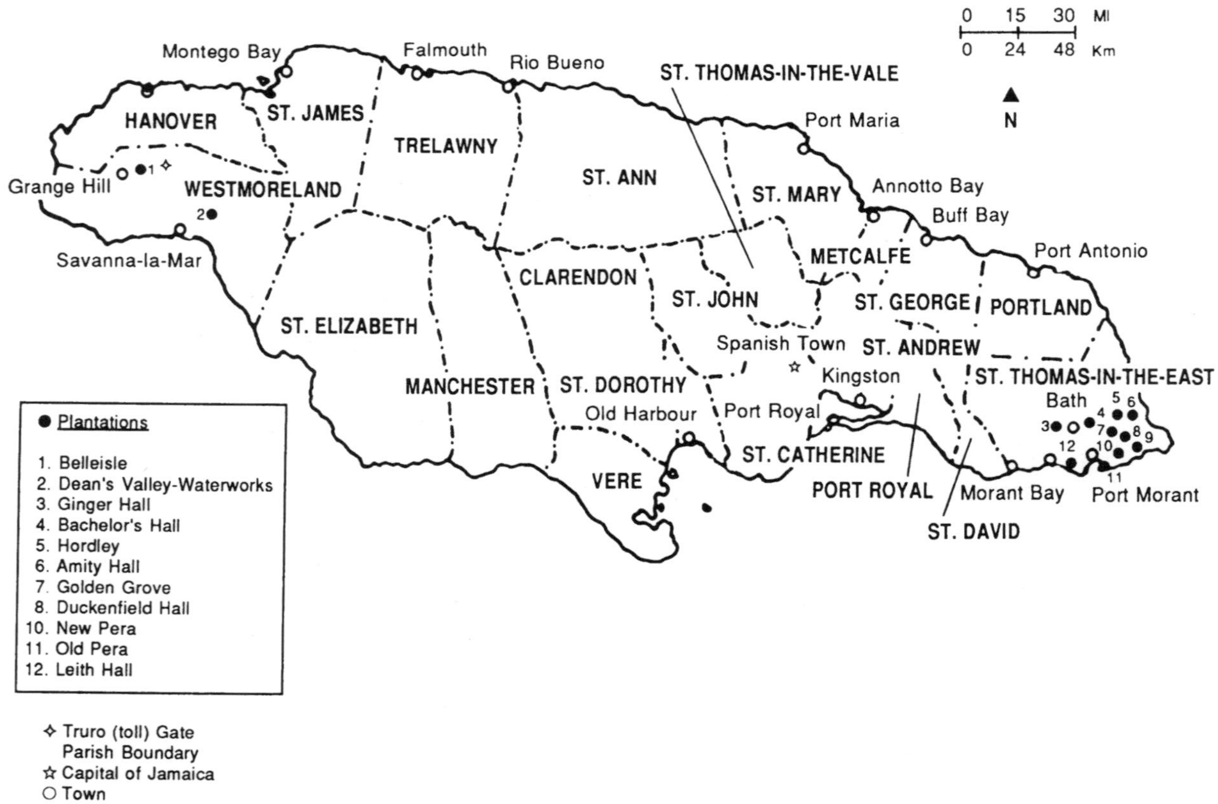

Map 10. Plantations Using African Indentured Labor in Jamaica, 1840–1865 (Schuler 1980: 49)

Map 11. German Settlements in Jamaica in the Nineteenth Century (after Drascher 1932)

Africa, the probable linguistic source of the chant (Monica Schuler, personal communication).

Therefore, as post-Emancipation Jamaica became more creole in many ways (that is, deculturated in African terms), it also became more African as the freed slaves formed their own social groups, pursued their lives after their own fashion, and chose between aspects of the cultures they knew. The influence of the myal man and the missionary left their mark on nineteenth-century Jamaica.

Another immigrant group that left its mark on regional usage consisted of some one thousand to fifteen hundred German colonists. These farm families settled in tiny communities (see Map 11). A high death rate and deculturation reduced the original group, but the survivors remained sufficiently isolated to preserve a recognizably German way of life until as late as the 1930s. Elizabeth Müller (1981: 30–31) reported that in 1945 "a child's prayer, typical of the time of the German immigration to Seaford Town was given to [her], almost word perfect but without any understanding of the text: 'Ich bin klein, / Min Herz ist rein / soll niemand drin wohnen / Als Jesus allein.' (I am small, / My heart is pure, / Nobody may live in it / But Jesus alone.)" For the most part, German influence (like that of the French, the Sierra Leonian, and the Congo groups) was one of reinforcement in lexicon and phonology. Other immigrant languages of the nineteenth century, such as Hindi, Chinese, and Lebanese Arabic, arrived too late to filter through the cultural barriers and consequently have left no mark on pre-twentieth-century records of Jamaican Creole.

A major change in the recording of JC, however, appears in the growing importance of native speakers among the recorders of the language. In the eighteenth century the work of Francis Williams alone survives to testify to the literacy of black Jamaicans, and his Latin verses are as far removed from the speech of the dockside, the plantation, and the street as it is possible to be. About a hundred years after Williams, the brown Jamaican Henry G. Murray not only made a name for himself as a performer of Jamaican-based dramatic readings but published his texts and so furnished later audiences with an insight into "the Manners and Customs of the country." In the succeeding chapter we will examine the nature of the texts that belong to the various stages of Jamaica's history—as fledgling colony, slave plantation, and new home to the descendants of exiles.

2

Source Materials

> A book is a life, and this
> White paper death,
> I roll it on the drum and write
> Rum-courage on my breath.
>
> Derek Walcott, "Greenwich Village, Winter"

Because Jamaican Creole grew out of folk usage and was thus an oral language, those who spoke it rarely wrote it down. Instead, most of its chroniclers were educated Britons who wrote in the metropolitan English of their times, employing a variety of genres, styles, and registers. In literary usage, JC can play an important part in dialogue, characterization, and setting. Fictional portraits of creole characters often reflect shifts in register as well as social variation. Similarly, different genres offer different perspectives on the creole speech of the time.

In this century collectors such as Walter Jekyll, Olive Lewin, and H. P. Jacobs have recorded the recollections of elderly and rural speakers. It is possible, using variants of tales and songs gleaned in this fashion, to reconstruct texts of earlier Jamaican Creole. Text 9, for example, the song "Quaco Sam," was reconstructed from variants derived from oral tradition and from widely distributed written fragments of the song.

The reconstruction of a single song, however, points up the complexity of the task facing anyone who attempts to document the history of Jamaican Creole. Our reconstructions of the oral tradition have therefore been supplemented by data from private collections and supported by material drawn from jottings in old newspapers and even from inscriptions on pottery (see Plate 3 in chapter 9).

Almost all surviving written records of Jamaican Creole, however, are scattered through substantial published works: histories, travelogues, journals, grammars, and novels; studies of African and creole character, of slavery, of obeah; commentaries on domestic manners; missionary records. Most of these works date no earlier than the last decade of the eighteenth century.

Such written sources present several difficulties. Many occurrences of creole speech are no more than fragmentary: a chance phrase that sounds quaint to its hearer; a word or two in the outlandish language of the slaves, used to add local color in a novel or travelogue; a vocabulary list or a memorable proverb. Several relatively recent texts record archaic proverbs in what must be seen as an older form of JC (Franck 1920: 425). Nineteenth-century collections such as Charles Rampini's and Thomas Banbury's include some proverbs that, by their very nature, illuminate usage of a generation earlier. Proverbs provide phonological information and some lexical data; they also yield some syntactic information, but such data is by its very nature circumscribed.

Where more substantial texts survive, other problems appear. A writer's unfamiliarity with the creole may cast doubt on the accuracy of the record. The writer's subjective attitude to JC and its speakers or interference from his or her own speech patterns may disrupt the accuracy of a text. Records of usage may be misleading because of an author's inclination to record the unusual rather than the truly representative. Some records may also be rendered more complex by the blending of historical changes with social variation. Influences from different periods of the language's history may complicate dating. Finally, the absence of a normalized spelling system for JC means that records must be analyzed and spelling patterns compared if the phonological structure is to be inferred.

An example of the difficulties inherent in recording and interpreting texts can be seen in a nineteenth-century polemic disguised as fiction. The anonymous author of *Marly; or, A Planter's Life in Jamaica* (1828) uses his characters as mouthpieces through which he gives his views on slavery and plantation economy. The experiences of the hero, Marly, are recounted with an ear for the quaint and unfamiliar (1828: 13): "When they thought he was beyond hearing, he heard one of them exclaim to the others, 'Eh! mosquitoes hab grandy nyamn on dat new buckra!' Marly being ignorant of the negro corrupted dialect, or the talkee talkee language, did not understand the expression."

Marly's embarrassment arises from the strangeness of his surroundings and from the reactions of the slaves. Their language is unintelligible and must be translated, but he is both interested in and resentful of their actual comments. If one assumes that the novel is partly autobiographical and that the hero's growing understanding of Jamaican life and language reflects that of the writer, one must still question the writer's competence in recording a language strange to him. The linguistic alienation of Marly may have been shared by his creator. Yet features identical to those in the creole sentence just quoted occur widely in other texts.

In his *Etymology of Jamaica Grammar* (1868), Thomas Russell makes two important claims that set him well ahead of other nineteenth- and twentieth-century evaluators of JC. He notes that despite its "corrupted" origins, JC functions according to "certain fixed rules." Although he uses the conventional English grammatical rules as his framework of analysis, he also observes that JC possesses "certain plain and distinct [rules], which are, in not a few instances, in direct opposition to those of the pure parent language." Russell's little work consists mainly of word lists and sentences arranged according to different grammatical categories. Like any of his contemporaries, Russell assumes that JC is merely a "corruption" of a "pure" language, and he ends his book with a warning that any attempt to analyze JC syntax may bring one to the brink of madness. So even a publication aimed specifically at recording and commenting on Jamaican speech preserves mainly fragmentary expressions selected, from all appearances, primarily for their strangeness.

Occasionally such fragments run to a few sentences, and grammatical structure alone is preserved. However, even such linguistic patterns as may emerge lack the supportive data necessary to analysis; the problems of fragmentation lie deeper than the superficial question of length. Fragments are often highly personal or specific in reference. They apply to particular situations and are addressed in registers exactly appropriate to these situations: the saying of a grace before a meal (Jacobs, unpublished notes); a reference to airing one's clothes as the "keeping of the passover" (Hamley 1862: 187); a greeting between friends with the assertion that the "heatment is very greatment" (Rampini 1873: 27). Such expressions are recalled because they are unusual. Therefore, while they may preserve interesting features of social variation, they cannot be termed representative of any demonstrable level of Jamaican usage.

In such examples, social variation or shifts of register may be indistinct from historical changes. The speech of a brown woman recorded by J. B. Moreton (1793: 130–31) displays known structures of the archaic language, together with others less familiar. The stressing of vowels in word-final position, the reduction of initial consonantal clusters and changes like [v] > [b] or [đ] > [d] are also unsurprising, but the appearance of *garl* rather than *gyal* may startle those familiar with modern JC and raise questions of authenticity or of social variation versus historical change.

Clearly specialized are the captions that accompany caricatures and sketches. Antislavery drawings like those lampooning West Indian luxury preserve minute scraps of JC. The "Black Man's Lub Song" (circa 1832), quite a long ditty, refers closely to the Reform Bill. It draws heavily on educated English usage, which is mingled with JC to produce a comically stilted, almost macaronic diction. The self-consciousness of such pieces suggests that the authors must have had command of acrolectal Jamaican speech and some acquaintance with JC.

Yet despite problems of destruction, dispersal, and fragmentation, substantial examples of JC have survived. These include lengthy songs and tales, sermons and prayers, speeches in self-defense, conversations, and miraculously enough, even letters. Tales, songs, and monologues may occur in uninterrupted JC. Dialogues and anecdotes frequently include educated English usage because of the context of the larger text in which they are embedded. Letters—often hypercorrect in usage—show the JC writer attempting to use the acrolect and to resist the basilect. These different genres are peculiarly related to the historical and social framework of Jamaica.

Linguistically, the songs are perhaps the most conservative in that they trap and preserve archaic features in rhyme and rhythm. Moreton's song (Text 4) reflects the influence of West African phonotaxis through the occurrence of intrusive vowels: "Hipsaw! my deaa! You no do like a-me." Similarly, British dialect features such as [v] > [w] and such JC archaisms as [f] ~ [p] variation survive side by side, entangled by restrictions of rhyme scheme in "The Woodpecka" (Text 11.C). An Early Modern English pronunciation of *yeye* may be implied by its place in the rhyme scheme of "Hi, De Buckra, Hi!" where it is paired with "sea" and "me" (but see Text 10.B and headnote). The stress patterns of *obisha*, the intermediate form between SE *overseer* and JC *busha*, are implied in verse (Moreton 1793: 153).

Songs tend to resist change and are therefore more clearly applicable to a specific historical context, provided that some term of reference can be found either within the text or in some comment by the writer. The dating of "Quaco Sam" is assisted by references to the whip and to the Regency period; by the term *dandy*, in vogue during the period 1813–1819 and retaining in JC its connotations of fashion; and by mention of dance movements such as the *shay-shay*, "sashay," a movement in the quadrille (see Text 9). The song for Captain Crow (Text 5) is dated in his *Memoirs* by the captain himself. Matthew G. Lewis (1834: 322) identifies the "massa" of one of the songs he preserves as Bedward of Spring Garden Estate, providing us with a historical reference not only for this particular song but for features of the Annancy tale "Dry-Bone." Recorded by Jekyll (1907: 48–51), the tale repeats a fragment of the song "Carry Him Along" (Jacobs 1972: 9; *Short Journey* 1790: 106; and Stewart 1808: 225).

On the other hand, the tales are far more subject to linguistic change than the songs, although many are quite as old. Such change is of course a problem common to any orally transmitted material. Brief, mnemonic items like proverbs or expressions preserved in verse structure are less susceptible than longer, looser pieces in which discourse can be changed at the whim of the narrator. Still, one may find—even in the tales—traditional formulas quite rigidly preserved. In very old tales the speech of particular characters often displays archaisms that have been lost to the rest of the text. A distinction between the narrator's voice and those of his characters may correspond largely to a difference between the language current at the time of recording and that of an older form preserved in folk tradition. In other words, features that appear to be stylistic differences associated with characterization may actually reflect historical differences in the language.

In many ways the tales are inconvenient to handle as historical records even where a topical reference is available. The problem is largely one of dating. No one can say how far back into the past the individual linguistic features should be traced. It is not clear when the most recent ones were adopted or how many of the original patterns were modified by the superimposition and mingling of features drawn from later stages of the language. The Annancy story provides a classic example. Annancy himself uses distinctive speech patterns, the "bungo talk" of the folk hero, which includes a high frequency of Africanisms (such as *dirty* < Twi *dɔté*) and archaic JC features like [r] ~ [j] variation in *b'ute,* "brute" (Text 6). The consonant [r] was relatively infrequent in Twi and cognate languages. Annancy's syntax also preserves obvious acrolectal features in his flattery of Tiger ("as you are such a big man") alongside archaic JC features such as the "so . . . so" relational clauses: "One day Annancy an' Bro'er Tiger go a river fe wash 'kin. Annancy said to Bro'er Tiger: —'Bro'er Tiger, as you are such a big man, if you go in a de blue hole with you fat you a go drownded, so you fe take out your fat so lef' it here'" (Jekyll 1907: 7).

Other familiar characters—Tiger, Ratta, and Tacoma, for example—may show fewer conservatisms, yet their speech may still contrast with that of the narrator. Of course, one narrator follows another, and features are lost or introduced as the language evolves, yet certain important terms or phrases from the original may well be faithfully kept. The narrators' changes and additions add to the historical complexity of the tale. Topical references may be added and retained even when their significance is no longer clear, as is the case of Mr. Winkler (Jekyll 1907: 48–51). A storyteller may embellish or standardize the narrative for the benefit of a writer who is present to record the tale. Again, the recorder's own speech patterns may intrude and be indistinguishable from the rest. Yet with all this, the extant tales seem unified to a modern reader: chronological variations are reinterpreted as idiosyncracies and absorbed into characterization. In such texts, the problems of dating individual features are practically insoluble.

Other monologues survive apart from the tales. There are orations by creole speakers made before white audiences composed of judges and juries, missionaries and planters, visitors from England. The occasions of these orations vary in formality and urgency, but whether an audience is black or white, the creole orator yields to the situational pressure to embellish his speech, adjusting it toward the acrolect. Several examples survive of quite lengthy discourses made in self-defense. Delivered in the presence of administrative and legal authorities, these are motivated by a desire to impress and persuade.

Comparable to defenses are the extended prayers recorded by missionaries. In both genres we encounter a special register: the language of petition aimed at an authority of immeasurable power ("O dow great and blessed God," Text 14.C). In these prayers, hypercorrect creole mingles with biblical expressions and archaic diction drawn from formal prayers of the seventeenth and eighteenth centuries.

In contrast to defenses and prayers, the sermons tend to reflect the speakers' sense of their own authority. Ebenezer's sermon on the afterlife (Text 10.A) is delivered in creole free of hypercorrection and marked by few acrolectal features. The speaker is unaware of his white observer, who has hidden in the servants' quarters so as to record the speech. However, another sermon recorded by Williams (1826: 105–6) shows a more even admixture of acrolectal and basilectal Jamaican speech. No doubt this mingling is reinforced by a conflict between the writer's native usage and the creole spoken by his source, a servant who reports this sermon to him. It is equally possible that a house servant might command a register approaching educated English usage. The monologues are useful, however, in preserving long stretches of a speaker's idiolect.

Unlike the orations (which seem to form rather a unified group in terms of social register), the dialogues recorded by early writers vary widely. There are differences of context, of social class of the speaker, and of the topics under discussion. A slave in a religious setting expresses himself in a widely different register from that which he uses when confined in the stocks.

Apart from these written records of mainly verbatim material, there exist fictional works, largely in educated English usage, which include JC dialogue. As imaginative pieces these works must be approached with caution. Their JC features are at best renditions by the educated writer of a second language with which he is familiar. At worst they may be a jumble of partially familiar creolisms, nonstandard forms, and deliberately incorrect English structures. In other words, writers who begin on the assumption that the creole is indeed "broken English" may attempt to represent JC by arbitrarily distorting English patterns. They may supplement their inventions with expressions familiar in American Black English or may draw on stereotyped expressions popularly conceived of as pidgin. Such a usage may be found in the "blackamoor language" of the English theater, a lingo that would have been familiar to educated writers. Finally, the writer may ornament the dialogue with a few characteristically Jamaican terms. Such may be the explanation of the following speech by Chakra the obeah man in Mayne Reid's *Maroon* (1862): "You sabbey ole Chakra? you know he *myal-man?* Doan care who know *now*—so long dey b'lieve um dead. . . . Dey no kill *him,* nebber! Neider de white folk nor de brack folk" (Text 20.A).

Certain of the unusual features in this passage may well be genuine archaisms unattested in other texts. For example, *brack* may be the result of lambdacism; *braka* in modern Maroon usage gives credibility to Reid (Bilby 1983: 72 and chap. 6). If so, can *glass snake* (Text 20.A) be equivalent to *grass snake* elsewhere? Even if the solution is lambdacism, is it based on actual observation of JC structure? Is it applicable to the particular item in which it occurs or is it little more than a lucky guess on the basis of stereotypes current at that time? Some novelists, of course, display familiarity with the language and an understanding intimate enough to allow for social and situational variation in speech among Jamaican characters. The idiolects of William Hamley's protagonists in *Captain Clutterbuck's Champagne,* for example, are consistent and credible, and Hamley's attention to language is so detailed as to indicate nuances of vowel quality not apparent in other texts.

As distinct from records of spoken JC, there survive a few letters actually written down by creole speakers. Rampini (Text 22) records seven love letters written in the early 1860s, and two decades earlier, Phillippo records two letters (Texts 14.A and B). Both sets reveal the creole background of their writers and the inadequately grasped acrolect to which they aspire. Linguistic insecurity is more marked in the love letters than in other genres and arises directly from the writers' association of "high," standard usage with the act of writing. Very derivative in form and diction, the letters plainly draw on the kind of model letters popular in the Victorian era, as F. G. Cassidy suggests (personal communication). The writers' poor education and their need to use a flowery style add to their uncertainty. The pressure of the oral tradition is apparent in spontaneous expressions such as, "Lard! I wish I never been barn. Poor me Garg!" But such shifts are constantly juxtaposed to a self-conscious style aimed at elegance: "I is wrote you a letter to beg of you to make me your lover but you is not wrote me again. It is with a perplexing heart of anxiety that I take up pen" (Text 22). In such letters, constructions that are neither English nor JC are imposed on sentences that elsewhere display the grammatical and phonological patterns of both languages.

Although these letters are not generally representative of creole structure, they preserve linguistic information because archaic creole features persist even in the speech of literate blacks determined to exchange their language for the prestige form. Other letters show a closer approximation to the standard. One, preserved by Richard Robert Madden (1835: 136–37), betrays few JC features. Not only is it largely Standard English, but as the writer himself reveals, it is the product of a mind educated in the established literary tradition of classical Arabic. The letter abounds in complex sentences, informed images, and carefully selected and ordered autobiographical details. Its writer, Abū Bakr al-Ṣiddīq, came from a highly educated family and was himself a student of Arabic letters when captured and sold into slavery. Contrasting with other letters, this text raises the question of how Jamaicans of this period may have adjusted their usage to fit a particular genre.

The fact that the texts vary in genre and in social context is important to historical analysis. All the synchronic variation exists within a chronological range of under two centuries. At first sparse and fragmented, the records gradually become more numerous toward the end of the period with the rise of social interest in the slaves as human beings.

Before interpreting the linguistic data gathered from within this range, we must resolve a number of difficulties. Classification either by chronology or by social variation remains problematic because of JC's continuing relationship to the official language, English, itself a living, changing form. In such circumstances, the dating of texts becomes difficult and at times impossible, for features derived from different diachronic stages of the language are continually superimposed. Phonological analysis must be attempted in the presence of an idiosyncratic and often amateur spelling system. Standard and nonstandard English dialectal features appear mixed with the creole because the writer's language intrudes or because the creole speaker switches register. These shifts reinforce difficulties in historical interpretation.

Consequently, social, chronological, regional, and generic variation become entangled as different British dialects and African languages influence the creole at different stages. The variety of the language also depends on context. Material pertaining to obeah practices may preserve more archaic features than records dealing with biblical events. The varied self-interest of the missionary, the antiabolitionist, and the slave trader permitted each to render a version of JC suited to a theme and an audience, and unregarding of the realities of the creole.

Because of such considerations, each piece must be examined individually in its own, almost unique context. Out of these difficulties of interpretation arise problems for the evaluator of such textual material. The usefulness of one text against another may be clear on one level of linguistic analysis but hazy on another; the accuracy of a record will depend on the nature and extent of interference between JC and other language structures. Equally important will be the motivation and hence the credibility of the writer and the length and degree of his or her involvement in the JC speech community.

Possibly no single text so well exemplifies the difficulties of assessment as *Manners and Customs of the Country a Generation Ago: Tom Kittle's Wake* (Murray 1877, extract, Text 17). In the first place, we conjecture an approximate date of 1844 on the basis of the date under the writer's preface (1869) and the writer's identification of the episode as belonging to a generation earlier. But *Tom Kittle's Wake* is a long and varied piece.

Its frame is a narrative in educated English of the later nineteenth century in which occur occasional hints of local pronunciation. This narrative is interrupted by fragments of JC, most of which cannot be isolated from the English frame without destroying their context. Of these fragments, the speeches and dialogues probably represent nineteenth-century JC, while the songs and tales may be more archaic. The obsolete features of one short song renders it mostly unintelligible to speakers of modern JC (see Text 17; also D'Costa and Lalla 1989: Text 20 and note).

Where the writer is less familiar with the language, our assessment becomes still more complex. Murray was a brown Jamaican and bidialectal, possessing an intimate knowledge of JC and a deep interest in it. In contrast, Captain Hugh Crow is distanced because of his background, his occupation and motives as a slave trader, and the remoteness of his situation from that in which intimate conversation with creole speakers is likely to have occurred. Yet Crow records unmistakable JC features, although they are affected by educated English usage. More interesting still are Crow's records of conversations between him and the King of Bonny (see Chapter 6).[1] Here, several features now familiar in JC emerge in the king's speech alongside others unfamiliar today, absent from other texts, and never repeated elsewhere by Crow. Significantly, some of these recall the compounding characteristic of pidgin (*big rogue man*); *good-belly pigeon* in the archaic tale of Mudfish and Watchman provides an interesting parallel. As distinct from such usage, Crow notes the creole speech of slaves whom he claims to have transported and for whom, therefore, JC must be an acquired rather than native language (1830: 128–29). The relationship of Guinea Coast Creole English to JC will be considered in subsequent chapters.

Such is the range of the sources and such the more obvious problems that attend them (Lalla 1979; cf. Jacobs 1945; Hancock 1977). Once we have passed the difficulties of layering, of interference from the writer's usage of written and spoken English, and of interpreting the writer's biases and intentions, however, we must admit that the implications of such records for our understanding of creole language history are enormous. The records document the variety of creole speech at different stages of its development. But before an interpretation of the language structure can be attempted, the material has to be read and the visual symbols correlated to linguistic systems. Far more subtle than many of the problems of fragmentation and ambiguity in dating are those of spelling inconsistency. There is, after all, no normalized system of orthography; most of the writers appear to make spontaneous decisions about how to represent creole sounds. However, a systematic analysis of these efforts must be attempted before the sound system of the creole can be understood, just as an interpretation of the historical and social background of Jamaica must provide a setting for linguistic analysis.

3

Reconstructing the Sound System

So yuh a de man me hear bout!
Ah yuh dem seh dah teck
Whole heap a English oat seh dat
Yuh gwine kill dialec!

Meck me get it straight, Mas Charlie,
For me no quite understan—
You gwine kill all English dialec
Or jus Jamaica one?
Louise Bennett, "Bans a Killin"

The phonological structure of early Jamaican Creole can be inferred only after detailed orthographical analysis. Such analysis is complicated by the problems that writers of the eighteenth and nineteenth centuries would have encountered in their efforts to set down an oral, nonstandard language that partially overlapped with their own. Early texts show that different writers made very different attempts at spelling the creole. The differing strategies of monolinguals, of native bilinguals, and of nonnative bilinguals in writing down a language, reflect the orthographical problems caused by differing language backgrounds. Differences in social class and regional origin must have affected the writers' interpretation and representation of the creole they heard.[1]

The creole they encountered was uncodified, unlike contemporary written English, which had acquired fixed conventions by the late eighteenth century. Then as now, however, English spelling allowed many alternative symbols for single sounds (e.g., "ie," "ea," "ee" in *grief, beat,* and *sleep*). Such variety does not help an English writer attempting to record JC. Unsurprisingly, eighteenth- and nineteenth-century texts abound with spelling variants that may or may not represent differences in pronunciation. The difficulties can be clearly observed by a glance at the range of forms possible for JC equivalents to English "negro." No less than thirteen forms occur: *nega*, *neger*, *negar*, *negur*, *neegar*, *neaga*, *nigger*, *nigga*, *niggar*, *niggah*, *naga*, *naygar*, *nagur*. Modern JC commonly uses [niega] or [nega], and *DJE* notes that the "influence of Sp *negro*, Fr *nègre*, Du *neger* in the Caribbean area may have contributed to the retention of this older sound." In using such variants the recorders may have unwittingly represented etymologically distinct forms.

Not only do different writers represent the sound patterns of JC in varying ways, but even within the work of a single author inexplicable shifts occur. A lack of understanding of JC structure, intrusion of English features, and simple carelessness born of contempt all affected spelling and must be taken into account in order to reconstruct phonological patterns. The writer's origin, education, grasp of languages and dialects, social class, and associated social dialect may affect his or her orthographical representation of JC. Besides, the actual ability to write the oral language systematically seems highly variable. One writer includes only a few local words and characteristic grammatical structures; another attempts a more precise rendition that indicates consonant changes like [θ] > [t] and [v] > [b]; yet another goes farther still to reflect details of vocalic pronunciation in *weaste* and *soart*. Some appear to achieve a systematic relationship between JC sounds and written symbols; others appear to make arbitrary and rather inconsistent choices of representation. In either case the writer's involvement with educated English almost certainly intrudes.

Such intrusions may be conscious or unconscious. It is clear that the writer cannot avoid using English conventions in spelling English-based words. The orthography of the official language is a nonlinguistic factor that influences the spelling of creole words (Hall 1966: 45–48; cf. Hancock 1977). It is not unreasonable for English orthographical practices to influence the spelling of JC, of course. Had eighteenth- and nineteenth-century writers attempted to avoid Standard English spelling, they could only have alienated their readers, most of whom would have been unfamiliar with JC.

On the other hand, some writers capitalized on the distinctiveness of JC from familiar English forms to develop setting and characterization and to heighten humor, sensationalism, and mood. As motives for recording the creole vary, so does its representation.

Different genres (and, within them, different registers) plainly elicited different orthographical effects. Dialogues sometimes display persistent hypercorrection because of Massa's presence. Tales may preserve highly deviant forms in the speech of a few select protagonists. Songs may reveal unusual patterns of hyphenation (for instance), in order to indicate their meter. Each shifting glimpse allows further insight into the phonological system of JC.

All of these problems in interpretation arise from the very real difficulties inherent in representing an oral, creole language. A phonemic orthography, providing a distinct sign for each significant sound, is frequently the practical and scientific choice for providing a spelling system (see Voorhoeve 1959: 436–45; Carrington 1971). Frederic Cassidy and Robert LePage (1961: 22) find a straightforward phonemic spelling ideal for a language never yet written down and only distantly related to any other language. They point out, however, that such a system is not the answer for JC, even today, because of its relationship to English dialects and their entrenched spelling systems and because of the occurrence of the creole in written records during the past two hundred years. The writers lacked a system they could follow. Contradictions were therefore inevitable not only between but within their documents. They might be aware that JC varied but might be unable to distinguish among the variants. They might be unfamiliar with the basilect. Almost certainly, most were unaware that structural differences between the creole and the standard frequently rendered the archaic spelling system of English inappropriate. SE orthography was the only familiar spelling system, so the writer was forced either to use it and misrepresent the creole or to ignore it and be unintelligible.

The fact is that most of the JC lexicon is drawn from English. It is therefore logical to retain the existing and universally familiar standard spellings for these items where pronunciation in English and JC is identical (e.g., *night*). Where limited but obvious differences occur, the educated writer modifies only that part of the word that reflects exclusively JC usage (e.g., *Garamighty* vs. *God Almighty*). So all words, including those of non-English origin (e.g., JC *say* < Twi *sé*) are respelled according to English conventions. As SE spelling is historical rather than phonemic (preserving long-lost features of early English), it hardly serves as an efficient orthography for English words reinterpreted according to West African sound laws, let alone providing a system for lexemes dependent on a very different phonology. Some writers, facing the conflict between SE spelling and an alien phonology, solve the problem by creating exotic orthographies so as to draw attention to the feature in question. Walter Jekyll produces "é" (*whé fe do*); William Hamley writes "ny" in *nyoung lady*; and J. B. Moreton spells JC *nyam* as *knaum*.

Even having accepted the necessity for some system that reflects the actual sound structure of JC, writers still differ on the question of how closely pronunciation is to be represented. In modern linguistic terms, the question is whether a broad or narrow transcription should be the basis of representation. Normally the broad transcription is chosen. Spelling systems are created on the basis of the native speakers' recognition of significant (contrastive) sound features in the language. Features that may not be significantly distinctive in JC, however, may well exist in the standard.

Ultimately, orthographical analysis involves a study of all the possible relationships of each graphic symbol to the sound structure of the language. In order to establish such relationships, one must identify all allographs and determine how they are conditioned. The areas of overlap between the graphemes must also be determined, for it is clear that several are used interchangeably. No exhaustive orthographical survey can be made in the space of this discussion, but certain important correspondences between sound and symbol must be established so as to assist the reader in approaching the texts.

Suprasegmentals are not indicated in records of JC any more than in written English. For example, the word *object* can be recognized only by its context as verb or noun, and by the structural markers of the sentence. Similarly, a notable crux arises in *Macbeth* I.vii.60 because of an inadequacy in English orthography to indicate patterns of intonation and stress. In early JC texts some features appear to be indicated by hyphenation but little else is done to indicate suprasegmentals (Thomas Russell alone makes a valiant attempt to indicate sentence melody). A noun formed by doubling the verb form, *yam-yamme,* probably contained the ʼ̀ stress patterns of an English compound. The unusual hyphenation of "you no wind like a-me" (rather than "like-a me") may indicate a disturbance of normal juncture in the rhythm of the song as well as the writer's ignorance of West African syllable structure. *Y-o-n-d-e-r,* on the other hand, seems to reflect extremes in quantity, probably for emphasis.

Doubling of vowel graphs in JC appears to be associated with quantity though it probably also denotes features of quality such as vowel height. Thus "ee" and "y" in final position for [i] appear to be in free variation, replaced at times with "ie" where the preceding syllable has "ee" (hence *eerie* and *yeerie*). What appears to be free variation between double or single graphs for vowel sounds is also indicated as in *dee* and *de* ("they") and *fee* and *fe* ("for").

We have no reason to suppose that doubling of consonant letters reflects lengthening of consonant sounds in JC any more than in modern English. Indeed there often appears to be free variation between single and double graphs. Some texts show *nebber* and others *neber* ("never"), and in one both *fuss* and *fus* ("first") are recorded. It seems that such a doubling frequently indicated a preceding short vowel as it may in SE. Hence JC *robuss, lilly, libba, saccomstance, togeddar, youseff.* In addition, doubling frequently seems to compensate for what an educated English speaker might interpret as an omission of a consonant. The fact that the [d], [t] or even [ř] that replace English [đ] and [θ] are often written as double does not conflict with this tendency, since educated writers associate the sounds [đ] and [θ] with the digraph "th" and persistently represent these sound changes as involving omissions, by use of the apostrophe as in *Deat'* and *t'ought*.

Use of the apostrophe itself varies. Some writers utilize it extensively to denote elided vowels or syllables (*'tate*, "estate"; *'blige*, "oblige"; *'member*, "remember"); syncopation (*p'raps*, *'spose*); deletion of initial [h] (*'andsome*); and simplification of consonantal clusters (*'corn*, *'trike*, *sen'*). Apart from indicating such omissions, the apostrophe is also used to indicate actual sound changes mistakenly interpreted as omissions (e.g., *sa'*, "say"; *cravin'* and *t'row*). On the other hand many writers represent such features without apostrophe, as in *blong*. Others use it apparently randomly: *ha't* ("heart"), but *geen* ("green"), *cull'd* ("curled") but *ollow* ("hollow"). To dispense with these variants would be to deny the heterogeneous and almost exclusively oral nature of the language.

The correspondences we shall note, therefore, cannot be consistently applied to each text. They represent merely the sounds that certain letters or ranges of letters generally represent in early records.

Consonants

In order to assess the influence of English in early JC phonology, one must compare the creole not with present-day RP but with EModE, nonstandard British dialects, and other contact varieties of English (see Chapter 6).

In the early seventeenth century, the consonants of English were similar to those of today, except that [x] still survived from Old English and [ž] had not yet arrived from French (Chart 1; see also Gill 1971; Dobson 1968, 2.379). The major difference between EModE and modern SE lies in the distribution of sounds and in the variation acceptable in polite usage. Thus the occurrence of [w] after stops was polite eighteenth-century English usage and survives today in JC phonology (*gwine*, "going"). Similarly, the palatalization of stops before front vowels was quite automatic in British English at that time and occurred in Scots dialect up to the first decades of this century, so much so that eighteenth- and nineteenth-century writers of JC fail to distinguish [gj] and [kj] from [g] and [k], although modern writers naturally do so. Hence nineteenth-century records show *gal/garl* where twentieth-century records show *gyal*.

Such conservative features in JC may have been strengthened by their survival in nonstandard dialects that maintained intimate contact with JC. The occurrence of [w] after stops, for example, was frequent in Scottish and northern English pronunciation. Other features such as lambdacism

Chart 1. English Consonants: Early Seventeenth Century

	Labial	Labio-dental	Dental	Alveolar	Alveo-palatal	Palatal	Velar	Glottal
Fricatives								
Voiceless		f	θ	s		š	x	h
Voiced		v	đ	z				
Stops and affricates								
Voiceless	p			t	č	[kj]	k	
Voiced	b			d	ǰ	[gj]	g	
Oral resonants								
Median	w			ř		j		
Lateral				l				
Nasals	m			n			ŋ	

often occur in pidgins and creoles. The [θ] > [t], [đ] > [d] substitution was common in Irish English: "De books are here: dat one is yours and dis is mine" (Joyce 1910: 2–3). Alan Bliss (1979: 189) discusses the complications for writers attempting to represent Hiberno-English dental stops:

> The consonant /θ/ does not occur in Irish, and the speaker of pure Hiberno-English renders it by the pure dental stop /T/; . . . the English-speaker is likely to interpret this /T/ as /t/. . . . Thus, though /θ/ and /t/ are hardly ever confused in Hiberno-English, the English-speaking listener may think that they are, and may use the symbol /t/ to represent the Hiberno-English articulation of both.

In the Jamaican situation, Irish usage must have added to the range of possible variants for the interdental fricatives.

P. W. Joyce also notes other features familiar in JC: the palatalization of [d + u], as in "Juke of Wellington"; svarabhakti in medial consonant clusters (e.g., *ferrum* for "firm"; note *feril,* "fern" in *DJE*); and the diphthongization of [o] before [-lt#], [-ld#], or [-rd#] as in *cowlt,* ("colt"), *cowld* ("cold"), *foord* ("ford") (Joyce 1910: 95–99). Single items such as *chaw* ("chew"), *ketch* ("catch") (Joyce 1910: 101) and *Caatholick* (Bliss 1979: 353) testify to the influence of Irish speakers on JC.

Some features of JC, quite unfamiliar in English of any period, are traceable back to West African sources (e.g., [ɲ] in *nyam*). West African influence may have reinforced some feature present in British English and encouraged its survival in JC long after it had disappeared from the standard (e.g., [#gj-]). However, many features familiar in West African languages have not become established in JC. Coarticulated stops appear in Johann Christaller's full table of Twi consonants and in Mervyn C. Alleyne's reconstruction of a phonological system for early Afro-American dialects, but if these or the prenasalized stops survived at all in early JC, they were only vestigial (note *congo saw, conconsa* < Twi *ŋkoŋkonsá* and *bakra, bacceroes* < Twi *mbakára*).

In early JC texts, voiced and voiceless stops are normally distinct but some variation is permitted between them. Variation between articulatory positions also occurs, as in the [t] > [k] change in *likle.* Affrication is usually significant but there is some fluctuation between affricates and fricatives (*wich,* "wish"; *witch/wish,* "which"), and affricates and stops (*codreel/catchreel,* "quadrille"). Palatalization may well have been conditioned at first but eventually becomes distinctive. Prenasalized stops cannot be inferred from the texts, but there is a tendency for nasals to be homorganic with stops that follow them (e.g., *sunting*).

There are far fewer fricatives in JC than stops; in fact the creole shows a

Chart 2. The Consonants of Nineteenth-Century Twi (with the exception of the coarticulated sounds)

	Labial	Labio-dental	Alveolar	Palatal	Velar	Glottal
Fricatives *Voiceless* *Voiced*		f ~ [p]	s ~ [š]	~ ç	[x] ~	h
Stops and affricates *Voiceless* *Voiced*	p b		t ~ [ts] d ~ [dz]	kj ~ ǵj ~	k ǵ	
Oral resonants	w		ř ~ [l] < [d]	j		
Nasals	m		n	ɲ	ŋ	

(See Christaller 1933: xvii; and 1964: 4.)

marked tendency to replace fricatives in the English-based lexicon with stops or affricated stops. Thus [θ] > [t], [đ] > [d], and [v] > [b] occur regularly, and [f] > [p], [s] or [š] > [č] and [ž] > [ǰ], less frequently. Those that are normally absent or infrequent in the creole are those that are absent or that vary in phonemic status in the influential African languages (Fante, Ewe, Twi).

The consonants of nineteenth-century Twi show clear similarities to early JC, especially among the fricatives (Chart 2). In addition, nonstandard English dialects and contact varieties of English would have reinforced the avoidance of dental sounds. Several pidgins and creoles substitute [ɸ] and [β] for [f] and [v]. Again, as in early JC and some English dialects, such as East Yorkshire,[2] initial [h] is often dropped.

Among the resonants there is extensive variation, again linked to phonological patterns in the West African languages and to those in EModE and nonstandard English ([j] ~ [ɲ], [n] ~ [ŋ]). There is also some fluctuation among the nasals and between nasals and homorganic stops (*bin*/*min*). The variation of [l] and [r] (see Table 10) is not only influenced by West African sound laws but may have been reinforced by the correspondence of Portuguese [r] to Spanish [l] (e.g., *branco* and *blanco*).

Throughout the consonant system, widespread fluctuation can be traced between significantly distinct sounds and between others that appear to have been nonsignificant and conditioned, such as the intervocalic alveolar stop and the flap, [d] > [ř]. That this variation is so widespread naturally reinforces the belief that the creole is unstructured and that differences from SE are errors. In fact, the extant texts suggest that the fluctuation itself is highly structured and occurs within certain linguistic constraints. Fluctuation between voiced and voiceless pairs, for example, seems to occur only among noncontinuants. Interaction between stops and fricatives may appear sporadic in recent creole speech, but continued

Chart 3. The Afro-American Consonant System Reconstructed by Alleyne (1980: 76)

kp ~ kw	p	t	tj	k	
gb ~ gw	b	d	dj	g	
	mb	nd	ñdj	ŋg	
	m	n	ñ		
	f	s ~ s	j		
		l ~ r			
	w		j		h

influence from educated English has introduced sounds like [v] into modern JC. Originally only [f] and [s] appear to have been well-established fricatives in JC, and even these could be replaced by stops or affricated stops close to them in articulatory position (e.g., [p] and [č]). Alleyne (1980: 76) reconstructs the earliest consonant system of Afro-American

Table 8. Jamaican Creole Stops

JC Sounds	Variants	Examples	Spelling	History
/b/	[b] < [v]	sa*be*/sa*bby*, de*bb*il, ne*bb*er, gi*b*, *b*ittle/*v*ittle	"b", "bb" ("v" rare)	EModE /b/ and /v/ Engl. dialect [v] ~ [b] Engl. 17th-c. nautical dial [v] > [b]
	SE/v/> ∅	(gie "give")		Twi—no /v/
/p/		*p*an/*f*an, lea*p*/lea*f*, '*p*on/u*pp*on, o*p*e, fi*pp*ence	"p", "pp"	<EModE /p/ and (rarely) EModE /f/ Twi [f] ~ [p]
/d/		fa*d*a, *d*em, toge*dd*er	"d", "dd"	< EModE /d/ and /đ/ Engl. dialectal [đ] > [d]
	[d] < [đ] occas.	*d*ere–*th*ere	("th" rare)	
	or SE /đ/ > ∅	bra ("brother")		In West Africa /đ/ rare.
	[ř] intervocalic	ga*r*amighty, bra*r*	"r"	Engl. dial. [ř]; Twi [r̃] ~ [d], Ewe [ɖ].
/t/		*t*anks, Me*tt*odis/ Me*t*ody, no*tt*ing	"t", "tt"	EModE /t/ and /θ/. In Engl. dialects frequently [θ] > [t] and [θ] rare in West Africa

dialects and represents it as in Chart 3. Again, variation between such pairs as [s] and [š], or [r] and [l], was probably originally conditioned in JC, especially in the basilect. Fluctuation, then, appears to have been a characteristic of Jamaican speech, but the consonants fall into clear categories and variation occurs within structural constraints.

Table 8. (*Continued*)

JC Sounds	Variants	Examples	Spelling	History
	[ř] intervocalic	wha*rr*a, "what" da*r*a, "that"	"r", "rr"	as above, /d/
/g/		*g*aramighty, ne*g*a/ni*gg*a/ ne*gg*ar	"g", "gg"	< EModE /g/
	possibly [gj]	*g*al/*g*arl (19th c.) but *gy*al (Mod. JC)	not attested	<18th c. British [gj] before [a] and [a:]. Twi [gj] before front vowels
/k/		li*k*e, *c*orpion, pi*cc*anniny/pi*ck*inniny, sa*cc*omstance, fa*ck*, condu*ck*	"k", "c", "cc", "ck"	< EModE /k/
	possibly [kj]	*c*ane (19th c.), but cyan' (Mod. JC "can't" [kjã:])	not attested	<18th-c. British [kj] before [a] and [a:]. Twi [kj] before front vowels
	Note /-ks/	a*x*/a*x*e, e*x*cape, be*x*/ve*x*	"x"	OE axian/ascian Metathesis
	Note [ŋk]	ta*nk*s, *conc*onsa/Co*ng*o Saw	"nk" "nc", "ng"	Usually EModE, see /ŋ/, but note Twi prenasalized stop, e.g., [ŋkoŋkonsá]

Table 9. Jamaican Creole Affricates and Fricatives

JC Sounds	Variants	Examples	Spelling	History
/ǰ/		*j*ig, *j*am, cu*dg*o, so*g*er/so*j*er *g*emman, 'bli*g*e, *j*ook, re*g*ester, ca*j*on,	"j", "dg" "g"	<EModE /ǰ/
	but note occas. [ǰ] ~ [ž]	cabba*g*e ("scavenge")		pre-17th-c. Engl., Twi and Ewe, no [ž].
/č/		*ch*o/*ch*a/*ch*aw, *ch*upid, *ch*ookoo	"ch"	< EModE /č/
	[č] ~ [s] [č] ~ [š]	differen*ch*, corro*s*is wi*tch*/wi*ch* ("wish"), suspi*ch*		
	and before [i], [t] > [č]	Pon*ch*y ("Pontius"), cut*ch*y, ("curtsey")		Fante affricate [ts] ~ [t] or [d] before [i]
/f/		*f*or, *f*um, nu*ff*in, le*f*, yourse*ff*, *F*illistones, *F*eesus ("Ephesus"), blas*f*ame	"f", "ff" (often replacing SE "ph")	< EModE /f/ but see /p/ (above). cf. Gullah, which substitutes [Φ] and [β] for [f] and [v].
/z/ uncertain		probably him*s*, I*s*e, han*s*, mi*ss*ery, '*z*ackly, '*z*emble, '*z*aman (examine), ra*z*a	"z" or indistinct from spellings for /s/ below	< EModE /z/
/s/ and /š/	frequently vary. Originally perhaps [š] before front vowels.	mi*ss*u*s*, ju*ss*i*s*, *s*ing/*sh*ing, pani*sh*, oba*s*eeah/obi*sh*a/ bu*sh*a, di*sh*a ya, *sh*ivel, fi*s*, ye*sh*terday, you*sh*ef	"s", "ss" "sh"	< EModE /s/ ~ /š/ esp. 17th-c. nautical cf. Gullah; Sranan: [s] ~ [š] and Twi: [s] ~ [š]
[h] not phonemic		*h*edication, *h*up, *h*onimal, im, ave. (Earliest JC texts show no [h] deletion or addition. First citation in the speech of a white planter.)	"h"	fluctuation common in Engl. dial. and contact varieties of Engl.

Table 10. Jamaican Creole Oral Resonants

JC Sounds	Variants	Examples	Spelling	History
/m/	~ [n] occ.	*m*ada, *m*us, ge*mm*an, *m*u*mm*a su*n*ting	"m", "mm"	< EModE /m/ and freq. assimilation
/n/		picke*n*i*n*y/pick*n*i*nn*y/ picki*nn*i*n*y, se*n*, gra*nn*ie, he*nn*emy *kn*ew/*n*ew ("knew")	"n", "nn" "kn" as in SE	< EModE /n/
	also [n] < [ŋ]	gwi*n*e, bei*n*, marni*n*	"n"	18th-c. Engl. dial. and Mod. Engl. dial. [ŋ] > [n].
/ŋ/		shi*ng*, childri*ng*	"ng"	< EModE /ŋ/
/ɲ/		*ny*am (*n'y*am/*kn*aum -rare)	"ny"	< West African /ɲ/
	occasionally replaces [j] or varies with it.	*ny*oung *y*am(me)/*ny*am		
/r/		*r*atta, ye*rr*y, c*r*uddle	"r", "rr"	< EModE /r/
	frequently vary			
/l/		*l*i*ll*y, gar*l*, g*l*ass, Wi*ll*yforce	"l", "ll"	< EModE /l/
	[r] ~ [l]	swa*rr*a/swa*ll*ow, f*l*agrant, b*r*ack folk		Ewe [r] and [l] in complimentary distribution. Fante [l] replaces [r]. Lambdacism frequent in contact varieties of Engl.
	[l] > ∅ [r] > ∅	b'a'pheme, gory ("glory") ems ("elms") swa ("swear"), massah, do ("door"), geen ("green"), g'acefully		Twi [l] only in loan words

Table 10. (*Continued*)

JC Sounds	Variants	Examples	Spelling	History
/j/		*y*am, *y*eye	"y" (see "ee", "ie", "i", "igh")	< EModE /j/
	[j] < [r]	b'ute, *y*abbit		
	[j] < [l]	*y*itty		
	[j] < [h]	*y*erry, ya		
	[j] > ∅	*y*es/iss/ess		
/w/		*wh*arra, *w*ind, *w*antee	"w", "wh"	< EModE /w/
	occasionally replaces [v]	*w*erry, *W*ily ("Violet"), *w*icious, *w*ittal; but *wh*ip/*v*ip		[v] ~ [w] in 17th-c. London dialect and nautical Engl.
	[w] > ∅	uman ("woman")		
	[w] freq. maintained as glide after [b] and [p]	b*w*ai, g*w*ine		17th-c. Engl.

Vowels

Fluctuation among the vowels is far more marked than among the consonants, but again there are structural constraints. It appears that extensive variation in quantity was possible; long and short vowels were frequently indistinct. Minor height distinctions (high/lower high, for example) were often disregarded also. Central vowels were absent from JC (and still are), although there appears to have been some centralization of mid and low vowels (*hot*, "hurt"). All vowels are stressed, with the possible exception of svarabhakti vowels mentioned below. The importance of West African influence on JC vowels can be inferred from Christaller's description (1933: xvi; 1964: 4). This influence seems to imply a structure rather like that in Chart 4. According to Mervyn Alleyne, the earliest Afro-American vowels were arranged in a four-tier system, and, like Christaller,

Chart 4. The Vowels of Nineteenth-Century Twi

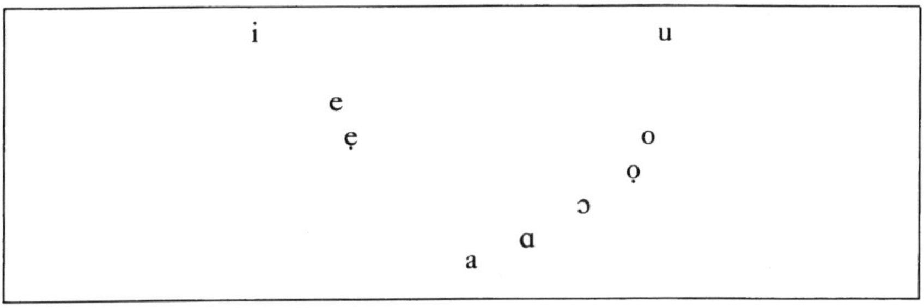

Chart 5. The Afro-American Vowel System Reconstructed by Alleyne (1980: 76)

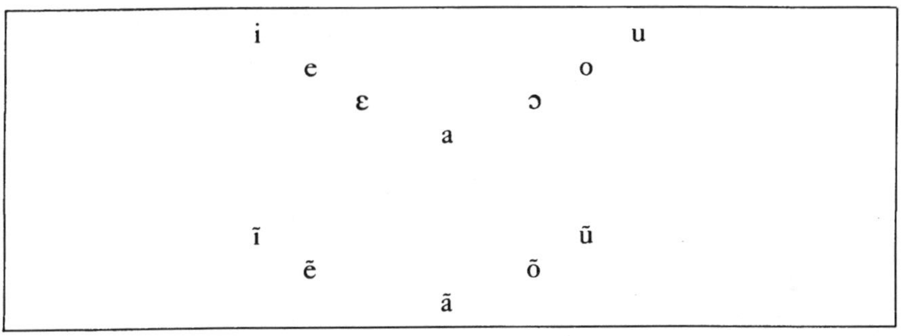

Alleyne displays a front-back distinction rather than a three-position system with central vowels (Chart 5). In Christaller's description, there are no central vowels. Christaller also notes that /e/ and /o/ are at times pronounced close to [u] and [I]. Commentators on seventeenth-century English reveal that in EModE there was frequent variation between [i] and [u], [i] and [e], and [o] and [u] (cf. Matthews 1935b: 199, 200).

Early JC differs from educated English in its loss or partial loss of quantity distinctions and the absence or irregularity of minor quality distinctions such as finer details of height and tense/lax (cf. Rickford 1981: 506–9, who summarizes findings about vowel laxing in the Guyanese Creole continuum). These changes appear to have reduced it to a three-tier system with a simple front-back distinction. Lengthening and diphthongization may then have expanded the system (*soart,* "sort"). Finally, changes in British English that did not affect the conservative and somewhat isolated creole of Jamaica served to separate the phonological system of JC farther from what was to become RP. Changes that had produced [ai] in the eighteenth century (from Middle English /oi/) were reversed or modified in RP, leaving /ai/ as a distinguishing feature (e.g., *pisen,* "poison") of the creole.[3]

Again, changes at work in educated British speech of the late seventeenth century were not necessarily complete or even present in JC by the eighteenth. Eighteenth-century British [r] was less strongly trilled and was being absorbed into RP [ɜ] in postvocalic position. Moreton's *garl* (probably reinforced by Scots dialect) suggests that in late eighteenth-century JC, vocalization was incomplete.

Table 11. Jamaican Creole Vowels

JC Sounds	Variants	Examples	Spelling	History
/i/	[i] ~ [iː]	l*ee*tle/l*i*lly, n*i*ggar/ n*ee*gar, bl*ee*ge, d*e*/d*ee*, f*e*/f*ee*, look*ie*, g*ie*/g*ae*/g*e*/g*e*b ("give") p*ea*k, h*earey*.	"i", "y" "e", "ee" "ie" "ae" "ea", "ey"	16th–17th-c. Engl. [i] ~ [I] and not phonemically distinct in Twi and Ewe.
	[i] ~ [e]	n*e*ber/n*i*ber, *e*f/*i*f p*e*rit/p*i*rit ("spirit")		17th-c. Engl. (educated); Ibo, Yoruba, Gullah [e] above cardinal also cf. Twi.
	[i] ~ [u] occas.	k*i*/k*u*, ob*u*sheer/ob*i*sha		17th-c. Engl.
/e/	[e] ~ [eː] see /i/ above	n*e*ga, y*e*re, '*e*m, br*ee*kfis, sab*ey*/sab*ay*, d*ey*, s*ay* (< Twi *se*), h*e*arey/y*e*are, d*ea*t', fr*ai*d, f*a*ba, b*ai*t, h*e*nkychi, t*e*nky	"e", "ee" "ey", "ay" "ea" "ai", "a"	EModE /e/ and /æ/ [æ] unacceptable before mid-17th-c. Eng. If in West Africa, [æ] > [e].
/a/		neb*ah*, br*ah*, c*a*tchreel, fell*ar*/fell*ah*, neg*ar*/ neg*er*, s*ar*vant, g*ar*l, s*ar*ve, neg*a*/neg*ur*, mass*a*, dinn*a*	"a", "-ah" "ar" "er" "ur"	EModeE /a/ > RP /æ/ and > JC /a/; [ɜ] unfamiliar in West African langs. and some creoles.

Partly because of massive variation and partly because of the inadequacy of orthographical representation, differences in quantity are difficult to infer. Even more tantalizing are those of rounding and nasalization. Evidence of nasalization is particularly limited but it is probable that rounding in early JC differed from that of today. For this sound change there is both orthographical evidence (such as the spelling variation between *obusheer* and *obisha*) and literary evidence (rhymes such as *misses* and *busses; dish* and *bush*).

Table 11. (*Continued*)

JC Sounds	Variants	Examples	Spelling	History
/a:/		yond*aa* l*ah*d bec*a*se cons*a*rn, w*a*ntee, c*a*ne *a*fta	"aa" "ah"+cons. "a"+cons.+ -e#, and before "r", "n", "f".	17th-c. Engl. /a:/ corresponds to Twi /a:/.
		m*au*gre, d*au*ter/d*ar*tar, ch*aw*	"au", "aw"	Cf. ME "au" which may represent /a:/ (ME daunce)
/o/	[o] ~ [o:]	*so*-*so*, ch*o*, d*o* ("door"), b*u*ckra/b*o*ckra, w*u*tless/w*o*rtless, m*u*squitto, s*u*nting	"o", "oo" "u"	Efik, Ibo, Yoruba, Twi, and Ewe [o] is above cardinal position. ME /u/ unrounded and centralized to [ɵ] as pronounced in JC; RP developed to [ʌ].
		ch*ur*ch, p*u*sson, b*u*d, h*o*t (?) ("hurt")		ME [er] [ir] [ur] ~ [or] } +CONS > in late 17th-c. educated Eng. [ər]. In RP [ər] > [ɜ]; in JC /ɜ/ > /o/.
/u/	[u] ~ [u:]	b*u*sha, b'*u*te, c*oo*p	"u," "oo"	EModE /u:/ and /ʊ/.

Table 12. Jamaican Creole Diphthongs

JC Sounds	Variants	Examples	Spelling	History
/ie/	[iɛ] or [ie]	w*ea*ste, n*ea*ga, d*ea*	"ea"	ME [a:] > 15–17th c. [æ:], ME [æI], ME [ɛI] } [ɛ:]; [ɛ:] 18th c. [aI] (later [ie] > [eI] in RP but JC retains [ie]
/ai/		dib*i*de, bl*i*ne, gw*i*ne j*ei*nts (toil, joy, etc. spelled as in SE but probably pronounced as in JC)	"i" "ei" "oi", "oy"	ME [i], ME [ɔ], ME [oI] } late 17th c. [əI] > 18th c. [aI] (later [ɔI] > [aI] change reversed
		garam*igh*ty	"igh"	[ɔI], [oI] } [aI] change modified to [ɔI] in RP, but JC retains [aI]
		h*uy*g ("hag") b*uy*g ("bag")	"uy"	EModE [æg] > JC [aIg]
/ou/		d*ow*, dr*ow*ny	"ow"	17th c. and later Northern Engl. dialects, originally < ME [u:] (later RP lowered further to [aʊ] but JC retains [ou])
/uo/		d*oa*nt, s*oa*rt, m*oa*st f*oa*	"oa"	British dialectal. cf. mwornin (Cumberland), and huope (Scottish)

Syllabic Structure and Suprasegmentals

Syllabic structure in early JC was West African, as obsolete terms such as *wharra*, *killee*, and *preachy* demonstrate: the existence of a similar syllabic formation in some EModE dialects (e.g., the well-established Devonshire infinitive marker *-ee* as in "hearee," "bannee," and "caree") ensured the reinforcement of this pattern.[4] The regular method of maintaining this structure was to add intrusive vowels in final position (*rassa*, *tenky*), or between the consonants of initial clusters (*sinicky*). Generally, vowel harmony appears to have been maintained (*winkie*, *junka*). Final consonants seem to have been added occasionally as well, possibly as hypercorrections (*sarmint*), but this feature also occurs in EModE (Wyld 1956: 309). Elision sometimes occurred, bringing a word of English origin in line with the preferred phonotaxis (*kimbo*). Finally, syncopation occasionally resulted in a sequence of consonants, but these were normally an accepted sequence; that is, the second consonant was a resonant. Hence *gubna*, *gubnis*, *begnet* ("governor," "governess," "bayonet").

The survival of lexical tone in the creole has been documented elsewhere.[5] This feature is the most difficult of all to infer from written records. Intonation patterns, however, are vaguely remarked on by early commentators and may be indicated by unusual punctuation. It is possible, for example, that the placing of question signs at the end of declarative sentences may mark a rising intonation unfamiliar to the educated English listener. Similarly, a period, comma or semicolon at the end of a rhetorical question may indicate falling intonation: "Me tink, you savee well, who thief me?" (Lewis 1834: 235) and "You no hearee, for you parson say we nigger for free aftah Christmas" ([Senior] 1835: 228). These intonational patterns also occur in other creoles, such as Gullah, and are similar to those of Ewe, Efik, Ibo, and Yoruba.

Syllables in JC remain level, owing to the absence of unstressed vowels. Where [ə] is obligatory in RP in final position JC shows [i], [e], [a], [o], and [u]. It is probable, though, that svarabhakti vowels carried reduced stress. Possibly vowels that were eventually elided, such as the initial sound in *overseer* > *busha*, also lost stress before they disappeared. This tendency is supported by metrical evidence in songs recorded by J. B. Moreton, in which the word *obisha* occurs. As Glen Alan Akers notes (1981: 28) vowel insertion after a final consonant is an alternative to deletion of the final consonant. In either case, the result of these deletion or insertion rules in conservative or archaic JC manifests itself in the syllabic structure that normally approximates to CVCV.

Chart 6. The Consonants of Early Jamaican Creole

	Labial	Labio-dental	Alveolar	Alveo-palatal	Palatal	Velar	Glottal
Fricatives							
Voiceless		f ~ (~p)	s ~		~ š		[h]
Voiced			(z)				
Stops and affricates							
Voiceless	p		t ~ [ř]	č	[kj]	k	
Voiced	b		d ~ [ř]	ǰ	[gj]	g	
Oral resonants	w		r l		j		
Nasals	m		n		ɲ	ŋ	

Chart 7. The Development of Jamaican Creole Vowels

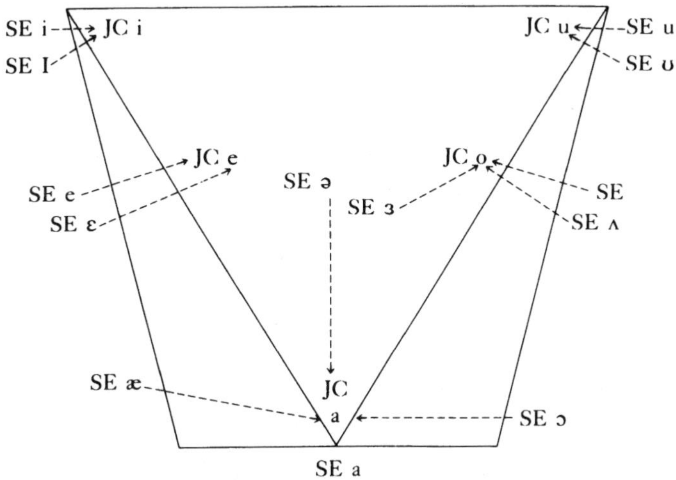

Chart 8. Tongue Movements in Jamaican Creole Diphthongs

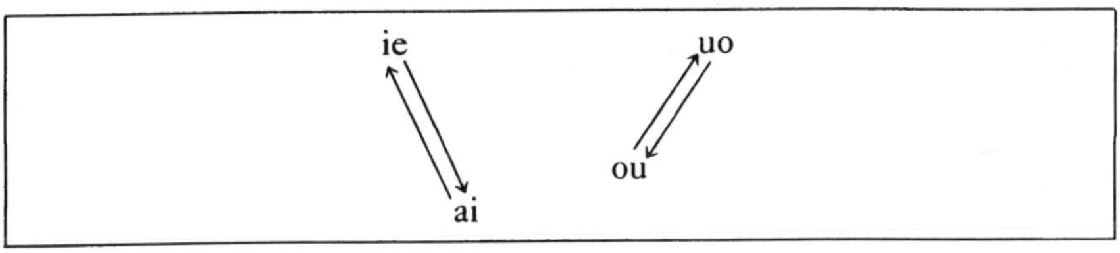

Summary

The phonological system of early JC, therefore, appears to have taken roughly the shape summarized in Charts 6–8. Chart 6 indicates consonants that appear in early records of JC. Note, for example, that [h] was unphonemic in JC but apparently frequent, and that neither the presence nor absence of [z], nor of the West African coarticulated stop [ŋk], can be inferred from written records with any certainty. Chart 7 illustrates vowel changes by loss or deemphasis of quantity distinction and by merging of vowels to reduce quality distinctions. Such spellings as *lilly* and *leetle* suggest such extensive overlap between high and lower-high vowels that these distinctions cannot be assumed to have phonemic status in early JC. We therefore summarize the contrast between significant vowel distinctions of early JC and EModE on Chart 7. The third, Chart 8, demonstrates the absence of central vowels from diphthongs.

4

Morphosyntax and Lexicon

> In their conversation, they confound all the moods, tenses, cases, and conjugations, without mercy.
>
> Edward Long lamenting the Jamaican vernacular, 1774

Extensive syntactic analysis lies well beyond the scope of this volume, partly because the data yields little that contrasts with twentieth-century JC. The texts collected in this volume have, with a single exception (Text 24), produced few surprises in the realm of syntax. Brevity of discourse, irregularity of citation, and (undoubtedly) the influence of the educated usage of each writer—as well as the probable influence of socially conditioned variation on each speaker—have all combined to deny us adequate evidence for exploring the formation of JC syntax. In any case, our earliest text in JC dates from 1740, nearly a century after English colonists occupied the island and well after the initial contact with West African speakers had laid the foundations of JC grammar.

Analysis in creole linguistics has so far focused largely on the African substratum, but within the morphosyntactic patterns of JC there may also be found distinct traces of EModE word building and morphosyntax; marked parallels exist between these and Barbadian usage (Niles 1980: 96–135). The present chapter offers some insight into this rather neglected branch of creole studies. Our description of early JC does not undertake pure syntactic analysis but looks at the conservatism of the morphology (*no mo so,* "no more than that"), and the lexicon (*infreshment,* "refreshment, a snack"). Naturally, many features failed to be recorded; others appear in the twentieth century as archaisms.

Among the archaisms, many reflect the archaic English usage from which early JC drew much of its material. For example, the terms *'nan* (literally "anon," or "what?") and *loblolly* ("a kind of gruel or porridge") appear in EModE texts, the latter in common usage in seventeenth-century Barbados where Richard Ligon (1657: 43) mentions it as part of the colonists' staple diet ("potatoes, loblolly, and Bonavist"). The term also occurs in nautical usage of the seventeenth and eighteenth centuries (*OED* "1. A thick gruel or spoon meat freq referred to as a rustic or nautical dish"). *OED* goes on to note that *lolly* derives from an obsolete Devonshire dialect term: the influence of the Southwest English dialects on Barbados English has been well established (Niles 1980). The case of EModE dialects in JC invites further elaboration.

Surprisingly few African-based archaisms have come to light in the data: the song in "Mudfish and Watchman" uses the now obsolete term *pempeny* ("many" or "plentiful"), which possibly derives from Twi *apem* ("a thousand"). Most of the terms unfamiliar to speakers of modern JC, however, turn out to be drawn from EModE regional usage. Such a low level of African archaisms may very well reflect the nature of the recorders, who would be more inclined to admit English dialectal features into their texts than unfamiliar African terms. Many African terms may also have escaped the attention of even such keen observers as the physicians Hans Sloane and John Atkins or may have been part of a slave-to-slave idiom never committed to writing or spoken to massa (Long 1774: 2.426). Certainly one may find evidence of African lexicon surviving as obsolescences in nineteenth- and twentieth-century JC.

An example of the latter appears in Text 24, a cumina chant recorded by Joseph G. Moore (1953) and etymologically analyzed by Mrs. Abena Enyonam Agbley-Odamtten. The chant constitutes the only text that suggests the structural and lexical signs of pidginization, but the pidginization is African, not African-English, and the structure of the chant suggests the accretions of ritual syncretism rather than workplace jargon. Setting aside matters of origin and transmission, one must note that the chant uses African words in a syntactic format unlike either English or JC, and closely akin to Ewe, the main source of African lexicon in the chant.

Because of many problems of translation and etymology in the cumina chant, a thorough and firm analysis of its structure is not possible here, but sufficient contrast with JC and English makes it clear that the syntax of the song belongs to neither of these and relies more on Kwa features and on a combination of phrases drawn from several languages. Mrs. Abena Enyonam Agbley-Odamtten recognizes in it not only the Ewe of inland Ghana but the classical Ewe of Dahomey, together with some items from Twi, Gã, and Yoruba.

The problem raised by the chant strikes at the heart of theories of language making in the Caribbean plantations: did the public, anglicized creole coexist alongside concealed African-based creoles? The Odamttens view the chant as an ancient product, remade and worn down by many generations of worshipers from different language groups. That Moore's English version of the chant (based on reports from informants) assumes that *Jeni* and *eva* must be English lexemes indicates how far the users of the chant have departed from any living knowledge of the original Ewe lexicon and structure.

The data represented by a single short chant cannot sustain extensive theorizing as to the origins and development of an African pidgin in Jamaica, but it does serve to highlight the systems of JC syntax and morphosyntax represented by the main body of eighteenth- and nineteenth-century texts. In contrast to the insights gained from comparing archaic and modern JC phonology, the data supply a few unexpected features instead of a set of rule-governed contrasts between the archaic and the modern. It is in this data (which represents the usage from basilectal to acrolectal) that the integrity of eighteenth- and nineteenth-century JC as a fully evolved system may be seen.

Morphosyntax

The following summary of the syntactic system found in the eighteenth- and nineteenth-century texts may provide a useful overview for those unfamiliar with JC structure and may be used to point up correspondences among JC, Barbadian English, and EModE dialects.

The sentence normally consists of subject-verb-object (SVO) in declarative sentences as well as in questions. Word order is an important determinant of the meaning of the sentence.

The VP of JC (Alleyne 1980: 78) is as follows:

(*mos bin wan kom yesidie*)
VP → (Modal) + (Particle) + (Auxiliary) +
(mos) (bin) (wan)
Predicate + (X)
(kom) (yesidie)
'(they) (must) (have wanted to) come (yesterday)'

Zero marking occurs in subject-verb combinations (inflexional features of educated English do not appear on nouns and verbs). Functional particles using the model familiar in Kwa syntax mark plurality (e.g., *-dem* the postposed pluralizer in later texts). Mervyn Alleyne (1980: 151) states, "In Twi the plural is . . . formed by the postposition of a word . . . [and] Jamaican follows Ewe and Twi" (but see Mufwene 1986). Preverbal markers such as *da, de, bin, bina* (Alleyne 1980: 162–72) function as indicators of aspect, tense, and mood.

In the verb phrase, tense and aspect reflect modern JC usage but also correspond in certain respects to EModE dialectal forms. Norma Niles (1980: 122–23) shows that EModE dialects provided models for the verb phrases that appear in Barbadian English. Unmarked verbs in the preterite parallel BE and JC (e.g., Somerset dialect *Uur kaech, Ee laarf, Jan wann all,* "he caught," "he laughed," "John wanted all").

Most fascinating are Niles's comments on *da* (1980: 124): "the *do* of the dialect present tense was *not* [our emphasis] the emphatic *do* of literary or modern Standard English." Instead, it functioned as a habitual marker in EModE dialects, and "in Somerset the construction became the most usual form of expression for the unemphatic indicative and subjunctive." Niles's examples suggest that a comparative analysis of EModE and Caribbean English creoles may reveal one of the major sources of *da na a,* often attributed by linguists exclusively to Kwa influence. Niles's examples of the EModE present habitual tense resemble the corresponding JC tense-aspect system closely:

I do labor
You da make a noise
I shall pick it up when I do goo home

The imperative formed by *to + infinitive* after *please* (Niles 1980: 128) occurs in EModE, BE, and JC. Niles's examples for BE are identical with JC usage: "Please to gi me di book." Not accounted for in BE or EModE is the parallel JC imperative *Please can gi me di book,* or *Im say please can come now,* in which *can* signifies willingness and ability on the part of the one commanded, a modality which politely diminishes the force of command.

Serial verbs are not attested in the earliest texts. By the nineteenth century, verb phrases containing *go* and *come* are documented: note *what you da go do,* and *pigeon come da waterside come drink water* in Text 17. A probable reinforcing element in the retention of these African substrate elements may exist in BE and EModE (Niles 1980: 131–32), where one finds the "verb + connective + verb construction where verb 1 is (a) of no semantic significance or (b) where verb 1 implies an initial action of verb 2, or has as its object the instrument effecting the action of verb 2."

Sentences include compound and compound-complex types and the classical creole structure: subject + nonverbal predicators (adjectival, nominal, or locative), verb patterns characteristic of West African languages. Functional elements such as verbal auxiliaries, connectives, determiners, and noun-phrase complementizers exist in the data as in modern JC.

Certain patterns of emphasis, such as the doubling of negatives and comparatives, are, of course, well attested in EModE literature, and EModE may have contributed to the marker *nuh* in sentence final position. Niles notes a sentence-final Old English *na* (1980: 130) that survived as an emphatic marker in the southeastern dialects, as in Kentish "He is not come yet-na." While JC uses the double and triple negatives common in OE, ME, and EModE, the few examples of sentence-final OE *na* that exist (cf. Battle of Maldon 1. 21 *ond ne forhtedon na,* "and not fear") suggest that more data is needed to prove a definite connection between British English and Caribbean English usage.

Throughout the data, sentence types show no signs of current or recent pidginization except in the sense suggested by Rickford (1984: 4) when he describes texts in which such markers as anterior past *bin* and plural *-dem* do not appear. Many do, however, display intrusions from educated English usage.

Many sentences display EModE structures such as inversion, the English pronoun system (but see Niles 1980: 115–17), and the SE apparatus of voice and tense markers (verbal auxiliaries in which EModE forms and West African forms have achieved a unique balance, as in *do da*). These structures occur in records made by writers (such as M. G. Lewis) through whom a strong English literary attitude prevails; in the letters of educated slaves sent to missionaries such as Phillippo; in the carefully distinguished usage of house servants and white creoles recorded by Moreton and Hamley; and in songs that may have been composed by speakers familiar with more acrolectal forms of the language (e.g., Moreton's "Me Know no Law, Me Know no Sin"). Certain of these features also appear in quite careful records of basilectal speech among field slaves, a fact which bears investigation.

A significant number of features (Lalla 1986b) suggests the influence of EModE syntax and morphosyntax (e.g., the use of *for* in place of JC *fe;* the use of EModE contractions such as *'tis* and *Ise;* and the use of inversion other than in questions, a notable feature in view of the resistance of JC to SE inversion).

These examples show influences from EModE on JC that have been well established at the phonological and lexical levels (e.g., *to go an hunting; wibble wabble loblolly*). It is probable that more research into the regional varieties of seventeenth-century English will reveal syntactic connections with JC unaccounted for by the African-base theory put forward by Alleyne.

While the short life-span and social backdrop of JC hinder attempts to track its internally determined changes, the English language provides evidence of certain types of change that are continued in JC either through reinforcement or through direct influence. In Lalla (1986b) a fuller discussion of the morphosyntactic data details those historical trends in ME and EModE that parallel features in JC. Chief among these established historical trends in English are the dialectal confusions that yielded standard and nonstandard variants in the marking of noun plurals and pronoun types; the use of ellipsis; the disappearance of grammatical gender; the erosion of inflectional endings leading to the extreme reduction of contrast in noun, verb, and pronoun paradigms; the increased use of word order as a syntactic device; and thus the absence of systematic distinctions between classes of lexemes.

The loss of grammatical gender in ME was not a sudden event but a high point in the process of inflectional decay that was already under way in early OE and continued well into the EModE period. It led to the decay of many types of bound morphemes, such as those which (for instance) distinguished weak from strong nouns and marked gender in both. As the morphological distinction among nouns, verbs, and adjectives eroded, English lexicon shifted such that Shakespeare might write "Thou leavest here, a better where to find" (*Lear* I.i.220). Textual analysis of JC records the continuation of morphological erosion and produces variants that may be of linguistic significance and not merely a sign of the recorders' failure to comprehend JC (Lalla: 1986b).

The following features and tendencies of EModE and JC show a parallelism worth further investigation.

Early Modern English	Jamaican Creole
Nouns	
1. Loss of grammatical gender	1. Zero features
2. Reduction of case markers to possessive	2. Zero inflection
3. Dialectal variation of plural marking (-s, -en)	3. Zero or *-dem* (*dem* attested only by 19th c.)
4. Compounding	4. Compounding
Pronouns	
1. Reduction of personal pronoun paradigm	1. Use of oblique SE forms
2. Variation in case (e.g., I ~ me, he ~ him after copula) and dialectal confusion in I ~ me usage after copula	2. Case unmarked and hypercorrections

Early Modern English	Jamaican Creole
3. Erosion of grammatical gender	3. Gender unmarked
4. Erosion of pronoun-verb agreement (e.g., "he don't" and "you was")	4. Zero agreement
5. "Them" as demonstrative	5. "Them" as *dem*
Articles	
1. Reduction of Old English se~seo~þaet to indeclinable *the*	1. Restriction of JC *de* to a limited number of NPs
2. Splitting of indefinite article and numeral (OE *an*) during 15th and 16th centuries into *a, an, one*	2. JC *wan* (numeral and article)
Verbs	
1. Reduction of subject-verb agreement (in the past tense to zero)	1. No agreement
2. Variation in pronoun-verb-agreement ("you pays," "He don't mean to have no clerk," "women gets themselves took in" [Trollope 1907: 1.86–87]	2. Similar variation
3. Dialectal confusion between present participial *-ing*/*-in*	3. *-in*
4. Reduction of number distinction save for *-s* of the third–person present tense	4. Unmarked
5. Reduction of person distinction	5. Unmarked
6. Use of *for to* and occasionally *for* as infinitive marker in ME and EModE	6. Use of *for* in early texts, later *fe*

Another important feature of EModE usage, ellipsis, may also connect with the creation of such JC sentences as "Five minutes the other one say:—Puppa!" (Jekyll 1907: 132). The unstressing of function words may be connected with the decay in the English inflectional system, but elision alone cannot account for the structure of the JC sentence.

Of all the features that demand commentary, *for* offers unusual possibilities (Winford 1985). The modern JC *fi fa fo* forms do not appear in early texts. "The form *fe* that resembles Twi appears relatively late. Certainly there are orthographical interpretations of JC in all records. Some are close enough to English in appearance to be taken as mesolectal . . . [b]ut the form *for* [appears] in records containing basilectal features [and in which] valiant attempts are being made to represent actual pronunciation" (Lalla 1986b).

The frequency with which *for* occurs leads one to question once again the absoluteness of a Kwa model for early JC syntax, especially in the absence of *fe* + noun as a possessive marker in the earliest texts. The occurrence of *for* in songs such as those recorded by Moreton (1793: 153) points to an English dialectal influence (see Chapter 6).

Table 13. A Comparison of Compound Words in Early Modern English, Jamaican Creole, and Barbadian English

EModE Dialects	JC	BE
hand-gloves	hand-socks hand stockings	—
nose-holes	nose-hole	—
day-morning	day-morning	—
morning-time	morning-time	morning-time
before-time	before-time	before-time
night-time	night-time	night-time
which-part	which-part	which-part
ram-cat	ram-puss	—
bull-stag	bull-dog	—
dark-night	dark-night	dark-night
—	rock-stone	rock-stone
little-small	—	little-small
self-same	self-same	self-same
—	said-same	said-same

Lexicon and Word Formation

Compounding, once a major source of word formation in OE, ME, and EModE, occurs frequently in JC (e.g., *man-crab, woman-crab, goodbelly, cornpiece*). Many similarities exist among the types of lexical expansion that occur in JC, BE, and EModE. In Table 13 appear JC, BE, and EModE dialectal compounds (Niles 1980: 101–3).

Niles's discussion of the types of compounding (iteratives, gender markers, time markers, and so on) offers a strong case for EModE dialect usage both as one important source and as a model for lexical expansion in JC, BE, and other English-based Caribbean dialects and creoles. The Jamaican historian Edward Long points up the importance of seventeenth-century English dialects in common Jamaican usage with special reference to nautical usage. Among the terms he cites (1774: 2.319) appear *cook-room, bread-kind,* and *kill-devil* ("kitchen," "such roots and fruits of the country as are used instead of bread," and "a rum-based drink"). In modern JC, parallels such as *meat-kind* and *fish-kind* occur, but many of Long's nautical terms have disappeared.

Long's list is well worth considering, particularly in the terms in which he presents his evidence:

> The many nautical, or sea-faring terms of expression, in use here among the planters from time out of mind, were probably introduced by the first English settlers; who, for some years, *alternately followed privateering, and planting* [our emphasis]. I shall enumerate a few of them, with their explanation:
>
> *Cook-room.* Kitchen.
>
> *Leeward.* Every place situated to the Westward.
>
> *Windward.* The contrary.
>
> *Store-room.* Warehouse for goods.
>
> *Stoaker.* The Negroe appointed to stuff fuel into the holes under the boilers. Probably from the word *stoaked* or stopped as a ship's pump.
>
> *Boatswain of the mill.* The Negroe who attends the mill-gang, or feeders.
>
> *To rig the mill.* To get it ready for putting about.
>
> *Sweeps.* The arms or levers belonging to the main roller.
>
> *Skids.* Poles, or levers used for putting casks into a boat from the shore.
>
> *Stanchions.* Upright pieces of timber in the curing-house.
>
> *Gangway.* Interval or space left for passage through the middle of the curing-house.
>
> *Cot.* A settee.
>
> *Awning.*
>
> *Bread-kind.* Such roots and fruits of the country as are used instead of bread.
>
> *To jerk.* To salt meat, and smoak-dry it.

Birth. An office, place, or employment.

Grog. / *Toddy.* / *Kill-devil.* } Liquors, whose choicest ingredient is rum.

Hand the mug. Carry or bring the mug.

Bowl. Instead of cup.—As a "bowl of tea," of chocolate, or both; which term expresses the large morning-potations of our ancestors here.

Cow. In the buccaneer term, to signify all sorts of horned cattle, &c.

Many of the items listed by Long have disappeared from Jamaican usage along with the technology they represented. Others (such as *cow*) have survived. One must wonder what other items might have appeared in the list, for Long is citing a few examples and not giving a full account of Jamaican usage. Most important, he affirms the existence in Jamaica of a lexicon derived from seafaring, which combines buccaneering, privateering, and ordinary sailors' jargon.

The lexicon that survives in the data includes not only Long's items but such nautical terms as *tafferel* and *stamp-an-go* (see Glossary). Other terms, which represent a Hispanic element in JC—preserved either by the Maroons or by the Sephardic Jews—must have an equally long history: *chakalata*, *carochies*, and *palaver* testify to the influence of Spanish and Portuguese in JC. Of the approximately two hundred and fifty terms identified in the entire data as needing etymological commentary, nearly three-quarters (one hundred and eighty) derive from dialects of English; thirty-six are of West African origin; fourteen are Hispanic; and twenty-five are either unknown or of multiple origin, such as Twi *se* and English *say* > JC *se*, "that" after verbs of knowing, telling, and hearing.

Quite aside from the question of provenance, an important aspect of lexical expansion resides in the semantic extension of terms already in the language. Compounds (such as *hard-ears*) achieve new meanings by combining old elements, but equally active in JC is semantic change in the absence of such combination. English-based verbs such as *wind* and *sweet* remain identical in form to SE equivalents while diverging in meaning (see Glossary). Where phonological and perhaps functional shifts accompany semantic changes, new extensions of meaning open up. *Massa-tenky* ("a gift") provides an example of several types of change occurring together. Semantic change may of course be tied to social attitudes as well; one sees the process at work in the pejoration of African terms such as *Kofi* ("day-name for male born on Friday" in Twi), to *Cuffee*, "a fool, a country bumpkin," and *nyam*, "to devour" rather than merely "to eat."

Textual evidence confirms that the JC lexicon has developed by way of items from EModE dialects and from West African and other languages, by compounding, by semantic change, and through multifunctionality. The investigator familiar with modern JC expects—and finds—little or no word formation through morphological processes such as affixation. The real surprise lies in the dearth of evidence regarding certain African elements in the earliest material. Only in the middle and later nineteenth century do such grammatically functional items as *unu*, *da*, and the plural marker *-dem* appear. At present one may only speculate as to whether this scarcity has linguistic significance or whether it results merely from inadequate or biased recording.

In Chapter 5 we examine problems of social variation that must have affected the recorders' knowledge of JC as well as their willingness to set it down on paper. Long gives no comment on the phonology of Jamaican usage and has little to say about JC lexicon and syntax. More information regarding the structure and demographic nature of seventeenth- and eighteenth-century Jamaican communities may shed light on the probable development of JC. In Chapter 6 we turn to the questions raised by the data regarding the origins and development of JC and its relationship to other vernaculars.

5

Language Variation

Bwoy, yuh no shame? Is so yuh come?
After yuh tan so lang!
Not even lickle language, bwoy?
Not even lickle twang?

An yuh sister what work ongle
One week wid Merican
She talk so nice now dat we have
De jooce fi understan?
Louise Bennett, "Bans a Killin"

Limited in many ways, the data of late eighteenth- and early nineteenth-century JC nonetheless point to the foundations of a speech continuum in Jamaica. Extensive language variation apparently existed between basilectal Jamaican Creole at one end of the spectrum and acrolectal Jamaican English at the other. Between these extremes, both interpersonal and intrapersonal variation can be distinguished. At what stage distinct intermediate varieties developed is yet to be made clear.

The Creole

The earliest Jamaican speech recorded is distinct from any pidgin or, at any rate, from a pidgin as defined by Whinnom (1971: 106), who sees it as a language that can be identified on the basis of linguistic criteria and is thus recognizable as a separate structural type. Creoles, on the other hand, can more easily be defined by reference to history than by structural criteria. Still, it is possible to distinguish between early and later JC by structural features as well as through sociohistorical factors.

The language preserved in early Jamaican records has arisen out of contact between linguistically diverse peoples—a contact that occurred first under conditions of trade and in the collection centers of West Africa and later under the economic system of plantation industry in the Caribbean. In this multilingual situation, contact was at once horizontal (between slaves) and vertical (between masters and slaves). European communities bore little cultural resemblance to West African ones. Important concepts of the prestige languages were therefore carried into JC in a lexicon that was largely British (given the disruption of West African traditions and the debatable extent of such disruption). Sustained interaction among large groups of socially diverse peoples provided the conditions essential to the long-term development of JC, especially as the proportion of Europeans to Africans in seventeenth-century Jamaica was larger than in later years.

We have seen that the development and spread of JC was not limited to transmission from one generation to the next, since continued importations brought Africans who learned the established creole, bringing to it their own linguistic backgrounds. Because these may have included African languages quite different from those of the early colonial period (as well as new varieties of GCCE), the developing creole would have been relearned subject to interference from the linguistic background of new groups.

While it is true to say that social and racial prejudice in Jamaica defined the development of the creole and associated it with caste, the situation was complicated by a number of factors. For example, English presented a diversity of social and regional varieties and it was the sum of these that made up the prestige tongue. At the same time, a far wider social and racial range of speakers than is normally acknowledged was apparently competent in the creole. In this case, an early JC speech community may not only have linked working-class blacks in a sort of "group solidarity" (Mühlhäusler 1974: 44) but would have included widely disparate age groups, social classes, and economic levels. Eventual isolation from British English fostered conservatism, especially in the rural creole, even while the continuing presence of acrolectal Jamaican speech exerted strong acculturative and decreolizing influences. The divergence between standard speech in Britain and in Jamaica (largely phonological) was neither absolute nor final, for SE has continued to influence acrolectal Jamaican English through small, elite groups.

Although the nature and components of the original contacts changed, it was a stable creole that survived in oral communication. Rather than testifying to the acceptance of JC as a literary language, the written records that follow merely document certain varieties of this oral language.

Fundamental restructuring of the languages that contributed to JC belongs to its prehistory, and linguists have speculated about it. A common view is that pidginization began with optimalization of rules. Next, creolization introduced new rules. Mühlhäusler (1974: 136) distinguishes simplification from descriptive simplicity in that the former expands the domain of grammatical rules. In any case, the end result is a language in which functional components of the grammar may be stressed more usefully than categorical components. As Mühlhäusler points out, the linguist can, therefore, describe such characteristic features as multifunctionality without becoming entangled in class overlap (1974: 138).

This restructuring has been multidimensional. It has not simply occurred in two stages or between two parties or at any one level of language structure. On the contrary, interference among many languages and varieties of these languages in the contact situation occurred and reoccurred at all linguistic levels of JC. Mühlhäusler's schematic representation of pidginization (1974: 58), based on a modified standard scheme for language acquisition, can perhaps be further modified to illustrate the process (see Chart 9).

As a result of rapid structural change, the creole emerged prior to those social conditions and attitudes likely to have produced or preserved written records of the language. The rate of change in the creole has apparently not been constant from one level of linguistic structure to another. Phonological change is more clearly discernible in texts of the eighteenth and nineteenth centuries than is morphosyntactic change (cf. Alleyne 1980: 138).

Because social attitudes have affected the compilation, survival, or extinction of written records, evidence of historical variation from one century to the next and of social variation at any one period is subtle and elusive. In most cases the type of material to be preserved depended entirely on the interests of an SE writer. In the rare case of a document written by a creole speaker, the writer typically made strenuous attempts to avoid the basilect in an effort to appear literary. A variant modeled on the acrolect was selected and, frequently, ornamented with hypercorrections (see Text 22). Yet it is possible to distinguish a stage at which several of the basilectal features of modern JC are unattested in situations where they might be expected to occur.

The descriptions in Chapters 3 and 4 have shown that anterior past tense markers, *fe* complements, occurrences of second-person pronoun plural (*unu*), *-dem* plurals, and deletion or insertion of [#h-] are all slow to appear in records of the eighteenth and early nineteenth centuries. Instead, the documents preserve a wealth of other features widely recognized as basilectal (for example, caseless and genderless pronouns, various forms of nonverbal predication, fricative replacement, and reduction of consonantal clusters).

Chart 9. Process of Pidginization

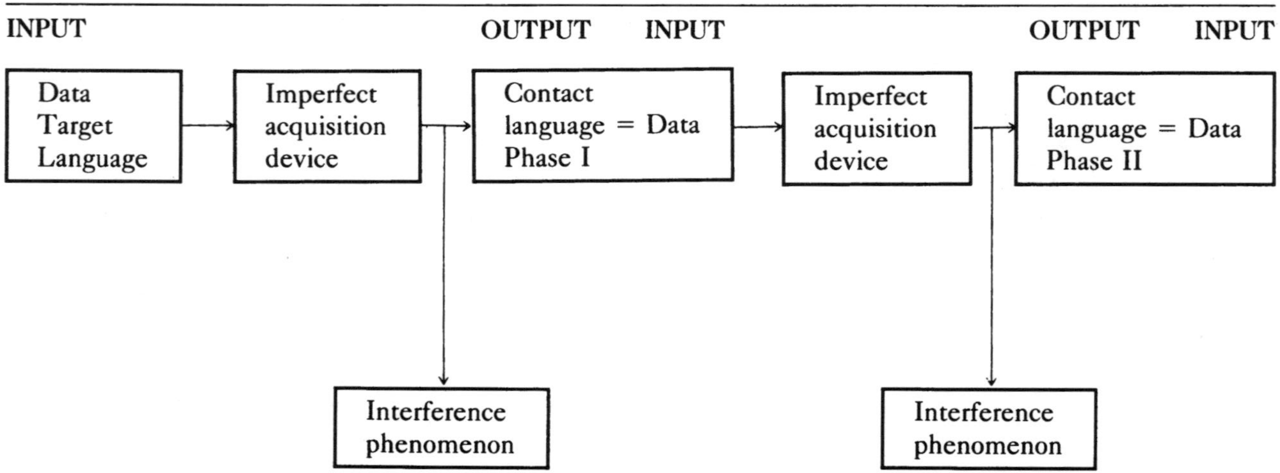

Carrington (1987 personal discussion) questions the salience of these features to persons recording Jamaican speech. As he points out, recorders might be inclined to note features that would give readers an indication of deviance in the language without blocking comprehension. He therefore questions whether the features marked (often present in English dialects) were recorded in preference to other, distinctly unfamiliar terms. This possibility should be borne in mind before drawing conclusions about language change. Frankly, more research on patterns of observation among recorders of JC and other creoles should be carried out before the issue can be satisfactorily resolved. Prolonged study of the texts, however, reveals a tendency on the part of recorders to note less-familiar features. The palatalization of velar stops (which survives in English dialects of the time) is not noted, nor is the equally familiar [#h-] deletion. On the other hand, early texts regularly record West African lexical items such as *cuntung, tatta* or *nyam/knaum* and include such phrases as *kackkaw foa you.*

The absence of features from the evidence does not of course mean that they did not occur in speech, but it does imply a possible infrequency of occurrence as compared to other well-attested features. The data gathered from the texts therefore promise clues to historical change and social conditioning in the basilectal features in early JC.

Mid-Seventeenth to Mid-Eighteenth Century

There is no written record of JC in the seventeenth century, and although it is clear that several highly variant language systems must have coexisted at the time, we have no documentary evidence of their nature or conditioning. We can visualize models for language interaction based on our knowledge of social organization at this time. Michael Craton (1978: 11–12) describes what may have been a typical community in 1680. Its upper stratum consisted of a white planter, Francis Price, his wife, and four children. Directly beneath were seven white servants, and at its base "fifty-seven adult and three child slaves." In the next seventy years the whites were to remain relatively stable in number but would rise socially from positions of bondsmen to those of managerial and specialist staff. During this time the number of slaves would quadruple.

Settled to the northwest of Spanish Town and the valleys of St.-Thomas-in-the-Vale, the Price household lived in isolation, far from town or neighbor. Craton (1978: 7) describes a lonely, sprawling plantation set in a "fertile dry valley" enclosed by "shaggy, craggy 'cockpits' " over which the road to the coast— "twenty-eight miles to the south and thirty-two to the north"—entails a climb to almost 2,000 feet in any direction.

In the 1680s, when Jamaica's population numbered about seven thousand whites and ten thousand slaves (according to Long), rural isolation imposed on communities such as Francis Price's a tight, hermetic structure in which several language systems were forced to interact. It was not until the middle of the next century, however, that evidence of linguistic variation based on the social organization of the developing language community was preserved (even fragmentarily) in written records.

Mid-Eighteenth to Early Nineteenth Century

The social organization of Jamaica in this period was effectively more complex than in the last. The plantation economy of the latter eighteenth century supported 710 plantations, worked by about two to three hundred thousand slaves. Islandwide population estimates for this period are normally broken down into the racial groups on which social classification was based, though conflicting estimates exist. Edward Brathwaite (1978: 105) counts 18,000 to 24,000 whites in 1786, depending on the system of calculation. He estimates 23,000 browns, 4,000 of them free, in 1774 (1978: 168, on the basis of G. W. Roberts and Long 1774: 2.337). Orlando Patterson estimates 217,584 blacks for 1787 (Table 5), while Brathwaite cites 229,000 for 1785 (1978: 152 after Moreton 1793: 38).

Within these major strata, a number of significant social classes can be defined. The white class was made up of locals (creoles) and of English, Scots, and Irish expatriates. The upper echelons of the group included administrators, wealthy merchants, and planters. The urban middle class comprised such groups as were noted by the Kingston Vestry Jury lists (Brathwaite 1978: 136) and included shopkeepers and other suppliers of goods, professionals, and artisans. Of the retailers, many were Sephardic Jews. The rural middle-class whites included smallholders and merchants, estate staff and professionals, craftsmen and coastal shipping captains. Soldiers and sailors stationed on the island formed another discrete and influential social group. Some white proprietors lived with no other family but their black housekeepers and resulting brown children (Nugent 1966: 68). Indeed, not only was a white housekeeper remarkable but white women in general were rarities (Nugent 1966: 72, 86).

At the level below, browns might be free or enslaved, and free browns might be privileged or nonprivileged. Privileged free browns were those who could gain concessions on such grounds as their baptism in the Anglican Christian faith. They were often financially independent and had opportunities for education. Most free browns, however, were nonprivileged and often existed barely above the poverty line. In contrast, brown slaves were usually more comfortably placed (as mistresses, for example) and were treated with some respect by blacks.

The vast majority of the black population were slaves, but here too social gradations could be distinguished. The plantation work force was headed by a slave elite which included skilled foremen (e.g., head cooper, potter, carpenter, or blacksmith), the drivers, and the important domestics. Beneath these stood another class made up of such specialists as hospital workers (doctor, midwife, and nurses); craftsmen (coopers, masons, etc.); factory laborers (sugar guards and distillers); stockworkers (the mulemen, cattlemen, poultry and hog tenders); upper servants such as the cook, washerwoman, seamstress, and groom; and some specialists in miscellaneous duties, such as the ratcatcher. Next came the field gangs, ordered according to their capacities from the Great or First Gang down to the fourth. Finally, there were marginal figures like the watchman. Among these levels there was relatively little mobility. The slave society was essentially static, and few changed jobs to move from one social level into another. Set apart from the workers were the unemployed (infants, invalids, child watchers, and women with six children), and the runaways. Craton provides a detailed picture of the minutiae of the plantation hierarchy in his study of slave life at Worthy Park, home of Francis Price (1978: 176–79).

Social and racial characteristics cut across each other. Skin color gradations were not as closely attended to as in the non-British colonies, except to distinguish between the mulatto, who was brown (any admixture of white and black), and the octoroon, who was legally white and so free (Brathwaite 1978: 168). Again, Jews, although white, were treated as a quite distinct group and were discriminated against. Among the blacks, not only was skin color a class-associated factor, but Africans were clearly distinguished from creoles. The importance of creole slaves to language acquisition and to acculturation of newly imported Africans is emphasized by Robert Chaudenson (1977). Brathwaite estimates that Africans made up 36 percent of the slave population even after the abolition of the slave trade (1978: 164; but see Patterson 1973: 275).

Wide as were the gulfs that separated social and racial groups, intimate interaction between them was inevitable. A sugar plantation constituted a sharply defined community of speakers of whom few, perhaps even within the white class, would speak upper-class English. A variety of regional and social dialects of EModE would combine with Jamaican Creole, and the creole in turn would be subject to continuous interference from the West African languages, Guinea Coast Creole English, and any other contact language spoken by the newly arrived slaves. The plantations themselves were separate enough to make intercourse between them difficult, and movement was restricted mainly—but not entirely—to the master's family and attendants. Slaves working their provision grounds on the outlying estate lands came in contact with Maroons, runaways, or slaves from the neighborhood, and slave markets became points of limited contact also.

The social organization of the period, in fact, fostered the establishment of distinct, isolated communities of various kinds. Of these, some (like the slave ship) were transitory; others, such as Maroon communities, proved long lasting. In the towns, interaction between groups must have become pronounced, especially among the free browns and blacks who were concentrated mostly in urban areas (twelve hundred browns were reported in Kingston alone). But models for sustained intimate contact continued on the plantations and in fact in most large households in which blacks and whites coexisted.

The governor's mansion itself was an extremely mixed community. In the 1800s Lady Maria Nugent reports having both French-Haitian and German menservants in her household. Her maid was an Englishwoman adrift among strangers: "Poor creature, I pity her very much; she has no associates, and no equals; she is left to the care of a parcel of blacks, and everything is new and strange to her." Yet even between the maid's extremely upper-class mistress and other groups there was some interaction. Lady Nugent habitually read to her black servants and recorded that under this instruction they became well versed in their prayers. Lady Nugent herself was at times less distant with black and brown classes than the local white elite considered wise (Nugent 1966: 156, 203).

It is clear from accounts in this period that JC was spoken by a variety of classes and colors. Lady Nugent's famous reference to the creole spoken by white ladies not educated abroad is only one testimony of several. Conversely, literary English is fluently handled by a black poet, Francis Williams, in the mid-eighteenth century. Simplistic equations of basilect with black and acrolect with white must clearly be abandoned.

In the late eighteenth to early nineteenth centuries, interpersonal variation can be distinguished between social classes where characteristics such as occupation and economic standing vary. Records of Jamaican speech by persons of differing class, age, sex, and race within a time span of only two decades demonstrate that basilectal Jamaican features were used by some upper-class speakers and in the white community.

The following selected samples, analyzed in Table 14, occur in different situations. Speakers 1 and 2 are young, white, upper-class women endeavoring to behave with propriety at a formal dinner:

> Tank you sir, wid all my heart . . . Sir, Ise don't love turkey rump. Ise love turkey bubby.
>
> Me quite sorry mamma, Ise went in a bush to-day to do my ——, and Yellow Legs come, and he knaum my ——, and him puke; O I'm quite sorry for poor Yellow Legs! (Moreton 1793: 117)

Identical in class, color, and situation, Speaker 3 (a boy) says, "Me wantee crab, me wantee crab" (Text 3.B), while Speaker 4 (a brown seamstress) threatens her black apprentice: "I will flog you libba out! . . . Kackkaw foa you" (Moreton 1793: 131). In a meeting with the governor of Nova Scotia, Speaker 5 (a Maroon) cries out, "Top Massa Governor . . . top lilly bit" (Dallas 1803: 1.113). Speaker 6, a recently arrived African, greets the captain who transported him:

> Cappy Crow . . . me sabby you very much when you live for you big ship for big water—when you look every day wit crooked tick for find da pass. (Crow 1830: 128–29)

Speaker 7 is an elderly slave in conversation with his master (Text 3.A). The data allow us to compare the speech of several social groups within the brief time frame of twenty years.

A number of phonological features characterize basilectal creole, but for reasons of convenience as well as space, only a few have been identified for tracing. For example, because of orthographical difficulties in representing and interpreting vowel length, diphthongization, and monophthongization and because of questions surrounding the significance of minor differences of tongue height, variation in such features cannot be accurately described in a limited corpus. Again, because glide formation (e.g., *gwine/gwain*) occurs in EModE and survives in English dialects, it has not been selected as a distinctively basilectal creole feature. The deletion of [#h-] is also omitted both because it too is an English dialectal feature and because it is unattested in the earliest JC texts. Similarly, a number of basilectal morphemes (such as *unu*), which do not become familiar until later, have not been selected. However, it is possible to distinguish the presence or absence of several representative features that (1) clearly contrast with acrolectal models of English; (2) even if familiar in English dialects, are also known in influential West African languages; (3) are unequivocally indicated by documentary evidence of JC during the period; and (4) are associated with basilect-modeled JC. In phonology we traced fricative replacement, reduction in initial or final consonant clus-

Table 14. Selected Basilectal Features in Jamaican Speech (Recorded 1790–1810)

Basilectal Features	Speakers						
	Proprietor Class			Artisan Class	Working Class		
	1. Adult Woman White	2. Adult Woman White	3. Child White	4. Adult Woman Brown	5. Adult Man Maroon	6. Newly Arrived Male Slave	7. Elderly Male Slave
Fricative replacement	+	–	+	+	+	+	+
Reduction of consonantal clusters	–	–	NA*	+	+	+	+
Intrusion of final vowel	–	+	+	–	+	+	+
Non-English lexeme	+	+	+	+	–	+	+
Unmarked pronoun case or tense	+	+	+	–	+	+	+
No auxiliary in negative VP	–	NA	+	+	+	NA	+
For/fe complement	NA	NA	NA	NA	+	+	+
Nonverbal predication	NA	+	+	NA	+	NA	+

*Denotes absence of occasion for use of feature.

ters, and vowel intrusion (cf. Akers 1981: 28–43). In lexicon, we noted items not derived from English. And in morphosyntax, we noted occurrences of *for*/*fe* complements, nonverbal predication, negative VP without auxiliaries, unmarked tense, and uninflected pronouns. As Table 14 shows, basilectal features occur in the usage of all classes sampled, though to varying extents. All the features selected appear in the speech of the elderly male slave, Speaker 7. Significantly fewer show in the samples for Speakers 1 and 2, and indeed some are replaced by acrolectal features.

It may not be possible to identify the Jamaican situation in the late eighteenth to early nineteenth centuries as clearly illustrating one model of variation rather than another, that is, as (1) coexistent but separate systems whose speakers may be bilingual or (2) functionally the same as a modern creole-English continuum, the nature or even existence of which is not universally accepted. Noting the existence of intermediate varieties in all the Afro-American creoles, Alleyne argues against seeing the Caribbean creoles as "typical examples of linguistic continuum situations" (1980: 186–87). He also hints that the nature of the original early-contact situation may have played a critical role in defining intermediate varieties (1980: 181–86, 192–98) *within each creole*. The Jamaican records show a clearly defined basilectal form of JC and an acrolectal English spoken by the Jamaican educated. We have no firm evidence of a continuous spectrum from basilectal JC to acrolectal Jamaican English spanned by discrete intermediate mesolects. Neither is it possible, within these earliest documents, to observe code switching in individual speech acts with certainty.

However, a certain degree of mixing is both documented and described. Some speakers from the more prestigious classes of society display basilectal features as surely as does the black slave population, just as educated Jamaicans can be traced who were fluent in the acrolect. When upper-class speakers use the basilect, they often display acrolectal or hypercorrect forms seldom found in the speech of the uneducated slave.

Although we lack data by which to define continua in the eighteenth century, suggestive descriptions of the language situation have survived and, in spite of the limited witness of the recorders, must be scrutinized. Writing in 1774, Edward Long urges the perfection of English and the grossness of Jamaican and African speech. He gives very little data: eight words of supposed African origin, of which "sangaree" derives from Spanish, "bumbo" may be American Spanish, three other items can be traced only to Long himself, and the remaining three are unattested. His examples of creole, on the other hand, are genuine: reduplication ("fum-fum", "talky-talky"), *for* infinitives, and uninflected pronouns ("me glad for see you"). His distinction between African and creole speech, however, suggests continuing pressure from African languages, on one hand, aspirations toward English, on the other, and a complicated set of attitudes in between:

> The Africans speak their respective dialects, with some mixture of broken English. The language of the Creoles is bad English, larded with the Guiney dialect, owing to their adopting the African words, in order to make themselves understood by the imported slaves; which they find much easier than teaching these strangers to learn English. The better sort are very fond of improving their language, by catching at any hard word that the Whites happen to let fall in their hearing; and they alter and misapply it in a strange manner; but a tolerable collection of them gives an air of knowledge in the eyes of their brethren. (Long 1774: 2.426–27)

The "broken English" of the new Africans contrasts with the "bad English" of the creole blacks, while the creole practice of "adopting the African words" for better communication suggests a slave-to-slave pidgin based on the West African languages.

Gradations of usage also occur in the "bad English" of the white creole population. "This sort of gibberish likewise infects many of the white Creoles, who . . . meet with much difficulty . . . to shake it entirely off" (ibid.). The incidence of "bad English," Long states, may be measured by the speaker's gender, educational level, and degree of exposure to urban or rural influence. White creole boys tended to be educated abroad or in local schools. No schools for girls existed in Jamaica. Those white children sent to England—along with a small but growing number of colored—lost their command of creole. Such speakers would, on their return, have helped to form the tiny community of acrolectal speakers. The majority of white creole girls were educated at home by tutors, and some not at all. Among the better educated were Jamaican "ladies who live in and about the towns, being often in company with Europeans and others brought up in Great Britain, [and who] copy imperceptibly their manners and address"; in contrast to these mesolectal speakers are those born and brought up on remote plantations. This group uses "bad English" identical to that of their "black servants, equally illiterate and unpolished" (ibid. 2.278–79).

The social and linguistic divisions implied in Long's description amount to more than a simple division into creole and upper-class English. Among whites, Long describes the usage of the landowning upper class alone, and there we see (1) a British-educated creole elite speaking RP; (2) others of the same socioeconomic class speaking a Jamaican version of RP; (3) others, less educated and less exposed to urban influence, speaking RP "with much difficulty," and creole with ease; and (4) monolingual, rural creole speakers, who were usually women born and brought up on plantations. Long is silent on the usage of middle- and lower-class creole whites (including the Jews). Among blacks, his description indicates (1) African speakers acquiring an Afro-creole pidgin in contact with creole blacks; (2) creole blacks speaking JC and pidgin; (3) creole blacks ("the better sort") acquiring some RP and altering their JC accordingly; (4) locally educated free blacks and coloreds using the Jamaican form of RP in schools such as Francis Williams's (Long 1774: 2.476); and (5) British-educated blacks and coloreds, such as Francis Williams himself, speaking RP (ibid. 2.328–29, 475–85).

We may trust Long's account of upper-class usage. Born in England, he came to Jamaica in 1757 at the age of twenty-one to inherit his father's property. The Longs were connected with the oldest, wealthiest creole families, and Long himself served as private secretary to the lieutenant governor and then became a judge. He left Jamaica in 1769 and published his *History* five years later (Brathwaite 1978: 73). Typical of his class, Long lists the schools set up for white boys (1774: 2.249–51) and omits from among them Francis Williams's school in Spanish Town. He may well have omitted schools run by the Quakers or the Moravians, by other sectarians, or by the Jews. He mentions Williams's school as an afterthought, a feature of the extraordinary business of educating a black man. He tells nothing of how the bookkeeper and apothecary class acquired their education, yet such literate groups existed. Brathwaite (1978: 268–77) gives a full account of Jamaican schooling in the late eighteenth and early nineteenth centuries, enlarging but not contradicting Long's account.

Further research may yield evidence of the extent and nature of private tutoring, dames' schools, religious instruction and ritual, business and governmental transactions, and other activities likely to affect language. Given Sir Nicholas Lawes's attempt in 1695 to set up a school (Long 1774: 2.251), and the pressing problem of educating white creole children, one may infer that the creole society described by Long in the mid–eighteenth century must hardly have differed in essentials from that which Sloane saw in the 1680s and Atkins visited in 1721. From Sloane's day we may trace the shape it retained for over two hundred years: a European and creole white elite living, for the most part, in intimate contact with African and creole blacks, their lives governed by the routine of plantation life with its Sunday markets, where all fresh produce could be bought from slave higglers; the Christmas carnivals, or bruckings; the growing Maroon settlements; the black, brown, and white militiamen hunting the runaways; and the racially mixed plantation households with their "Gypsy Gibberish" (Atkins 1736: 245). The embedding of the creole, the slave language, lay deep in the consciousness of creoles of all colors and shades. Whether it yielded a continuum from the earliest days can be neither proven nor disproven. Only new evidence may disclose the daily lives of those households and settlements which shaped Jamaica's culture. Such evidence may reveal the extent of bilingualism and multilingualism. The use of Spanish and Portuguese survived among the Sephardic Jews for centuries, as the inscriptions in their ancient cemeteries show (Gabriel Coulthard 1968: 8–10). Among whites, fluency in one or more African languages may have been less rare than we might expect, given the competence of slave traders such as Captain Crow (1830) and of Aaron Bang, a planter in Michael Scott's novel (1834: 2.67). Letters and journals dating back to the seventeenth and early eighteenth centuries may betray creole interference and indicate that earlier generations experienced greater variability between dialects and languages—both vertically and horizontally—than our sparse records presently reveal.

Study of official records has, in fact, yielded small traces of creole interference in the SE usage of the educated upper class. The Vestry Minutes for February 14, 1789, in the parish of St. Thomas-in-the-Vale notes that "the Allotment of the said Road [should] be one Slave out every Fifty and one out every fifteen on all other Roads" (Jamaica: Government Archives). Slave Court Records of the early nineteenth century occasionally betray creole usage, but while such passages may reveal the stenographer's momentary response to a witness's actual words, creole usage by whites tells even more about the nature of variation.

The Early to Later Nineteenth Century

In the nineteenth century enough evidence exists to enable us to collect more informative samples. Within clearly defined communities, social hierarchies can be traced as in the preceding period, although there are some differences in population.

By 1830 whites numbered about 18,902, with half the number resident in Kingston. Of these, about 15 percent formed the upper class and the remainder a middle class ranging from merchants and tradesmen down to servants. The all-island ratio of slaves to whites is assessed by B. W. Higman (1976) as nearly 20 : 1. In the plantations the ratio is of course much higher, over 26 : 1. Higman estimates the slave population at 319,074 (1976: 55 and 1984: 77).

Browns had risen in number also, to approximately 40,000 of which a quarter were free. By 1844 this brown population was about 68,500 strong and concentrated mostly in Kingston (Brathwaite 1978: 135, 151, 168). One must bear in mind that all these figures derive from the educated estimates of historians, there being no census figures for Jamaica until 1844.

Still, one may link social organization with the linguistic variation shown in longer and more frequent records of direct speech. For example, in this period it is possible to analyze variation between participants at a single event as well as variation within the discourse of one individual. Even in situations for which no record of actual usage exists, one may trace the shape of a context that would elicit variations known to exist in JC usage.

One such event appears in the Jamaican Slave Court Records for October 31, 1822, in the parish of Hanover (Jamaica Government Archives). The standardized text describes the events at a party held in the house of one Georgiana Hall, a slave at Knockalva Penn. Entertaining themselves with dancing to the fiddle, drinking, eating, dicing, and playing backgammon were a large number of slaves from Knockalva and neighboring estates. It appears that at least one bookkeeper was present and certainly some runaways. One man was charged with stealing from the dicers' table and two Christian slaves (respectfully acknowledged by the court reporter), testified as to the happenings of the night. Georgiana Hall allegedly attacked the accused as a troublemaker come to discover runaways and was quoted as saying that "him one can't prove [nothing] against the whole Penn."

The social and cultural mix of this event illustrates what must have been a commonplace of Jamaican life: well-defined opportunities for language mixing and language variation as groups within this small, hierarchical society strove to merge and to separate linguistic identities.

A mid-nineteenth century record preserves extensive documentation of social variation in speech at a single event (Murray 1877). The setting is a wake held about 1844 for a fisherman. His "massnegers" (friends and neighbors of his own standing) have gathered, along with a few landowners from the area, to eat, sing, gossip, tell stories, and celebrate the dead man's life. All persons present are described as uneducated except Speaker 1, identified as the "executrix" of a will. As Table 15 indicates, this speaker shows none of the phonological or morphosyntactic features of the basilect selected (the same as those used in Table 14), while Speakers 2 to 5 show all. Although the basilectal features identified in this table exist in the language of Speakers 2 to 5, they do appear with varying frequency (Table 16). When the occurrence of two basilectal features is traced, for example, Speaker 2 (an uneducated woman of the landowner class) shows a more limited usage than Speaker 4, who is lower in the social scale. The occurrence of each feature is expressed as a percentage of the number of words in the sample.

Within the tightly knit structure of the wake, gossip, greetings, and storytelling unite the speakers in a single speech event in which such variations are normal and correct aspects of Jamaican language behavior.

Table 15. Selected Basilectal Features in Jamaican Speech at a Single Event, ca. 1850

Basilectal Features	Speakers				
	Landowners			"Massnegers"	
	1. Adult Man Educated, Color Unknown	2. Adult Woman Uneducated, Color Unknown	3. Adult Man Uneducated, Brown	4. Adult Woman Uneducated, Black	5. Adult Man Storyteller Uneducated, Black
Fricative replacement	−	+	+	+	+
Reduction of consonantal clusters	−	+	+	+	+
Intrusion of final vowel	−	+	+	+	+
Non-English lexeme	+	+	+	+	+
Unmarked pronoun case or tense	−	+	+	+	+
No auxiliary in negative VP	−	+	+	+	+
For/fe complement	−	+	+	+	+
Nonverbal predication	−	+	+	+	+

Table 16. Frequency of Basilectal Features among Jamaican Speakers of Differing Social Classes, ca. 1850

Speakers	Occurrence of Basilectal Features		
	Fricative Replacement	Intrusive Final Vowel	Nonverbal Predication
Landowners			
1. Adult man, educated, color unknown	0	0	0
2. Adult woman, uneducated, color unknown	2.40	0.22	1.31
3. Adult man, uneducated, brown	2.87	1.11	0.48
"Massnegers"			
4. Adult man, uneducated, storyteller, black	1.58	1.22	0.97
5. Adult woman, uneducated, black	3.99	3.26	1.81

In the data, paradigms such as sex, age, and color can be related to that of social class in terms of educational opportunity. A wide variety of idiolects are indicated and appear to be significantly related to a definable spectrum of variation between JC basilect and acrolect. By the late nineteenth century, it is clear that this acrolect (Standard Jamaican English) differs from the British standard mainly in pronunciation and details of lexicon.

Intrapersonal (stylistic) variation is also well attested in the nineteenth century. Records testify to speakers who can produce two codes, one modeled on the basilect and one on the acrolect. For example, in a single discourse from one speaker (a black apprentice) variations were observed in acrolectal subject marking of pronouns (*I, he, they*) as distinct from basilectal pronouns unmarked for subject (*me, him, them*), and in acrolectal tense marking of affix {-D} as distinct from basilectal unmarked stems.

The opening 250 words of the extract from the narrative of James

Williams (Text 16) produce 4 pronouns unmarked for subject (vs. 27 marked), and 15 verbs unmarked {-D} for tense (vs. 27 marked). The 250 words closing the account, however, show 11 pronouns unmarked for subject (vs. 3 marked) and 22 verbs unmarked for tense {-D} (vs. 1 marked).

The opening 250 words differ from the closing sample in ways typical of Jamaican language behavior. These first words begin a section of narrative. They are explanatory, setting the stage for action, and they therefore elicit a more formal register, closer to acrolectal Jamaican English. By contrast, the last 250 words belong to the climactic moments of the episode. Jamaican language behavior requires a code switch to features that identify the speaker's emotional and personal involvement and his rhetorical striving for absolute accuracy. Williams's use of basilectal register at this point encodes his experience directly. Situation, topic, narrative structure, and white official audience combine to produce code switching.

Written records of JC can thus be said to represent the speech of a wide range of social groups. Field and domestic slaves, locally born and newly arrived, are recorded. Free brown women include a basilectal speaker (Murray 1877) and a Sunday school teacher of the "niggar children," who displays a hypercorrect form mixed with acrolectal Jamaican English (Trollope 1860: 32–38). Local whites of the proprietor class are recorded or referred to repeatedly. A wide social spectrum is also represented—the Baptist deacon, the Maroon, the rebel, the lady's maid, the obeah man, the sailor and the nurse-housekeeper. Discourses also vary according to situation and according to topic. Most likely to be recorded in the basilect were songs of ridicule, ritual, protest, or eroticism; tales of cunning; tales with morals. Then as now, a storyteller adjusted his speech stylistically as he warmed to his topic. Slaves adjusted their speech to the acrolect (or to their perceptions of it) in addressing white owners, magistrates, or clergy or a formal gathering of other slaves. Social variation is common enough for novelists and journalists to distinguish between the speech of different social groups in their accounts (Text 20.A).

Apart from preserving basilectal Jamaican Creole and acrolectal Jamaican English, the language of many records shows a mixing of features not wholly explicable in terms of interference from educated English writers. There is no reason why a writer should be reliable in recording basilectal features in one text and the same writer be unreliable in recording a mix of basilectal and acrolectal features in another. Some samples are closely modeled on basilect or acrolect, but in others the language perceptibly shifts between or draws from both according to the needs of its speakers. Discrete mesolects may not be clear in the data, but what appears to be at least the foundation of a creole continuum is recognizable.

Attitudes

Attitudes associated with creole language situations are also everywhere apparent in the literature. White visitors and residents recorded JC mainly out of interest in the quaint or absurd, in exotic ritual, bawdiness, or folk moralizing. Speakers and observers alike appear to have shared a similar view of the creole and of the situations in which it was appropriate. The disapproving comments of foreign visitors and local residents confirm that the local white population, especially women, frequently spoke the creole (*Marly* 1828: 210). The white child of the proprietor class (whose speech is analyzed in Table 14) does not shock or embarrass his mother by the use of basilect in the presence of a visitor; in fact, the anonymous writer compares the mother's speech to that of her black servant (Text 3). Major Alan Chambre (1858: 129) sums up the situation in disgust: "There is scarcely a black in a hundred who speaks pure English, and the white people take no pains to correct them. Sometimes they even adopt the barbarous idiom of the negro, thinking to make themselves understood. The consequence is, their pronunciation is abominable, and the rising generation, notwithstanding the pains taken to educate them, retain the villainous patois of their parents." This attitude can be traced back to the early eighteenth century, when John Atkins (1736: 244–45) and others made similar comments. Acrolectal Jamaican English was the prestige form, as it is today. Variant features were considered contaminations, especially if they were loans, phonological reinterpretations, or syntactic structures perceived as slave-associated and African (D'Costa 1968). Some of the forms that occur in early texts later become impolite, rare, archaic, or obsolete (e.g., *nyam*, *wharra*, *congo saw*).

The consequence of such pejoration appears in the speech of the folk hero Annancy. Annancy (Twi *Anànse*, originally an African deity) is a trickster in Jamaican folktales—sometimes a spider, sometimes a man. He is cunning and immoral, and in early texts he speaks basilectal JC. In modern tales his odd speech is explained as a distortion caused by physical deformity, usually identified as a cleft palate. In other words, what is today classified as the "bungo talk" of Annancy is actually stigmatized archaic basilectal creole, fossilized in the traditional characterization of the folk hero.

Variation: A Postscript

It is important to recognize that the geographical domain of JC lies within a larger Caribbean language area (cf. Rickford 1981: 483). One of the parameters of variability now being stressed in creole linguistics is the heterogenous nature of the English that was carried into the slave trade and the colonies (LePage and Tabouret-Keller 1985: 22, 26). The linguistic varieties used by the white population of Barbados at the time of the mid-seventeenth-century migration to Jamaica would have helped to reinforce a tendency to linguistic diffusion already present in the language behavior of African slaves such as the Manding (Dalby 1970/71). The shifting of slaves through a rapid sequence of language situations must also have reinforced the inherent variability of the basilect. John Rickford comments (1981: 514–15): "The problems of linguistic variation with which creole continua confront us are not easy, and some of the more difficult problems—such as how we will be able to move beyond the usual analysis of variants within a single subsystem and tackle the analysis of varieties involving several subsystems simultaneously—have hardly begun to be addressed."

Historical reconstruction requires us to resolve an added complexity: the distinction of synchronic from diachronic variants. The corpus does not prove that the variant lects of early JC speakers at any particular stage (e.g., 1790–1810) do or do not represent "interrelated stages of a general change in progress" (Rickford 1981: 47). However, it does establish the existence, from the eighteenth century, of extensive variation (among speakers and within individual usage) in features of basilectal and acrolectal models of Jamaican speech. The data also confirm considerable mixing of such features. By this period, the focusing of speakers on either of these coexistent systems and the mixing of features drawn from them was apparently conditioned by social and economic characteristics and by situational requirements.

6

Implications of the Data

Wan tru puëma na den wortu d'e tan abra
Te ala trawan n'in yu libi wasi gwe . . .
[A true poem is made of words that linger on
When all the others in one's life are washed away]
Henny F. de Ziel ("Trefossa"), first Sranan poet of Surinam

Textual records of Jamaican Creole suggest that the language in its earliest form resembled other Caribbean English creoles and West African anglophone creoles more than it does today. It is difficult to evade the issue of common ancestry. The nature of those contributions described in the external language history must now be explored in the light of phonological and morphosyntactic descriptions of language in the texts.

The West African Coast

So far it has not been possible to identify any West African–derived lingua franca as the parent language of Caribbean Creole English, nor has any reconstruction of an ancestral anglophone creole on the West African coast been put forward. Mervyn Alleyne's reconstruction reveals a specifically African base spread over many languages and does not include English dialectal influences or GCCE origins. It is clear, however, that the circumstances under which such an anglophone creole could develop were present from the early seventeenth century. An English presence was established in the Gambia from 1618, spread to the Gold Coast by 1631–1650 and toward Bonny from 1662 onward (see Map 6). Ian F. Hancock (1986b: 83) suggests that during this time GCCE was transmitted to slaves being loaded for the Caribbean.

Table 17. Phonological Features of Nautical English and Jamaican Creole

Common Features	17-Century Nautical English	18th- and 19th-Century JC
[i] ~ [u]	*Bushop*	*busses* / *misses* (rhyming pair)
[e] ~ [i]	*twinty*	*perit* / *pirit*
[ɜ˞] ~ [ar]	*A starn*	*sarvant*
[ɜ˞] ~ [o] or [ʊ]	*churchyard*	*chutch*
[ɔ] > [a]	*drap*	*Garamighty*
[ɔj] > [aj]	*confayes* (convoys)	*jeints*
[e:] > [ie]	*clier*	*weaste*
[#h-] > ∅	*ospotall*	*im*
∅ > [#h-]	*hiland*	*honimal*
CC > C	*yeserday*	*tan* (stand)
[v] > [w]	*wery*	*werry*
[j] > ∅	*isterday*	*iss* (yes)
[ŋ] > [n]	*lightnin*	*marnin*
[v] > ∅	*grasend* (Gravesend)	*gie* (give)
[v] > [b]	*cobe*	*bittle*
[θ] and [đ] > ∅	*close* (clothes)	*bra* (brother)
[θ] > [t]	*Turse Day*	*tanks*
[đ] > [d]	*furder*	*dere*
[s] <> [š]	*portshmoth* *Spanis*	*shing, fis*
Variation among stops such as [t] > [k] and [d] > [g]	*Carickfardus* (Carrickfergus, Ireland)	*likkle, miggle*

GCCE would probably have had its earliest influences on the West African side from such languages as Kru, Manding, and Kwa. The nautical jargon of the trade ships must also have been crucial to the formation of this anglophone creole in the early seventeenth century.

Orthographical evidence of sailors' pronunciation in the seventeenth century confirms that nautical jargon shares several features with early JC. A study by William Matthews (1935a) of the phonetic spelling of unschooled sailors, as recorded in ships' logs, reveals a substantial overlap with the phonology of eighteenth- and nineteenth-century JC (Table 17). We have already seen that early JC texts preserve nautical terms (*tafferel, windward, stamp-an-go*, and *grog*).

West African anglophone creoles today preserve much of this "ship-talk," as Hancock demonstrates in an analysis of its influence on Krio (1976: 24–36). Several writers—from Schuchardt to Fyle and Jones (1980: xviii)—trace the beginnings of Krio to the repatriated Maroons from Jamaica, who were transported to Sierra Leone from as early as 1787. However, it appears more likely that Krio descended from GCCE of the seventeenth century (Hancock 1986b), was substantially modified by resettlement from Jamaica in the late eighteenth century, and was constantly subjected to West African influence. Those recaptives who settled in Sierra Leone after the ending of the slave trade in 1810 increased the West African input.

One may adduce many reasons why Krio should be distinct from JC and yet preserve numerous common features. An examination of the phonological similarities between Krio and seventeenth-century nautical jargon reveals substantial overlap between these shared features of pronunciation and the sound system of JC. In addition, Hancock (1976) identifies a number of Krio words—apparently derived from nautical English—which are also known in JC (e.g., *ganzi*, "thick sweater worn by seamen" [but see *DJE*]; *kotlas* / *kotlaš*, "machete"; *tsokɔp*, "chock full"). The *fɔ* possessive and *fɔ* infinitive marker are also common to all three.

Guinea Coast Creole English

A number of eighteenth- and nineteenth-century references point to the appearance, establishment and spread of GCCE, and some textual evidence of the language survives. John Atkins, who traveled in 1721 to both Guinea and the Caribbean, briefly quotes remarks made by native Guineans in an anglophone contact language that demonstrates nonverbal predication, *for* + pronoun possessive, *me* subject, intrusive final vowel, and ellipsis.

> John Conny, who is the principal Cabiceer, exacts a Duty from all Ships, of an Ounce of Gold, for this Privilege; and sends off a Servant with his Commission, a large Gold-headed Cane, engraved John Conny, to demand it. Our Neglect herein, with some opprobrious Treatment of the Agent, occasioned John Conny next day to come down with a Posse and seize our Water-casks ashore, carrying away ten or a dozen of our Men Prisoners to his Town. The Officer among them endeavouring to distinguish to John the Difference of a King's Ship from others, got his Head broke: John (who understood English enough to swear) saying, by G-- me King here, not only for my Water, but the Trouble has been given me in collecting it. (1736: 75)

> They use Circumcision, Prayers, and Washings, and seem to have an obscure Notion of Futurity; for when I used to charge my acquaintance with any thing of Dishonesty, they would reply, That after Death the honest goodee Man go to Godee, livee very well, have a goodee Wife, goodee Victuals, &c. but if a Rogue and Cheatee, he must be tossed here and there, never still. To this agrees the vulgar Notion of some, returning after Death to their own Country. (1736: 104–5).

William Smith's voyage in the early eighteenth century refers to GCCE even more briefly, yet also preserves very strong patterns of nonverbal predication:

> When I was at Sherbro, one Mr. Cummerbus, whom I shall have Occasion hereafter to mention, made me a Present of one of these Strange Animals, which are call'd by the Natives Boggoe: It was a She-Cub of six Months Age, but was then larger than a Baboon. I gave it in Charge to one of the Slaves, who knew how to feed and nurse it, being a very tender Sort of Animal, but whenever I went off of the Deck, the Sailors began to teaze it; some lov'd to see its Tears, and hear it cry; others hated its snotty Nose; one who hurt it, being check'd by the Negroe that took Care of it, told the Slave he was very fond of his Country-woman, and ask'd him, if he should not like her for a Wife? To which the Slave very readily replied, No this, no my Wife, this a white Woman, this fit Wife for you. This unlucky Wit of the Negroe's I fancy hasten'd the Death of the Beast, for the next Morning it was found dead under the Windless [*sic*]. (1744: 52–53)

Apart from recording actual texts, both Atkins and Smith comment on the language situation. Atkins, for example, lists "negrish words" (1736: 60). He also notes the names of Africans involved in the trade, and it is significant that some of these have English names, which may reflect a prolonged cultural contact (1736: 175). Smith mentions that in Sierra Leone, the slaves rowing his boat could all speak English, as could the brother of the local king (1744: 16, 22). On the British side, Smith records that Governor Rogers was able to understand the language of the local king. Familiarity with the Europeans was much greater in Sierra Leone than in the Gambia at this time, according to Smith (1744: 41). The company "linguist," or translator, defended himself when involved in a betrayal of the whites (75): "I have two Tongues; Tongue for White Man and Tongue for Black Man, I deserve to die, but I came that White Men should not kill Black but be Friends." Antonio, the linguist, had a good relationship with the Royal African Company and was far more Europeanized than the man at Cetra-Crue who "spoke a little English" and told Smith's crew that he "had too much Goats, too much Hogs and Hens" (107).

An account of three years in the life of an Efik chief, Antera Duke of Old Calabar (Map 5), is preserved in GCCE. Covering the period 1785–1788, the diary displays several features unlike JC, but a number of familiar patterns emerge: ellipses, tenseless verbs, *for* infinitives, *for* (directional) preposition, and the inconsistent marking of pronoun case (Forde 1968: 95, 100):

> 21.3.1786
> . . . Duk call all wee to com for his plaver house to hear Ephrim Egbo Daught with his . . . and Dick Ephrim and he say will not marry Long Duk so wee find Everry bob be true for him and wee hav Ephrim Duk women com and Break Duke god Bason about he Will not marry Ephrim after 7 clock night I have my wif Offiong Brother Dead by his father yard and putt his 8 yds fine clothe Did putt his in grown in 6 clock time
>
> 2.11.1786
> about 5 am in aqua Landing with fine morning wee have all us family went to Creek town for mak play first for Creek town cutt one women slave head of one cow be killd and goat and firs 7 great guns so wee com back in 5 clock time after 9 clock night I have Esim Duk com to my cobin for break one punchon Brandy for share to all Duke and sister so wee have us cason go up to guin Company with apandam for fetch wood plaver house Drun

Henry Bolingbroke's account of an African sailor (ca. 1798) is quoted by Hancock (1986b: 71, 84), who believes the man to be a *grumetto*. The African, a Mandinka speaker, had come from the Gambia to Demerara two years before. The creole he speaks closely resembles archaic JC, although anterior past *bin* is not attested in the earliest JC records: "The sentences Bolingbroke gives are "Kie, massa, you sabbe talk me country" (i.e. the Mandinka language), and "massa, me been see that white man in me country, in de town where me live, he been come dere one night for sleep, one blacksmith countreyman for me been with him, me been give him rice for he supper, and soon, soon in the morning he been go towards the Moor's country."

Several texts of Jamaican speech in the early nineteenth century are preserved by Captain Hugh Crow, who also records conversations between himself and African traders on the coast of Bonny. Published posthumously in 1830, Crow's *Memoirs* records his visits to West Africa ca. 1785–1808. Although this GCCE resembles JC, Crow's complete records preserve several differences of lexicon and morphology between JC and GCCE:[1]

> I one day on a visit to King Pepple found him in company with a chief named Calabar Foobra, a man who pretended to be a great warrior. He

> stated that having made war with his chief he was obliged to fly his country, and had come to Bonny for protection. When I had taken my seat, Pepple requested me to relate before this persecuted stranger what I knew about our great wars in Europe. I accordingly told him of the tens of thousands who in our wars were killed in one day on the field of battle, and of the vast numbers who were wounded. Pepple and his guest expressed some surprise, and after their inquiries were satisfied the king shrewdly remarked, "What is the matter, Crow, that you big man for you gran Palaver-house make all dat noise for we country and we trade? We no kill too much man all same you, and 'spose we black, and no sabby book, God A'mighty make we so, and we b'lieve God make we all and make white man sabby book; but you country want for pass all country, and now dem stop we trade, and want for pass God A'mighty, but all you big man and all you country neber can pass God A'mighty." I endeavoured to make some reply to this charge when Calabar said, "Crow you please hold you mouth a lilley. We big warm [glossed as "war" by Crow] passey you big warm two time; for dat time me fight for me country too much man go dead." I inquired, "How many men did you kill?" He replied, "Three men go dead, and too much man lose him foot and him fingers." Pepple here fell on a sofa in a roar of laughter that completely silenced the expatriated warrior, who looked somewhat disconcerted. The king thus addressed him, "You be poor fool man, for Crow tell you too much big thousand go dead for he country warm, and you tell him three man go dead for you fight, and som man lose he foot and he finger. What wo wo palaver ["silly talk," according to Crow] you make!" Poor Foobra was quite crest-fallen at this jeer, and was glad to dismiss the subject. (Crow 1830: 141–42)

Among the lexical items JC shares with both modern Krio and the GCCE of the seventeenth and eighteenth centuries are *fitis*, JC *fetish; pikin*, JC *pikni; tumos*, JC *to moch* ("too much"); *wantem*, JC *wan taim* ("one time"); *was-mot* ("liquor"), JC *wash-mout* ("early morning tea"); *bogbog*, archaic JC *bug-a-bugs* (see Hancock 1987: 277–78). Captain Crow (1830: 45) reports the remarks made in GCCE by a fifteen-year-old boy from Bonny: "Massa Crow, something bite me too much and me no can see 'im; and me want you for give me some was mouth."

Slaves who had learned GCCE on the coast and were loaded aboard slave ships would again be exposed to the nautical jargon described earlier, as well as to direct and multiple influences of many different West African languages. Linguistic innovations toward a new and recognizably Caribbean creole would thus include, first, substantial transfers from the slaves' own West African language patterns, such as those reconstructed by Alleyne (1980); second, other contributions from the English-oriented contact language already encountered; and third, inputs drawn from other varieties of English, especially "ship-talk."

The Caribbean

Even those Africans shipped directly to Jamaica encountered incoming settlers from other islands. Whether these speakers brought with them a creole recognizable as Caribbean or a creole established enough to exert significant influence on Jamaican speech is not known. In the past, considerable influence has been ascribed to Barbadian immigrants, but its nature is by no means clear. The lexical and morphological parallels linking BE and JC might arise as easily from a common, separate English dialectal ancestry as from transmission from Barbados to Jamaica. The third possibility—that *both* processes were at work in seventeenth-century JC—may provide the most useful line of inquiry. Norma Niles's insistence (1980) that Barbadian speech of the seventeenth century constituted a dialect of English and not a creole is consequently of great importance in unraveling this puzzle.

The relationship of Barbadian to an archaic creole form is discussed by Alleyne (1980: 182) in his study of the Afro-American creoles. "Barbados," he writes, "is rather unique in the context of the non-Hispanic West Indies since it is not considered an area where a creole dialect or language is spoken. Bajan is a regional, non-standard variety of English, but there is some evidence that in the late 19th century there was a Barbadian register analogous to so-called 'Jamaican Creole.' This 19th-century Barbadian 'creole' has disappeared." Alleyne assumes that traces of nineteenth-century Barbadian speech must be a continuation of a lost seventeenth-century ancestor. The regular demographic strength of the whites, the topography of the island, and the early development of secular and religious education all contributed to rapid movement through the stages of linguistic acculturation, he says, "but few relics remain from the earliest stage." He lists second-person plural *unu* and habitual aspect *da* as Barbadian dialect's most direct link with a creole past (1980: 186). For Alleyne, the present form of Barbadian speech is the result of decreolization. For Niles (1980: 124), the evidence of BE *da* points directly to English dialectal sources; the very low number of African-based lexemes also argues against a creole base for modern Bajan.

Actually, the evidence usually cited for a Barbadian creole is concentrated in texts of the nineteenth century, by which time there had been ample opportunity for linguistic interchange between Barbados and islands with established creoles and for inputs through later imports from West Africa. So far no traces of a seventeenth-century creole in this island have come to light, and Niles (1980) argues persuasively that a nonstandard variety of English was created early through the contact of a profusion of English dialects.

Burrowes and Allsopp (1983) argue strongly for an early Barbadian creole: "This accumulation of co-occurrence and correspondences in the everyday speech of the majority of Barbadians, is enough, [we] think, to establish a strong genetic relation between Barbadian Creole and other established Creoles." Burrowes and Allsopp acknowledge that some important creole features (front focusing and serial verbs, for instance) are missing from Barbadian speech, but they list many other features that are present. Actually, the majority of these happen to be features attested in seventeenth-century British dialects: reduction of consonantal clusters; [θ] > [t] and [đ] > [d]; palatalization of velar stops; reduction in inflection for tense, number, case, gender; infinitive marker *fo*. A few features (notably *wuna*) are exclusively associated with West African languages but are not necessarily seventeenth-century inputs into Bajan. JC records, for example, do not show JC *unu* until well into the nineteenth century.

Some nineteenth-century writers refer to a characteristic Barbadian speech quite distinct from educated English. The terms of reference ("a sad drawl," "lisping") recall descriptions of JC at this very time (Pinckard 1806: 244–94; and cf. Nugent 1966: 77). Still, it is impossible to conclude anything from these comments but that early Barbadian speech was distinct from educated English usage and that nonstandard British dialects (such as Cornish or Hiberno-English) could well have produced features later to become specifically associated with Caribbean English creoles. Niles estimates, for example, that over half of the British colonizers in Barbados (ca. 1670) were from southwestern England (1980: 77).

Apart from contact with the speech of incoming settlers and slaves from other Caribbean territories, however, Jamaican slaves would have encountered varieties of EModE dialects directly, and several features of these appear in JC. Even literary English of the EModE period, which few slaves could possibly encounter, shows features familiar in JC, although they no longer survive in modern Standard English. In the language of Shakespeare and his contemporaries adjectives frequently overlapped with adverbs; comparative morphemes and negatives were doubled for emphasis; prepositions were functionally variable (for example, the *for to* infinitive was relatively common); elision and functional shifts were frequent; auxiliaries were not required before negative verb phrases; pronoun case was at times indistinct enough for *me* and *him* to occur in subject functions. Even elision of "it is," "there is," and "is" can occur (and see *II Henry IV,* IV.i.98; *Tempest,* I.ii. 218–19). This literary register cannot be dismissed simply because it was inaccessible to the majority. It is significant that educated blacks, such as Francis Williams (Long 1774: 2.475–85), mastered it as a matter of course. But Williams is a unique example.

Not until the nineteenth century does substantial evidence of the language of literate blacks appear.

The accessible dialects of EModE were of course the nonstandard and regional forms. For example, the southwestern dialect bears many resemblances both to early JC and to the nautical jargon of the seventeenth century. Matthews (1935a) records familiar features: the raising of [e] (*sicond*), [ɜ] > [ar] (*marchant*), [i] ~ [u] (*busshoppe*), [ɔ] > [a] (*saft*), [#h-] > Ø (*aspetall*), reduction of consonant clusters (*husban*). He also draws attention to metathesis (*dexis*, "desks") recollective of JC *axe*, "ask," both from other English dialects.

Southwestern English, and specifically Western Cornish, also preserves [v] > [b] (*ob*, "of"); glide insertion (*gwine*); elision of initial vowels (*'pon*); and syncopation (*s'poase*). It shares lexical items with early JC, such as *thankee*, *liard*, and *yeri*. It shows morphosyntactic features well known in other English dialects (continuative prefix *a-doen*) and somewhat rarer but recognizable features such as *ketcht* for "caught," *me* in possessive function, and the negative verb phrase without auxiliary. Hancock (1986a) reproduces an example of southwestern dialect from Trevaylor 1935:

> "Deear, deear, Mister Bill—wot 'r' 'e tellan' av! —oall th' tripe 'n' hunyans clane waasted like 'at theere, jis' w'en . . ."
>
> "Noa, Thoph'lus—aw warn't waasted nuther, 'zactly; fer me 'n' th' oul' wumman 'n' th' cat, h'm—stroogl't, like, 'tween es fer t' maade a meal ob'm aaft'w'rds. I'm gwain a bit 'foore m' stoory, f'r oall. W'en th' tripe 'n' traade flied like 'at theere, I thoft—h'm—that I 'eeard a soort av a scraapen' kind av a nooise 'pon th' slats av th' roof, luk: so I quately awp'md th' back dooar (aw wor 'pon th' letch, 'knaw), mainin' fer to try fer t' see, ef I cud, wot wus hup theere. But wot fust ketcht me heye wes a peer av boots—'ha -right 'long-side th' waater-bar'l—h'm."
>
> "Peer av boots, Mister Bill—ha!"

Although this sample uses *fer to* as the infinitive marker, Hancock shows that northern Cornish often displays infinitives marked solely with *for*. Hancock maps the distribution of *to*, *for to*, and *for* infinitives (1986a) and shows *for* (without *to*) as also occurring in North Devonshire and Liverpool. Both areas, as he points out, were important places of embarkation for Africa and the Caribbean. Contact between dialects of English in Britain itself would have reinforced features that have survived in Caribbean usage.

Hiberno-English and southwestern English preserved such a relationship outside of the Afro-Caribbean area (Hancock 1986a). Not only did the two fertilize each other but Hiberno-English influenced JC both directly and indirectly through settlers from other islands. Seventeenth-century Hiberno-English recorded in the texts assembled by Alan Bliss (1979) displays both phonological and morphological features attested by records of early JC: [e] > [i] (*wint,* "went"); [θ] > [T] (indistinguishable from [t] to speakers of other dialects, as in *eleavent,* "eleventh"); [đ] > [d], but occasionally the lack of distinction between dental fricatives, dental stops and alveolar stops is indicated by the spelling of "t" as "th"; [v] > [w] (*Waacancy, owercome*); [s] > [š] (*shwering, anshwerd*), and sometimes [č] (*fenche*); [ŋ] > [n] so that *choosing* rhymes with *cousin;* loss of [t#] and [d#] also appears in Irish texts as well as in seventeenth-century English (cf. Joyce 1910: 2–3, 99).

Dem sometimes occurs as demonstrative, *me* as subject, *him* as equivalent to educated English *it;* plurals, past tense, possessives, and third-person singular may all be unmarked in this dialect; *for* can be directional (equivalent to SE "to") in "speak for you" but also survives as infinitive marker in Belfast English today, where it is used in a wider range of circumstances than in other present-day English dialects (Davis 1984). Several of these features occur in the rowdy dialogue of a play by Richard Head, *Ubi et Ubique* (1663) edited by Bliss (1979: 112, 115).

> *Patr.* Fuy by St. Patrick agra, he put de fuckation upon my weef. I will tell dee tale if thou wilt Glun ta mee. I came in wid my pishfork upon my back, thou know'st, and I see a greyshy [greasy, ugly] guddy hang [gallows bird] upon my weef, and I did creep in like a michear [thief], to the wattles upon de loft abow thou know'st, and there I did see putting the great fuck upon my weef, as if thy own shelf was there Moister; and because I wu'd make haste, I fell down upon 'em, and leek to have more than half break my neck; then wid my pishfork I clap him upon de Narsum, and I did make sharge for him in the Kings name, thou know'st, to stay dere til I fetch the Cunt——stable; but before I came, this chureeh crave Ruagh [Red Branch Knight] make run away for himself: and looky there Moister.
>
> *Kilt.* Sirrah leave thy howling.
>
> *Path.* My shelf no howle, me make speak for you: By St. Pathrick and St. Shone Batty, my shelf will make no servant for de.
>
> *Thrive.* Come, come, Sign, sign:
>
> Kiltory delivers the writings to Mrs. Hopewell
>
> So, so.
>
> . . . .
>
> *Path.* Shoole a crogh, [get hanged], manam a dioule, [my soul to the Devil], thou greisie micheer, by my soulwation joy a chree, y told dee, de English vil put de sheat [cheat] pon efry podyes.
>
> *Kilt.* Woman was the first that ever took the Devils counsil, and first communicated it to man, to the ruine of both their terrestrial happinesse; . . . 'twas well she had not cheated me out of my soul too. [*Exit.*

> *Path.* May starfing come to her sheeks, strepoh granach, [loathsome whore], and may her fader's shild make dye in de prishon. [*Exit.*

The significance of a Scottish input is also documented by historians and indicated by evidence of phonological development. This influence was sufficiently intense to produce not only a host of minor place names (e.g., Dumfries, Grants Pen, Blauwearie, and Glengoffe) as well as scattered lexical items but to affect phonology through innovation or reinforcement.

Heinrich Mutschmann (1909: 69–78) reports that glides may be lost (*amen* "woman") or may be inserted before rounded vowels, which then unround (*guid* "good"); [v] > [w] occurs in *wermen,* "vermin"; [s] > [š] in [šna] "snow," or before [t], as in [brišt], "breast"; [đ] > [d] in *de,* "the," while [d] may be lost in final position, as in *θuzn* "thousand," and [t] become [k] after [l], as in *kikkle,* "kittle" ("tickle"). Murray lists features familiar in JC, such as the diphthongs [ie] and [uo] in *eable, theare, my'ed* ("maid"), and *cluose, buore* (1873: 103–11), all of which occur in southern Scottish speech.

Creoles of Neighboring Territories

Extensive historical research underlies the lexicographical achievements of such pioneers as Cassidy and LePage, Holm and Schilling, Allsopp, and others. These linguists began the work of studying early documents to illuminate creole languages, and the work continues. Rickford (1987) has recently produced such a work based on early Guyanese texts. Until these records become generally available, however, and are analyzed for each area, much historical discussion of these languages will remain speculative. In the absence of exhaustive collections, a few samples of early creole texts from other territories may serve to highlight the similarities of these with early JC and to stimulate further comparative work outside the scope of this study.

Surinam, 1783

The following passage from Voorhoeve's discussion of the formation of creoles in Surinam (1973: 133–45) points up the importance of comparative work. The *sowtwatra nengre* ("saltwater negro") of Saramaccan (SM), Sranan (SN), and Ndjuka shares important features with JC:

> From 1779 onwards SM and SN were both studied by the same missionary, Christian Ludwig Schumann, who wrote a SM dictionary in 1779 (pub-

> lished in Schuchardt 1914), and a SN dictionary in 1783 (still unpublished). The latter is a remarkable piece of work, in which Schumann sometimes cites at length (and in Creole) remarks of his informant, who must have been keenly aware of dialectal differences. In speaking about the now obsolete item *bringi* (to bear) he says that this word is seldom used in town, that it is used in SM and on many of the plantations, but that he had heard a town Negro say: mi kau bringi wan mannpikin (my cow got a male child). I do not suppose that such a well-informed man would have been unaware of the existence of an established variety of Creole on Jewish plantations. (Voorhoeve 1973: 141)

To these remarks, Voorhoeve appends the following note, giving the full extract:

> 'Na Fotto dem no habi da muffe so menni; da Dju tongo: ma nuffe Plantasi habe hem. Tog wan reti Fotto-kriolo ben takki: isredeh mi kau bringi wan mannpikin, gestern had meine Kuh ein Junges, ein Oechsgen geworfen' (in town one does not use this word so much; it is Jews language (=SM): but many plantations use it. A real Creole from town said: yesterday did my cow get a male child). (Voorhoeve 1973: 141)

Gullah, 1799

Donald R. Kloe edited the following poem, titled "Buddy Quow," and reproduced it in *Southern Folklore Quarterly*. It is a Gullah poem, dating, Kloe says, from 1799:

1.
Was matter Buddy Quow?
I ble Obesha bang you,
You tan no sabby how,
Dan Backrow Man go wrong you, Buddy Quow,
Dan Backrow &

2.
No hawte pun morrowgo,
Nusso grandy hungry do you,
I hab som Barbaracco,
I bring dem all for you morrowgo
I bring dem all &

3.
No hungry nor so dry
For true now no me yerry

Make vawter for me yie
I cry so, tell me vary vipe me yie
I cry so tell &

4.
Pshaw tan way la me lone,
No so trouble begin now?
I goo mine take you tone,
So knock you rottin skin, so break you bone
So knock &

5.
Dah time Quasheba tell,
De Pickney he bin coming
I now go for to sell,
Dah hog me mommo gib me, berry well
Dah hog &

6.
Von coat I buy um new,
Von ropper I bin bring come
Von new hankisha too
I nebo bin go tink um nusso true.
I nebo bin &

7.
When Unco Quaco say,
De Pickney he was come now,
I no go morrow stay
My harete bin knock pum pum on true grangie
My harete &

8.
Gor Mighty da nah Buf
See how Quasheba do me
Dah Backrow Man he luf
He bring molatto for me Gor nah Buf
He bring &

9.
He yie, he nose, he mout,
(I bin good mine for hit um)
Tun ebry mossel bout
lak Obesha bin pit um out he mout.
Lak Obesha &

Guyana, 1797

The following letter, from Demerara, dated February 1797, appears in Pinckard (1806: 3.266–67). For discussions of these and other early Guyanese texts, see Rickford (1987).

> On the morning of January 13th, a well-looking robust negro, unexpectedly presented himself at my door, tendering his services, and begging that he might be allowed to work for me. Upon my going out to speak with him, his countenance gladdened with joy, and looking animated and cheerful, he said he would "do ebery ting to 'blige Massa, wait upon Massa, clean Massa's horse, and do all de work Massa tell him."
>
> Not immediately recollecting his features, I asked who he was, whence he came, and how it happened that he addressed himself to me? When he replied—"Ah Massa, if you no remember Prince, Prince no forget dat Massa tell 'em soldiers for break one great iron collar off Prince's neck, and gave him for gnyaam when Massa at Mahaica." This brought him to my recollection, and I recognized an unhappy slave, whom, in one of my walks at Mahaica, I had met wandering in a cottonfield, bearing a heavy iron collar upon his neck, with three long iron spikes projecting from it.

St. Kitts, 1822

The following poem, titled "Shatterday Nite," appears in Mathews (1822: 75–80).

> Shatterday nite aw bin daw my house man,
> Bin daw my house man, shed down so softly,
> Tank long Sabina, mit mommy Cumba,
> Mit unco Quaco, eh ha ha ha me haut
> Bin so grad now, hungry foo true now,
> Shunting foo yeat day, herrin and fish man.
> Pot bin daw bile man, bile um so sweet man,
> Set down so softly no tink pon notin,
> Massa daw caw me, Massa daw caw me,
> Kum yaw Sabina, wha you daw do da, eh ha ha ha,
> Kum yaw me boy, go charry de paper foo Missy Tonsy
> Go law Baksar, cookly my boy go,
> Bring kum de haunser, eh ha ha ha,
> Wha me muss do now, hungry daw kill me,
> Massa go sen me, run law Baksar man;
> Paw bin so furer, yaw me da go now,
> Yaw me da run now, eh ha ha ha,

Foot wha aw year now, no bin run furer man,
Meet missy Tonsy, bin pon von hoss man,
Gee um de paper, tay me, me boy
You run law you Massa, tay um to-morrow
Bring kum de haunsur, eh ha ha ha ha,
Me haut bin so grad now, hungry da kin me,
Yaw me da run now, yaw me da kum now,
Kum law me house man, house bin so dark now,
Chan see you han man, chan see you nose man,
Chan see you yie man, eh ha ha ha ha,
Caw pon Sabina, caw mommy Cumba,
Caw unco Quaco, no yerry notin, eh ha ha ha,
Wha me muss do now, go law me house man,
Sabina da sleep day, caun um, aw caun um,
Push um, aw shub um, shub um, aw push um,
Ee won gim me haunser, eh ha ha ha ha,
Wha me muss do now, hungry da kin me,
Tink say poo cretur, bex long ee Massa,
Dat time ee sen me, run naw Baksar man,
Paw bin so furer too, wha me muss do now,
Look foo de naunnom, dat time aw fine
So me da set down, yaw me da set down,
Naunnom so sweet now, dat time ee sweet me,
Set down so softly, no tink pon notin,
Aw yerry von sunting, sunting da walk man,
Da walk law me house man, tink say da jumbie,
Me haut bin so fraid now, jumbie go kin me,
Jumbie go yeat me, eh ha ha ha ha,
Dat time aw fine so, trow down de naunnom,
Run pon de bed man, caw pon Sabina,
Mek um budge up man, dat time ee budge up,
Tay um, Sabina, sunting da walk yaw,
You no sauby da wha he, eh ha ha ha ha,
Sabina bin tay me, bree say da jumbie,
Dat time ee tay me, me haut bin so fraid now,
Look foo de bamboa, kibber me head man,
Kibber me face man, kibber me yie man,
Dat time aw fraid so, jumbie da walk now,
Aw yerry ee foot man, yerry ee shoe man,
Since aw bin bawn man, aw nebber bin yerry
Jumbie bin hab on shoe pon ee foot man,
Dat time aw yerry, aw caw pon Sabina,
Aw tay um, Sabina, wha binness jumbie
Da law me house man, aw no owe um notin,
Aw look foo me tink [*sic*] now, dat time aw fine um,
Lick way pon jumbie, yaw me da lick way,

Jumbie da bawl man, jumbie da run man,
Since aw bin bawn man, aw nebber bin yerry
Jumbie bon bawl so, yaw ee da run now,
Run close de doa man, opin de doa man,
Yaw ee da run now, yaw ee daw bawl now,
Aw hit um, aw tump um, dat time ee run so,
Jumbie he fall man, me haut ee so grad now,
Aw hit um, aw tump um, tay aw bin weary,
Dat time aw wearyo, aw meet unco Quaco,
Ee begin foo tay me, ee tay me,
You sauby who you dau bong day,
Aw tay um aw sauby, you no see dau jumbie,
Who sa dau jumbie, debbil da jumbie,
You no see dau Massa.

St. Vincent, ca. 1833

Mrs. A. C. Carmichael (1833: 1.317–18) recorded many interviews with Africans in the islands of St. Vincent and Trinidad. In several of the interviews, the Africans use the term *bamboo* ("clothing," "clothes"), which occurs as *bamboa* ("clothes," "bedclothes") in the previous text. The interviews took place over a period of many months in which Carmichael traveled around the eastern Caribbean to observe and report on the manners and customs of all levels of society.

"How old were you when you came to St. Vincent?" "One big man, so big me be now." "What nation were you of?" "The Mandingo." "Were you free or slave?" "Misses, me be one very great grandee; not one grandee massa, but one great grandee; me hae slave to wash me, me hae yams for eat, fresh pork; me hae no vorck for do, only me go fire at bird in a bush, for yam: well, misses, one grandee massa send always hunting for people; so dey take me in a bush, make me vorck hard,—me nevre vorck afore, me no know'd how to vorck; dey flog me, say me no good for noting, send me a Guinea coast, sell me Buckra capin." "But surely you would like to go back to Mandingo?" "No, misses, Mandingo one very bad country; me no have vorck too much now, me hae yam, tanias, plantains, every ting very good."

St. Thomas, ca. 1834

The following text from Wentworth (1834: 1.241–42) is one of the few samples from that island.

Hurra, my jolly boys, Fine time o' day.

We pull for San Thamas boys, Fine time o' day.
San Thamas hab de fine girl, Fine time o' day.
Nancy Gibbs and Betsy Braid, Fine time o' day.
Massa cum fra London town, Fine time o' day.
Massa is a hansome man, Fine time o' day.
Massa is a dandy-man, Fine time o' day.
Him hab de dollar, plenty too, Fine time o' day.
Massa lub a pretty girl, Fine time o' day.
Him lub 'em much, him lub 'em true, Fine time o' day.
Him hunt 'em round de guaba bush, Fine time o' day.
Him catch 'em in de cane piece, Fine time o' day, &c.

Barbados, ca. 1834

Like the St. Thomas text, the following song, recorded by Wentworth, probably represents Bajan usage of a few years previous to the time of publication, 1834 (1.284–85).

Ante Nanny, Open da door,
Pater want da soursop soup,
Ante Nanny, open da door,
Pater want da soursop soup,
Run, Mr. Cunningham,
run for you life,
run Mr. Cunningham,
run for you life,
run Mr. Cunningham,
run for you life,
Pater da come wid a open knife.

Ante Nanny, open da door,
Pater want da soursop soup,
Ante Nanny, open da door
Pater really want da soup. — (pause, ad libitum)
Run, Mr. Cunningham, run, run, run,
Run, Mr. Cunningham, run, run, run,
Run, Mr. Cunningham, run, run, run,
Pater da come wid a loaded gun!

North America, 1840, 1842

Mende rebels held in Connecticut, 1840–1842, are described in Blassingame (1977: 30 n. 23) as recaptives destined for Cuba. Captured by a U.S. schooner and taken to New Haven, Connecticut, in 1839, the Africans quickly learned to read and write under the tutorship of Yale University students "because the Mendians [already] had a written language" (ibid.). The following letters provide examples of their English usage. Apparently, communication with the group was first carried out through an interpreter, James Covey, a Mende sailor on an English ship. Their Sierra Leone background would probably have exposed the Mende to Krio, and that language may have played a role both in the kind of English these letters contain and in the recaptives' willingness to acquire literacy in English. The first letter (Blassingame 1977: 30) was written in the United States and the second (43–44) on the return journey to Sierra Leone. (Blassingame quotes it from the *American and Foreign Anti-Slavery Reporter,* June 2, 1842, 63).

Westville, [September, 1840]

Mr. [Lewis] Tappan   I going write you letter   I want tell you some thing   I bless you because I love you   I want pray for you every night and every morning and evening and I want love you too much   I will write letter for my thing for you from that time Jesus began to preach and to say repent for the kingdom of heaven is at hand   my friend I write this paper for you because I love you too much   I pray for you   Love us pray our father who art in heaven hallowed be   Mr. Tappen I bless you because I love you and I love write you letter my friend

I want love all teachers who teach me and all my people good things about Jesus Christ God and heaven and every things   I bless them that teach me good   I pray for them   I want write some   thy name thy kingdom come thy will be done in earth as it is in heaven give us this day our daily bread and forgive us our debts as and we forgive forgive our debtors and lead us not into temptation but deliver us from evil for thine is the kingdom and the power and the glory for ever Amen   O God keep all my teachers and all friend and all my enemy that no love me   all I love them   I try to write letter of paper for Mr. Tappan   and Jesus said unto him foxes have holes and birds of the air have nests but the son of man hath not where to lay his head   and Jesus said unto him No man having put his hand to the plough and looking back is fit for the kingdom of God.

my name Kale J
send your letter by James Birney

BARQUE GENTLEMAN, at sea, near Sierra Leone.)
January 13th, 1842)

Mr. Tappen—Dear Sir: Captain good—no touch Mendi people. All Mendi people love Mr. Tappan. Mr. Tappan pray for Cinque and all Mendi people all time, and Cinque, and all Mendi people pray for Mr. Tappan all time. You give Cinque two white men and one colored man to go with Cinque. We stay Sierra Leone; Cinque can't help, because it no my country; we go my country I help very much. Cinque love Mr. Tappan, and all Mendi people love Mr. Tappan very much. I no forget Mr. Tappan for ever and ever; and I no forget God, because God help Mr. Tappan for Mendi people. All Mendi people glad for Mr. Steele, and Mr. Raymond and his wife, and for colored man and his wife. All good—no touch Mendi people. Cinque no forget Mr. Williams, because he love Mendi people very much. We catch Sierra Leone very quick now—I think to-morrow morning: I very glad. Two years gone, Cinque see ship. Mr. Raymond glad, Mr. Steele glad; then I go back to see 'Merica; I go my country—I make house and take care of white man. I thank J. Q. Adams, Mr. Norton, Mr. Williams, Mr. Denning, Mr. Lucius Cowles, Mr. Solomon Cowles, Mr. Ludlow and Mr. Townsend. I pray for all men all time. I no forget them   Cinque tell Mr. Tappan to make letters for all these men. I thank all 'merica people, for they send Mendi people home. I shall never forget 'merica people.

Your friend, CINQUE

Trinidad, 1858

A mid-nineteenth-century sample from Trinidad displays many features found in archaic JC: *fou* infinitive, *me* as subject pronoun, and lexical items such as *sabby, Garra,* and *na.* The resemblances and contrasts between this sample and the JC of the same period put difficult questions to the Caribbean creolist. The following passage appeared in the *Trinidad Sentinel,* April 8, 1858, under the title "Foo massa Headhitter Sentiwel."

Massa Squire,
Tarra maarnin me walk in lek a decent fella wid me battle a Ginger Beer fou tek me maarnin da Jacobson, lek backra da tek fou he da Ice House wid Soda. Traat, no bin hab time go dung, when me see da Bajian nagar "Cuffey Tom" cum in wid big Gaazette na he han—he begin fou read gib naga; how one poor Backra bin dey de look bex, he go out. Me say, warra disha? Da true wha French nagar say, "baton changez boutte" . . . eh, eh, did time na lek Merriky War. Me tek seat, sid dung-pan bench. By Garra, da nagar read en paper lek so me hin nuise lang time fou yerry backra read Proclamation when dem bin da gie nagar "quatre piquet." Me say, Bajian nagar da debble fou true! Da fella read letter, day da massa Hinde write em na Market da time he da watch butcher fou he no sell rattin beef gie awee.

Cho! da massa wha da command Port a Spain Gazette, he no hab sabby nuf fou massa Hinde. Oui foutre! massa Hinde chap he up lek me bin nuise fou chap beef fo! Cotch man—call em "Cotch collop." Chou massa Chewrd mus go hide he self no Woodbrook hilin house. But dat no all; directly, Jacky Brach, he cum in wid narra newspaper he call em Sentiwell—da fella read better agen. He begin he nancy torey, say, da "maarnin Poce" write em na blue water no England; den me buddy cum yerry backra chark—me bin shake—me hart go bip! bip! bip!—tree time me say, warra dish ya? pas possible, backra cuntry lang me no rope; spose backra no look sharp, maratta lang nagar go sen newspaper Africay fou learn all nagar fou read em. "Quacoo, cum see mud fish?" Ya de wurk wen dem nagar yerry news, dem no go, cum ya fou plantez cane baye boque. Den how dem go manage? Portugue all da keep shap—Coolie no fit, nomo fou weed grass. Awee free man lek a wee so no blige fou work two bit a day when no hab sweet patata: no hab yam, no hab cush cush, no hab caan, no hab punkin, no hab dry pease, no hab nuttin da grung, me donkey, me go wuk garden fou meself fou plant ebry ting. Ebery Satiday me go buy newspaper fou vite Cuffey Tom lang Jackey Roach fou pen de ebenin, and read the news fou me and my wife Naancy. me go sen narra letter nex week.

You begent saarvant,
Sam Ricketts

Continuity and Convergence

Alleyne's position on the relationship of substratal to other influences (1980: 140) is an important one. He believes that substratal influences "cannot be automatically invalidated by the existence of similar forms elsewhere which are subject to other historical causal factors." Textual evidence supports and enlarges on this view in that it demonstrates the importance of converging forces whose shared features tend to reinforce each other. It cannot be coincidental that so many of the features that flourished in the fully developed and conservative creole of nineteenth-century Jamaica can be related to multiple sources (Cassidy, 1966). Nor does it seem unnatural that in the language-learning process the repertoire acquired by a child in a multilingual situation might be shaped most profoundly by features that recur through a number of the many language models available to him (cf. Carrington 1982a: 56; 1982b; 1987: 12–13). Carrington (1987) considers methodologically hazardous Bickerton's argument that rules are acquired in creoles because they are required by the structure of the creole rather than because they exist in the input (1981: 51). Certainly it seems rash to pass lightly over the presence of features common to JC and to one or more of the languages whose contact is a fundamental stimulant to creolization (but see Bickerton 1984a and 1984c). And having found these features in the developing creole, how may one not relate them to it in terms of historical continuity?

Mufwene (1986: 129–62) argues persuasively for an integration of universalist and substrate hypotheses and demonstrates that neither provides a full answer to questions about creole genesis. Analyses of African substratal features have not sufficiently accounted for the isolating systems of creoles in which one or more of the contact languages were agglutinative. Equally, they fail to explain why the system selected for description should be compared to the Kwa rather than to some other group such as Mende or Kru (Mufwene 1986; Huttar 1981). In a description of development, one must seek those aspects of language making likely to be demanded by the language-learning process in the context of the slave trade.

According to Bickerton (1977: 55), "the difference between arriving at a pidgin and arriving at a reasonably accurate version of a standard language lies mainly in the availability of target models and the amount of interaction with speakers of the target language. . . . If . . . target models are scarce, and if he or she speaks mainly to non-native speakers who suffer a similar restriction of access to the target, the end product will be a pidgin." Such conditions as these may have prevailed to a greater degree in eighteenth- than in seventeenth-century Jamaica. The notion of a standard language is not applicable to seventeenth-century Jamaica, and at that time, whites outnumbered blacks. The conditions required by Bickerton's hypothesis (a high ratio of blacks to whites) did not arise until about 1700, long after the period commonly regarded as the time for the rapid and violent birth of a pidgin.

Many creolists dispute this view for a variety of reasons. In any case, the models of English available at this period would be the sum of Early Modern English varieties, and a number of slaves would have been repeatedly exposed to these dialects even before arriving in the Caribbean. The creole obviously formed in order to fill a communication gap, but textual evidence of the languages in exile in Jamaica confirms that the situation was neither a vacuum nor a total disruption of West African memory nor yet one in which Early Modern English was inaccessible. On the contrary, JC appears to have been the logical result of a continuity of both West African and English dialectal structures. Chart 10 displays the position of JC among the anglophone creoles and in relation to its contributing languages and dialects. On the subject of West African continuity, Alleyne (1980: 141) points out that despite pressures to discontinue the use of African languages, several of these languages continued, in some form or other, into the twentieth century. He points to Yoruba and Kikongo survivals in Jamaica and to the "Kromanti" of the Maroons. Gilman (1979: 36–43) relates the introduction of the [r]-deletion rule and the variable heights in midvowels of seventeenth-century British English to probable variation in early creole speech communities.

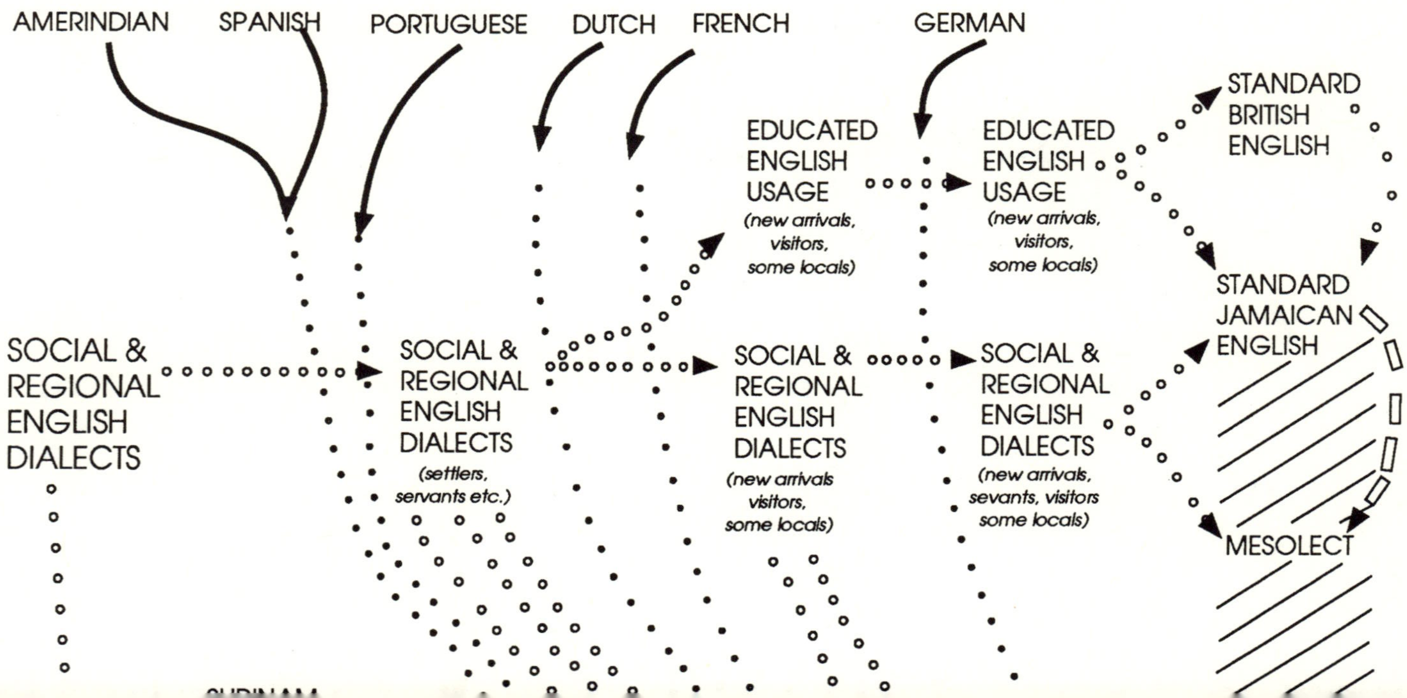
AMERINDIAN
SPANISH
PORTUGUESE
DUTCH
FRENCH
GERMAN
SOCIAL & REGIONAL ENGLISH DIALECTS
SOCIAL & REGIONAL ENGLISH DIALECTS (settlers, servants etc.)
EDUCATED ENGLISH USAGE (new arrivals, visitors, some locals)
SOCIAL & REGIONAL ENGLISH DIALECTS (new arrivals visitors, some locals)
EDUCATED ENGLISH USAGE (new arrivals, visitors, some locals)
SOCIAL & REGIONAL ENGLISH DIALECTS (new arrivals, sevants, visitors some locals)
STANDARD BRITISH ENGLISH
STANDARD JAMAICAN ENGLISH
MESOLECT

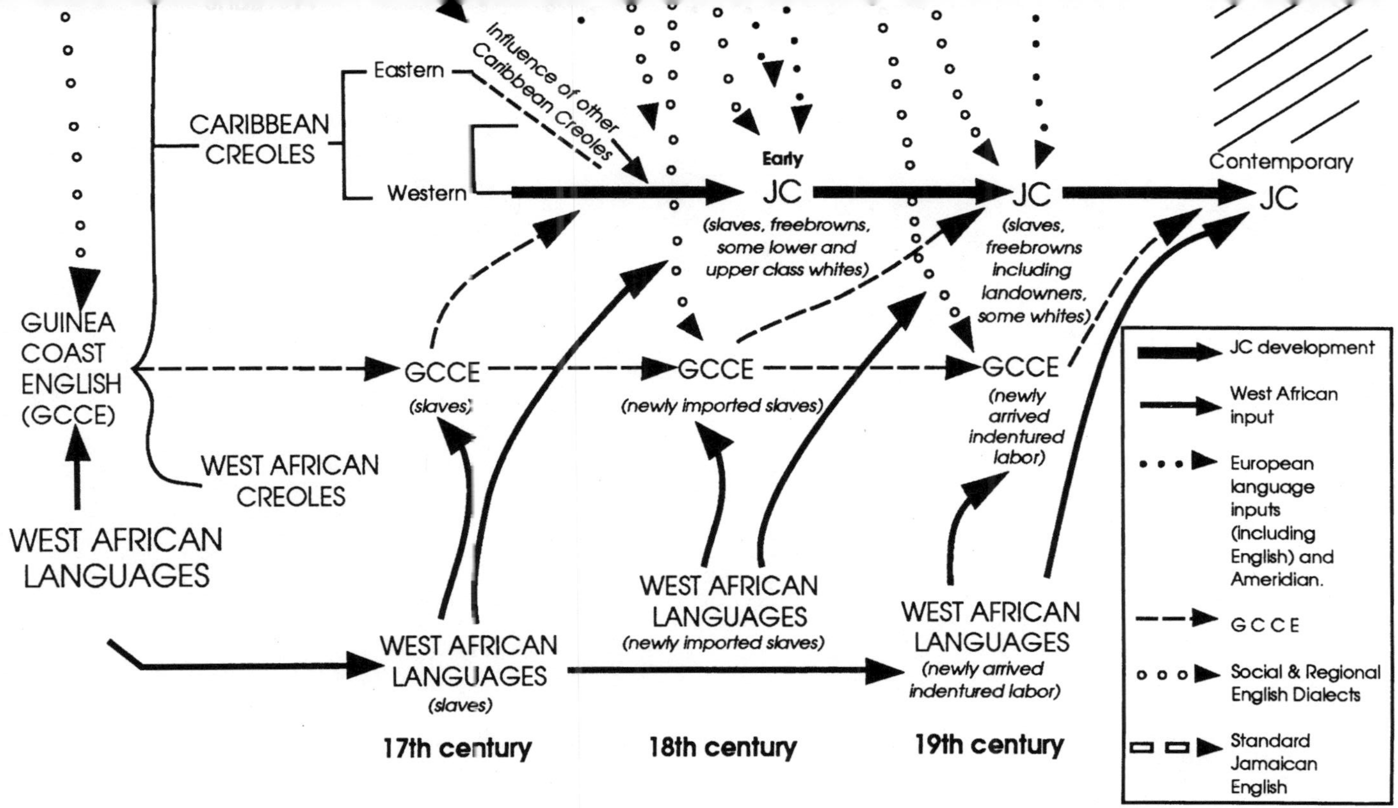

Chart 10. Sources of Language Influence on Jamaican Creole

Holm (1980) focuses on the creole copula to demonstrate the reinforcement of one historical input by another. He postulates a syntactic category, "highlighter," in a number of contributing West African languages and relates this form to a Hiberno-English structure influenced by an Irish introductory copula. Holm also demonstrates that "both African and Afro-European languages of the New World have a variety of 'copulas,' and the use of each is restricted to specific semantic and syntactic categories" (1984: 297); linguistic ancestry may account for variants both *within* and *between* creole languages. Hancock's research into the existence of GCCE and the input of English dialects and nautical English at the same time draws back other veils from the mystery of the creole past and reveals further levels of complexity.

Historical theory and, in particular, theoretical reconstruction of language structure must be credible when judged in the light of known languages. The reconstruction must sustain comparison with related languages and with later stages of the same language. Our findings demonstrate extensive similarities not only to other Caribbean creoles and to an early creole English fragmentarily recorded on the West African coast, but also to the most conservative, archaic, and isolated variety of JC to survive into the twentieth century.

This variety is the so-called "deep language" of the Maroons, described by Kenneth Bilby (1983) as a special register of JC used in Kromanti ceremonies during possession by ancestral spirits. Bilby clearly distinguishes this register from the most basilectal forms of contemporary JC as being only partially intelligible to non-Maroons. He also separates it from a third linguistic form, Kromanti, the invocational African language itself.

Among the features preserved in Bilby's sample are vowel epenthesis (*bigi* "big"); elision of syllables (*sonti* "something"); variation such as [ɲ] ~ [j] (*nyũman* "youngman"), [r] ~ [l] (*pre* "place"), and possible [s] ~ [š] (*manis* "mannish"); regular sound change [h] > [j] (*ya* "here"); and archaic/conservative usage of *da*, *bin*, and *na*. His material also demonstrates features—such as vowel nasalization (*grãfa*)—that we have suspected but have so far been unable to document (Bilby 1983: 72):

> yes, bigi suma, da nyũman ya bin fram big īsho, bin fram abrouni, bot afa im bin a yangkungku pre, grãfa, da man de a manis. di nyũman a manis. wi tuk tek na im na wi kaban. grãfa, wi tuk tek na wi kaban tel i about yangkungku sonti.

> . . . Yes, old one, this man came from (across) the sea, came from outside, but after he came to the Maroon place, Grandfather, that man is (showed himself to be) a man. Grandfather, the man is a man. We took him into our home. Grandfather, we took him into our home and told him about Maroon things.

Bilby's study lends credence to isolated and unusual features in the data that might otherwise have remained suspect. Perhaps the most notable example occurs in Bilby's variants *blaka, baka, braka:* the last matches the phrase *brack folk* from Mayne Reid's nineteenth-century novel *The Maroon*. In this way documentary evidence, histories, and social commentaries interlock with linguistic analysis to form a picture of the developing creole.

The language history of Jamaica bears the impress of Amerindian, Spanish, Portuguese, Dutch, French, and German, but at its center unfolds phase after phase of West African encounters, metropolitan English encounters, and encounters with GCCE and creoles from other colonies (see Chart 10). Direct African input occurred through many kinds of contact and through many discernible stages of JC history: on African coastal trade posts, on board the ships of the middle passage, in the seasoning of new slaves to plantation life, on the plantations where "saltwater Africans" and (later) indentured Africans mixed with creoles, in the markets and provision grounds where blacks could meet. The African influence continued indirectly through GCCE, which could have entered the scene through any of these settings.

English dialects filtered in through GCCE but also exerted direct influence in the coastal settlements, on shipboard, on arrival in Jamaica, through the continued influx of English speakers, and ultimately through missionary activity, education, and the wider forces of acculturation. Under these circumstances, socially conditioned variation must have been inevitable.

From the interaction of all these models comes the selective total of linguistic continuities which we recognize as Jamaican Creole. We have no evidence that this total was arrived at as early as the seventeenth century, but the earliest JC texts extant provide data for description and display obvious resemblances to JC's major sources and to its sister languages in the Caribbean. The texts also demonstrate the ethnic complexity of its speakers and reflect considerable social and situational variety. Finally, the written records preserved in this chapter, together with the JC texts that follow, suggest a view of JC history as not so much a set of survivals, losses, and interferences as an intermeshing web of continuities that often reinforced each other in the establishment of a new language. Sifting the data of the past, researchers of today and tomorrow may come to a better understanding of how human consciousness contrives to create harmony out of disorder and meaning out of chaos.

Part Two
Data and Commentary

7

The Late Seventeenth Century

Text 1. Sir Hans Sloane, *A Voyage to . . . the Islands Madera, Barbados, . . . and Jamaica*

Sir Hans Sloane visited Jamaica in 1687–1689, making his famous botanical survey of the island and compiling material used in his description of the Caribbean region. Although the first volume of his account of his stay in Jamaica was published eighteen years after his sojourn as personal physician to the governor of Jamaica, Sloane based his great work on careful journal entries made on the spot. We may regard his account of Jamaica as reflecting the state of the island in the latter part of the seventeenth century.

He makes no direct comment about language in the island, although he interviewed and treated scores of white and black patients and traveled across the island, stopping for visits at remote plantations in St. Thomas-in-the-Vale. His account of the population of seventeenth-century Jamaica suggests that JC may have come into being from the usage of servants, slaves, and planter families brought to Jamaica from Barbados, the Windward Islands, and Surinam. He describes the African slaves in some detail, noting diseases, child-rearing practices, habits of dress, religious beliefs, musical instruments, songs, and dances. Of the following two short texts, Sloane remarks that "upon one of their Festivals when a great many of the Negro Musicians were gathered together, I desired Mr. Baptiste, the best Musician there to take the Words they sung and set them to Musick, which follows" (Sloane 1707–25: 2.1).

We have been unable to trace the first of the two songs but gratefully acknowledge the help of Vincent Odamtten, formerly of the University of Cape Coast and a speaker of both Ewe and Twi, in assessing the texts.

A. Angolan Chant

Sloane informs us that "you must clap hands when the Base is plaid, and cry, 'Alla, Alla' " (2.1). Vincent Odamtten suggests that the term *Alla* is unlikely to be Arabic *allah* and notes that the morphemic boundaries and phonology may not have been accurately represented by the European transcriber.

Ho-baognion, Ho-baognion,
Ho-ba, Ho-ba Ognion, Ognion.

B. Koromanti Chant

Identified by Vincent Odamtten as a children's play song in archaic Twi, the chant may be roughly translated as "I am coming, we are coming." There is a version still current in Ghana, a song for very young children: "Michi langa / Kofi so langa" (I am coming / Kofi is coming). The child claps an accompaniment to words and tune, with a kick-shuffle-step in time.

In Sloane's version most of the elements are repetitions of nonsense words typical of play songs. Odamtten suggests that such a song would by its very nature survive in the memories of exiled Africans when the more sophisticated and complex knowledge of adult life perished.

Meri Bonbo mich langa meri wa langa.

8

The Eighteenth Century

Text 2. *The Importance of Jamaica to Great Britain Consider'd in a Letter to a Gentleman*

Eighteenth-century writers in Jamaica seldom recorded any verbatim nonstandard speech. The speech of Africans and creoles is represented by sparse word lists, and few writers even attempted to comment on the language usage of the island. The following excerpt from *The Importance* (1740: 18–20) gives the earliest traceable account of connected creole usage of the period. The writer's attitude suggests that he is a supporter of slavery.

Early Fragment

The Slaves do the Offices of Servants, either [in] the House or Field; the House Negroes live as old Servants in *England,* and some will refuse their Freedom, when offer'd them, saying, *Why should they leave goodee Master, and goodee Mistress, where every Thing is provided for them, to meet with Troubles, and starvee starvee about the Streets.* The others work in the Field, Men and Women; but their Labour is not so hard as our poor People's in *England;* the Creol Negroes greatly value themselves for being born in the Island, and think themselves as much superior upon that account, as an ancient *Britain* [*sic*] would himself to a *Norman,* and are afraid of the wild Negroes. . . .

. . . When they are severely corrected, they will tell their Masters, *if you killee me, you lose Negroe,* sensible that their Labour is their Master's Riches. The old *Greek* . . . took a milder but more effectual Method to expose one of his [slaves] than stripes; he had him tarr'd all over, and then roll'd in Feathers. Imagine what a Figure he made.

They make odd but natural Reflections. They say, Ships come from *England*, from *Pensilvania*, *New-York*, *New-England*, *Bristol* (which they don't think is in *England;*) but none come from *Jew land*, and they wonder where it is. *England* must be a large place and *Scotland* a small one; for *Scots Bacceroes* (which they call all white Men) all know one another, but *English Bacceroes no know one another.*

Text 3. *A Short Journey in the West Indies*

The anonymous author, himself the owner of an estate and two hundred slaves (*Short Journey* 1790: 1.66), considered slavery a disgrace to nature and reason (92). His description reveals an interest in the condition of the slaves and especially in their language.

In the first excerpt, the narrator gives his views of Jamaican Creole (1.69). These are followed by a conversation with an old man named Cudjoe[1] (1.72).

A. An Old Man of the Late Eighteenth Century

He speaks his mind, and advancing years have had their wonted effect upon his tongue. He loves to talk, and I love to hear him talk. Our colloquies would divert you, could I remember them verbatim, for his remarks are often proverbial, and his allusions keen and novel. . . .

The language of the negroes is more expressive than I could have supposed, and conveys their ideas most forcibly. Cudjoe has gained experience, and he tells stories with humour."

. . . .

"Massa," said old Cudjoe to me, some days after my arrival, "you no dey go in a plantation? all you nega dey come down, if you no go see 'em soon. You been tan here in a dis country, so long you no shame for no go see dem yet?"[2] Very true, Cudjoe, said I to him, I ought to be ashamed of myself. Well, old man, we'll set out to-morrow morning. "Gar a mighty in a top! Massa, dem nega dey go run mad wid joy for see you."

. . . When shall we get there Cudjoe? "Massa will come dere for nyam dinna, if massa no nyam dinna, a Panish Town in a pass." But at what time Cudjoe? "Massa muss top lilly bit for bait in a Panish Town, den we will catch de 'tate 'bout four or twelve o'clock."

B. White Creole Child

A white planter family at Prospect Penn provided the setting for the following scene between a white Jamaican boy of about seven and his mother (2.36). Both mother and son use creole forms such as "woman crab"; the child's speech is entirely basilectal.

The text is of particular sociolinguistic interest, supporting the view that JC was commonly spoken as a first language by white as well as black Jamaicans. The child's speech is obviously acceptable to his mother despite several features that are creole rather than Standard English (e.g., *him* and *me* as subject pronouns [cf. Lewis 1834: 120], the [v] > [b] sound change, the lexical curiosity *blue maugre* [see Glossary], and West African phonotaxis in *wantee*).

There was a little urchin, about seven years old, who constantly stunned my ears with—"*me wantee crab, me wantee crab:*"—to stop his noise, I took up the first that came to my hand and gave it to him; but he immediately examined it, and, finding it had no eggs, he roared out, "Him no hab egg, him blue maugre to hell, me no *wantee man crab,* me wantee *woman crab;*"—so he had heard his mother and the negroes distinguish the sexes of crabs. I would have taught the little scoundrel better manners, but his mother called him to her, kissed him a dozen times, and picked him out the best *woman crab.*

Text 4. J. B. Moreton, *West India Customs and Manners*

J. B. Moreton's work provides an outsider's view of creole society while capturing the language behavior of the planter class as well as that of their servants and slaves. A sympathetic observer, Moreton attempts to record both the syntax and the pronunciation of white and black creoles. The following song (Moreton 1793: 157) celebrates the provocative body movements characteristic of the slave dances held frequently on the estates. Moreton tries to convey rhythm and details of vowel quality and quantity (*deaa, yondaa, hipsaw*), which are often unrepresented in JC records (cf. Allen 1893; and Moreton 1793: 157).

Song: Hipsaw! My Deaa!

Hipsaw! my deaa! you no do like a-me!

You no jig like a-me! you no twist like a-me!
Hipsaw! my deaa! you no shake like a-me!
You no wind like a-me! Go, yondaa!
Hipsaw!
Hipsaw! my deaa! you no jig like a-me!
You no work him like a-me! You no sweet him like a-me!

9

The Early Nineteenth Century

Text 5. Captain Hugh Crow, *Memoirs*

Hugh Crow (1765–1829) of Liverpool, a captain active in the triangular trade, retired after making his final journey from Bonny in 1807–1808. His *Memoirs* (begun in 1815 and continued up to shortly before his death) were edited by his executors chiefly from his manuscript and from anecdotes fresh in their recollections (Crow 1830: 179). Such evidence, together with the fact that he began writing after retirement, makes the authenticity of his work uncertain at some points. However, he is described as having "a memory uncommonly quick and retentive" and as being scrupulous about the veracity of his material (xiii).

Crow's linguistic abilities may have been considerable. In Liverpool he was seen to address in the man's own language an African whom he encountered by chance and whose origin he recognized by tribal marks (xxxii–xxxiii). He was acquainted with the "soft and pleasing" form of the Ibo language spoken in Bonny (229). His record of the English-based creole spoken there provides one of the few clues as to the nature of trade languages of that time and place; defective as his account of the usage of King Pepple and King Holiday may be, it allows some comparison with Jamaican Creole of the period, especially as Crow records both forms. Crow was himself bilingual in Manx and English.

Song Made by the People of Colour in Jamaica on Captn Hugh Crow

Although it seems hardly credible, Crow claimed a proven reputa-

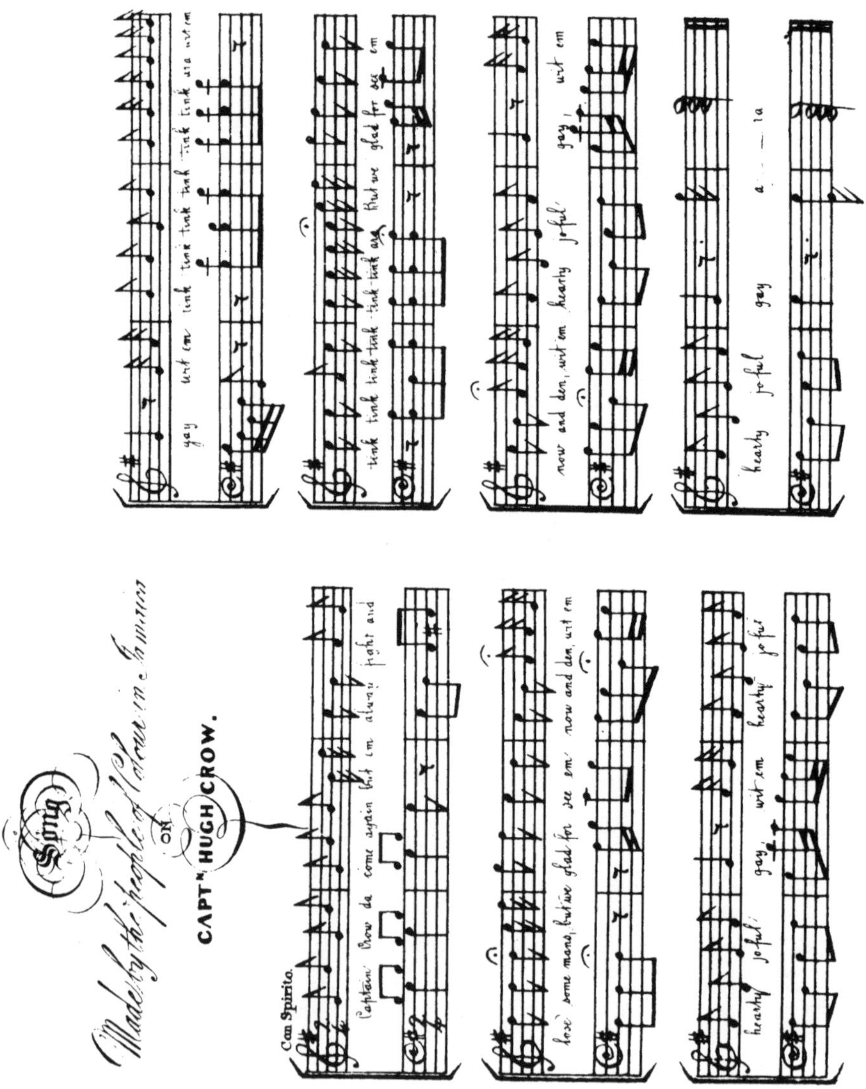

Plate 2. Song for Captain Hugh Crow (Crow 1830)

tion both for his treatment of his human cargoes and for their good condition on arrival in the Caribbean, "as plump as cotton bags" (73). Regular exercise, fresh air, sanitation, and proper diet formed the regimen on board Crow's ship. Blacks on his ship not only were released on more than one occasion to assist in saving the vessel when it was leaking or keeling over but were armed and fought for Crow against enemy ships (102). He consistently refers to the blacks of his acquaintance with affection and admiration and at times physically defended them at his own risk.

Nevertheless, he considered the slave trade a necessary evil, beneficial to the prosperity and safety of Britain, as well as the colonies, the navy, and the slaves themselves (xvi, 158–59). He strongly criticized Wilberforce and other abolitionists for ignoring the suffering of white sailors, prisoners, coal miners, factory workers, and the Irish peasantry while they opposed a system of which they had no experience. Crow himself knew Jamaica mainly from its wharves, and his compilers note that he never saw real plantation life (287–90). He never mentioned the conditions of want and degradation noted by contemporaries such as Henry Whiteley.

Crow claims to have recorded the following song (125–26) verbatim, but there are several unfamiliar features (*da em sorry* and *for to see*) that raise suspicion. According to his own account (126–27), pills are "large shot taken out of the ship's hold"; "Mrs Mann was a white woman who kept a turtle crawl in Port Royal"; "a man by the name of Goodall kept a famous house there for good beef steak; and as Captain Mann and myself were constantly together we were called by the blacks 'the two partners.'"

After getting in our mainmast and bowsprit and repairing the ship, we began to take in a cargo of sugar and coffee for England. While this was going on I received an additional testimony of the friendly disposition towards me of a number of individuals of the humbler classes in Jamaica, and of which I was not a little proud. This was an original song, of which the following is a copy, verbatim, and which is submitted to the reader as a specimen of the literary abilities and good humour of the blacks.

i. Captain Crow da come again,
But em alway fight and lose some mans,
But we glad for see em now and den,
Wit em hearty joful gay, wit em hearty joful gay
wit em tink tink tink tink tink tink ara,

wit em tink tink tink tink tink tink ara,
But we glad for see em now and den,
Wit em hearty joful gay, wit em hearty joful gay ara

ii. But da em sorry and bery sick,
For em da fight the two man-of-war ship;
But we glad em gae dem tat for tit,
Wit em hearty joful gay, wit em hearty joful gay.
Wit em tink tink tink tink tink tink ara.
Wit em tink tink tink tink tink tink ara.
But we glad em gae dem tat for tit,
Wit em hearty joful gay, wit em hearty joful gay.

iii. But did you ever see dem pills,
Dat dem send to cure em ill?
But of dat dem got dem fill.
Wit em hearty joful gay, wit em hearty joful gay.
Wit em tink tink, &c.
But of dat dem got dem fill,
Wit em hearty joful gay, wit em hearty joful gay.

iv. Then up to the hospital em da go, hay hay,
For to see em wounded boys,
And sat down and talk and pity and say.
Wit em hearty joful gay, wit em hearty joful gay.
Wit em tink tink, &c.
And sat down and talk and pity and say,
Wit em hearty joful gay, wit em hearty joful gay.

v. The Captain Mann and em da go
To Port Royal to Missey Man's crawl,
To get a beef take at Goodall's;
Den dem call for the bill, and pay for all.
Wit em hearty joful gay, wit em hearty joful gay.
Wit em tink tink, &c.
Den dem call for the bill, and pay for all,
Wit em hearty joful gay, wit em hearty joful gay.

vi. For none like dem from Guinea come,
For dem always joful never glum,
And never gae dem boys fum fum,
Wit em hearty joful gay, wit em hearty joful gay.

Wit em tink tink, &c.
And never gae dem boys fum fum,
Wit em hearty joful gay, wit em hearty joful gay.

vii. But did you eber the governor see
When em went on board of he.
Den em say Sir Hugh you must be,
Wit you hearty joful gay, wit you hearty joful gay.
Wit em tink tink, &c.
Den em say Sir Hugh you must be,
Wit you hearty joful gay, wit you hearty joful gay.

Text 6. Walter Jekyll, Editor, *Jamaican Song and Story*

Walter Jekyll recorded songs and tales directly "from the mouths of men and boys in [his] employ. The method has in every case been to sit them down and make them dictate slowly; so the stories are in their ipsissima verba" (Jekyll 1907: Author's Preface). At the end of the tale he adds copious glosses and notes, which throw light on features of morphology, semantics, and phonology.

It is important to note that Jekyll's orthography, though at times unusually accurate, is not consistently maintained. For example, *dirty* is orthographically assimilated to SE *dirty* but is in fact *doti* < Twi [dɔ̀té], "soil, earth, clay, mud," possibly influenced by the SE word (*DJE*). The pronunciation of *vittle* is uncertain, for the *v* may indicate either a phonological variation or simply a failure to record the usual [v] > [b] change.

Jekyll's work is, nonetheless, one of the most informative sources of Jamaican folk materials. Because of certain details in the following text (Jekyll 1907: 31–34), it has been ascribed to the early nineteenth century.

Brother Annancy and Brother Death

One day Brother Annancy sen' gal Annancy fe go a Brother Deat' yard fe go beg fire.

When the gal go, him go meet Brother Deat' dis a eat fe him breakfas' enough eggs. Brother Deat' give gal Annancy one. Gal Annancy take the egg an', after eat done, put the shell 'pon him finger.

Brother Annancy wait an' wait but can't get the fire, till at last he sees the gal a come.

When him see the gal with the egg shell 'pon him finger, him run an' bit off the gal finger slap to the hand. Him take 'way the fire, out it, an' go back to Deat' say: —"Bro'er Deat', de fire out."

Brother Deat' give him fire an' one egg, tell him fe go home.

"Say, Bro'er Deat', I goin' to give you me daughter fe marry to."

So Annancy do marry off Deat' an' him daughter the same day. So him lef' them gone for a week, then come back again fe come see him son-in-law.

When him come him say: —"Bro'er Deat', me son, me hungry."

Brother Deat' no 'peak.

So Annancy begin fe talk to himself: "Bro'er Deat' say me fe go make up fire, but no mo so me no yerry."

After five minutes him call out: —"Bro'er Deat', me make up de fire."

Deat' no 'peak.

"Bro'er Deat' say me fe wash de pot, but no mo so me no yerry.

When the pot wash done, him call out: —"Pot wash."

Deat' no 'peak.

"Bro'er Deat' say me fe to put him on, but no mo so me no yerry."

Soon him say: —"Bro'er Deat', where de vittle?"

Deat' no 'peak.

"Him say me fe look somewhé dé me see enough yam, me fe peel dem put dem a fire, but no mo so me no yerry."

Annancy cook all Deat' food.

When it boil, him take it off. Him say: —"Bro'er Deat', him boil."

Deat' no 'peak.

"Bro'er Deat' say me fe share, but no mo so me no yerry."

Annancy eat fe him share, then turn back say: —"Bro'er Deat', you no come come eat?"

Deat' no 'peak.

"Bro'er Deat' say him no want none, but no mo so me no yerry."

So Annancy eat off all the food him one.

Then Deat' get vex in a him heart, and him run into the kitchen.

"Bro'er Annancy a whé you mean fe do me, say a come you come fe kill me?"

So Deat' catch Annancy an' say: "Me no a go let you go again, no use, no use."

Then, after, Deat' carry Annancy in a him house an' leave him, gone to get his lance to kill him.

So, after Annancy sit a time an' about to go away, him say: "Bro'er

Deat' say me fe go take piece a meat, but no mo so me no yerry."

When Annancy go to the meat cask, him see the cask full with meat. Him take out two big piece of meat. Then he see fe him daughter hand with the missing finger. Him jump out of the house an' bawl out: —"Bro'er Deat', you b'ute, you b'ute, you kill me daughter."

Deat' catch him again an' was going to kill him, but the feller get 'way, run home a fe him yard.

Brother Deat' follow him when him go home.

Annancy take all him children an' go up a house-top, go hang up on the rafter. Brother Deat' come in a de house, see them up a de house-top.

Annancy say to his family—there was two boy an' the mumma: —"Bear up! If you drop de man a dirty dé a go nyam you."

Here come one of the boy say: —"Puppa, me han' tired."

Annancy say: —"Bear up!"

The boy cry out fe de better.

Annancy say: —"Drop, you b'ute! No see you dada a dirty dé?"

Him drop.

Deat' take him and put him aside.

Five minutes the other one say: —"Puppa, me han' tired."

Annancy say again —"Drop, you b'ute! No see you dada a dirty dé?"

Him drop.

Deat' take him an' put him aside.

Soon the wife get tired, say: —"Me husban', me han' tired."

Annancy say: —"Bear up, me good wife!"

When she cry she couldn' bear no more, Annancy bawl again: —"Drop you b'ute! No see you husban' a dirty dé?"

She drop.

Deat' take her.

At last Annancy get tired. Das de man, Bro'er Deat' been want. Annancy was so smart, no want fe Deat' catch him, so he say: — "Bro'er Deat', I goin' to drop, an' bein' me so fat, if you no want me fat fe waste, go and fetch somet'ing fe catch me."

"What me can take fe catch you?"

"Go in a room you will see a barrel of flour an' you fe take it so fe me drop in dé."

Deat' never know that this flour was temper lime.

Deat' bring the barrel an', just as he fixing it up under where Annancy hanging, Annancy drop on Deat' head PUM, and jam him head in a the temper lime an' blind him. So he an' all him family get 'way.

Jack Mantora me no choose any.

dis a eat, just as he had eaten.
no mo so me no yerry, I must have failed to hear.
Deat' no 'peak, Death won't speak. The comedy is well sustained. Annancy goes through the various stages of preparation for breakfast, pretending that he is carrying out orders from Death which he fails to hear.
put him on, put the pot on the fire.
somewhé dé, somewhere there. The *e*'s are like French *é*, and *dé* is said with a strong accent and made very short.
enough yam, plenty of yams.
say a come you a come, say do you come.
me no a go etc., I am not going to let you go again.
no use, no mistake about it this time.
bawl. Remember to pronounce it *bahl*.
b'ute, brute, pronounced like the island Bute.
a fe him yard, to his yard.
a dirty dé, etc., on the ground there will eat you.
fe de better, all the more.
Das, that's.
temper lime, tempered lime originally no doubt, but now meaning quick lime. Temper, I am told, means cross. And in further explanation my informant adds: "You can't fingle (finger) temper lime as you have a mind; it cut up your hand."
pum with the shortest possible vowel represents the thud of Annancy's fall upon Death's head.

Text 7. *Montgomery; or, The West Indian Adventure*

The anonymous writer of this fictive study of West Indian life disclaims any association between real persons and incidents and his own characters and plot, insisting that one of his aims is to expose vice and prejudice (*Montgomery* 1812–13: 1.vi, ix). The narrative reveals the writer's sympathy toward blacks and his skill at observing the intricacies of creole attitudes in all classes of Jamaicans. His interest and sympathy dispose him to closer observation than might otherwise be the case, but his discursive prose style is often highly ornamental, with only occasional creole phrases occurring in the dialogue.

The following conversation (2.91–94) takes place as Montgomery, the hero, is traveling to the Retreat, an estate where he is to take up the position of bookkeeper.

The Slave and the New Buckera

He was repeatedly urged, too, by Quaco,[1] his companion, to accelerate his pace, and not to stop so often, as *"obusheer[2] say we must catch home by dinner to-morrow, and if we no catch, he will fum me."* Though this jargon was somewhat unintelligible to our hero, yet he made a shift to comprehend the negro's meaning, and asked him "if he was afraid of his overseer's punishing him for his delay, if it was explained to him that it was not his fault."

"*Him no mind that, sometime,*" said Quaco; "*him cann't fum buckera, but he will fum me, if we tand too long in a pass.*"

"Why, that's impossible, Quaco," said our hero, "at that rate your overseer can have no sense of justice."

"*Nan?*" said Quaco, not understanding either the language or the *nature* of this sentiment.

"I say, your overseer cann't be a good man if he punishes you for nothing."

"*Lookee massa, you look like a good young buckera,* but no talk so when you go upon plantation—obusheer will vex with you; he will say you saucy, and he will make you go away."

"And Quaco, if he should do so, if what you say of him is true, I cannot say I should much regret the separation."

Quaco seemed a negro of a mild disposition, and felt for the suffering of our hero from the heat, fatigue, and the musquittoes; but still the dread of *fum-fum* overcame in some measure this sympathy, and the poor fellow could not help at times evincing great uneasiness at the slow progress they made.

About one o'clock they came to an estate near the road, where they heard a shell blowing to call the negroes to dinner. This Montgomery's guide explained to him, and proposed their stopping and dining there.

"You know, Quaco," said Montgomery, "I am an utter stranger to the people on this estate, and they may think me guilty of a piece of presumption to obtrude myself, unasked, on their company."

"Never mind ask," said Quaco, "never mind ask—*buckera* in this country just go up and sit down in 'tother house, and go *n'yam* with them, and no body ask where they come from. Tavern no de in a country place."

Text 8. Matthew G. Lewis, *Journal of a West India Proprietor*

Matthew G. Lewis (1775–1818), or "Monk" Lewis, best known for his gothic novel *The Monk,* visited Jamaica in 1815 and again in 1817 to inspect his two properties, one in the southeast and one in the extreme west of the island. His journal shows that he had close contact with the slaves on his estates, that he made an effort to study their conditions and customs, and that he effected certain reforms that earned him the disapproval of the planter class. His accounts of Jamaican blacks are mainly rendered in standard English but he attempts to bring out such features of Jamaican usage as seemed to him to characterize the culture. At times he was plainly baffled by Jamaican creole, as the following extracts demonstrate.

The brevity of his visits must also have limited his usefulness as a student of creole. Nonetheless his journal is notable for preserving—among other features—one of the very few records of [#hV] variation in early nineteenth-century Jamaican speech. On the passage out he meets "a planter in the May Day Mountains," who states that "hedicating the negroes is the only way to make them appy; indeed, in his umble hopinion, hedication his hall in hall" (Lewis 1834: 2–30).

Several editions of Lewis's journal exist, and different publications vary both in the material actually included and in the order in which entries occur. Thus, Text A occurs on page 201 in the 1834 edition but on page 102 in the 1861 edition; Text B appears on page 233 in the 1834 edition but on page 118 in the 1861 edition. The structure of the 1861 edition suggests that many changes were introduced (some perhaps drawn from Lewis's manuscript) without any notice to the reader or any reference to the first edition. For background information on Lewis, see Peck (1961) and Baron-Wilson (1839). Margaret Baron-Wilson acted as a kind of literary executor for Lewis.

A. Eerie

The term *eerie* (meaning "buckish" or "happy") has a startling resemblance to modern Rastafarian *irie* (see Glossary).

Just now Prince came to me with a request of his own. "Massa, please, me want one little coat." —"A little coat! For what?" "Massa, please, for wear when me go down to the Bay." "And why should you wear a little coat when you go to the Bay?" "Massa, please, make me look eerie (buckish) when me go abroad." So I assured him that he looked quite *eerie* enough already; and that, as I was going away too soon to admit of my seeing him in his little coat, there could not be the slightest occasion for his being a bit *eerier* than he was.

B. Song at Cornwall Estate

The interjections in parentheses are Lewis's explanations of the text.

Hey-ho-day! me no care a dammee! (i.e. a damn)
Me acquire a house, (i.e. I have a solid
foundation to build on,)
Since massa come see we—oh!

Hey-ho-day! neger now quite eerie,
(i.e. hearty,)
For once me see massa—hey-ho-day!
When massa go, me no care a dammee,
For how them usy we—hey-ho-day!

Text 9. Song: "Quaco Sam"

This reconstruction originally appeared in Lalla (1981), with a full account of the fragments from which it was reconstructed and detailed comments. The sources include versions from the private collection of H. P. Jacobs, who had interviewed elderly informants in Trelawny; a variant printed by Mr. James Chandler in the *Welfare Reporter* (January 1947); scattered fragments such as that reproduced in Richard Hughes's novel, *A High Wind in Jamaica* (1949: 11); those versions painted on a series of ornamental dishes commissioned by Mrs. Rebecca Brandon of Kingston in 1838; together with others recalled by Olive Lewin (Olwin Cultural Services, Kingston) along with their musical score.

On the basis of these as well as internal linguistic and cultural evidence, the song can be roughly dated to a period between 1814 and 1823. Today, variants survive in the hills of Trelawny and Clarendon; F. G. Cassidy learned one version during his childhood in Jamaica (personal communication).

Plate 3. Pottery with Creole verse, "Quaco Sam." National Library of Jamaica. This version reads

> . . . regan gown, me hab me gin'am cloak,
> . . . henkychi tie me head, massa-tenky tie me troat.
>
> An da warra mo me wanty, me hab me junka pan
> Fe go da Berry Hill fe go see Quaco Sam
> Wid a ring ding ding and a pam pam pam

---

1. Howdy, Cousin Cubba,[3] me yerry lilly news,
Me yerry-se yo buy one new pair a-shoes,
Me yerry-se yo buy one dandy[4] hat.
Come tell me, Cousin Cubba, wha yo pay fe dat?

Chorus

Wid a ring ding ding an a pam pam pam,
Me nebba see a man lak-a Quaco Sam.
Wedda rain or-a breeze or-a storm or-a sun,
Me nebba see a man lak-a Quaco Sam.

2. Me yerry-se one dance de a Berry Hill,[5]
Unco Jack play de fiddly-an wan hag fe kill,
Come tell me, Cousin Cubba, how ebry ting tan,
Mek me ax Sista Susan, mek me call Sista Ann.

Chorus

3. Me hab me Regan gown, me hab me gin'am cloak,
Swalla-henkychi tie me head, massa-tenky tie me troat.
Da warra mo me wanty? Me hab me junka pan[6]
Fe go a Berry Hill fe go-see Quaco Sam.

Chorus

4. Laad! How me wi dance when me yerry fiddly-an drum!
Me no tink pon backra wo'k, me no ca' fe fum-fum
Me wi dance de shay-shay, me wi dance de Catchreel,[7]
Me wi dance till ebry craps a me foot-battam peel.

Chorus

5. Monday mawning Driba Harry, whan de cock da crow,
'Tek him cudjo a him han, knock him whip a Busha do.
Wi me hoe a me shoulda, wi me bill da me back,
Me da mash putta-putta, me da tink pan Unca Jack.

Chorus

6. Me tek me row a cane-piece side, de naygar—dem all da run
An ebryone come behin me, him ketch de fum-fum.
Wi me hoe da me shoulda, chackalata da me pan,
Me da wo'k, me da nyam, me da tink pan Quaco Sam.

Chorus

Text 10. Cynric R. Williams, *A Tour through the Island of Jamaica in the Year 1823*

Cynric Williams's account is based on observations made during a stay of less than three months in Jamaica. He records terms such as "wibble wabble loblolly," which derive from EModE and must have entered the creole through contact between Africans and white servants, soldiers, and laborers. Williams recorded two sermons. One, reported by a house servant, is mesolectal in form (Williams 1826: 104–6). To record the other, Williams hid himself and eavesdropped on the ceremony. The speaker was unaware of his presence. The sermon, taken down verbatim, is marked by basilectal and archaic JC morphology and sound laws (e.g., "deadee," "Garamighty," "gib"). It appears to preserve archaic JC with an unusually low degree of SE interference, probably because the writer was competent in JC and his presence (undetected by speaker or audience) gave no cause for upward shifting or hypercorrection. This sermon (Williams 1826: 108–10), reproduced as Text A, testifies to Williams's skill as a recorder of JC. The usage he reports is borne out by other sources as well as by reconstructions of archaic Afro-American morphology by Alleyne and others.

A. Sermon at a Funeral

[Ebenezer] had given out that he would preach to the slaves at the negro houses yesterday morning, and I went in consequence, incognito, and took my post in the house of the servant who had repeated to me the funeral oration, where I copied down as he delivered it the sermon which follows.

Most of the negroes (between two and three hundred) assembled to hear him, and arranged themselves on the ground beneath some coconut trees, in a ring, leaving a space for him to move about, and for a stool, on which he first mounted, then sat down a little, then mounted again, and began to pray a heap of unintelligible matter; in the midst of which he rushed into his sermon without text, and exclaimed—

"Brar! You tink say when you die, you dead for true? No such ting—nebba see de day—dat time no mo you begin for lib—You tink say—Deady come, trouble come no mo? Ha! man, tan lilly bit, you no bin dead six minutes before debbil catch you, put you na bilbo, set twenty thousand driba pon you. Dem no hab cattle whip, but dem poke you wid fire stick, tay you teet grind to de root. Deady no come no mo. You hungry tay you gut twist to pieces,—dem no gib you plantain—no so lead, no mo hot like hell, burn hole in you belly. You tongue roast wid feeba,—dem no gib you water—no one drop day—no so boiling brimstone, nuttin else for drink, tay de flame come trough you nose. You tink for run away!—nebba see de day—you foot roast in red hot bilbo for twenty tousand year. De tear in you yeye boil like a pot, yet deady no come—Sleep no come, nebba for cool you yeye. —Brar, me sorry for you. De sinful soul go ebery one straight to hell—you all sinful, you born so—you born in sin— You tink dat no you fault? Cha! no you fader do it? Pickninny must pay him fader debt. —You must hab wif no mo— No so, dem roast you pickninny— Brar, me sorry for you. You tink wha for Garamighty gib you black girl? No more for rat trap for catch you sinful soul. De bible say dem painted puckerie—dem cheat you yeyes— dem all rotten."

Here a [woman's] voice cried out, "Sneezer, you lie—you puckerie yourself—you good for nutten wibble wabble loblolly.—"

B. Song: Hi! De Buckra, Hi!

Williams reports that the following song was sung by Magdalene, a Christian slave. If one assumes a rhyme scheme of ABBBBA for the first verse and ABCCBA for the second, one accommodates the "yeye" and "sea" rhymes in a fairly plausible symmetry, but ABABBA and ABCCAA are of course possible. The diction of the song combines JC and literary SE ("tender look") as well as gestures that would have surprised William Wilberforce, the "Massa W—f——e" of stanza 2.

1. Hi! de Buckra, hi!
You sabby wha for he da cross de sea,
Wid him long white face and him twinkling yeye;
He lub, make lub, as he preach to we,
He fall on his knees, but he pray for me,
Hi! de Buckra, hi!

2. Hi! de Buckra, hi!
Massa W—f——e da come ober de sea,
Wid him roguish heart and him tender look;
And while he palaver and preach him book,
At the negro girl he'll winkie him yeye.
Hi! de Buckra, hi!

Text 11. *Marly; or, A Planter's Life in Jamaica*

This anonymous novel shows the writer's intimate knowledge of Jamaican society at all levels: the narrator, a young man from Edinburgh, hired as a bookkeeper on a plantation, describes his duties and his encounters with field and house slaves, white overseers, creole whites of high and middle estate, and two Gaelic-speaking Campbells, who refuse to employ him because of his ignorance of their mother tongue (*Marly* 1828: 9).

The narrative abounds with terms such as "sugar ground" and "coffee mountain" (used by white creoles, 58) and with JC expressions such as the field slaves' request to the bookkeeper for permission to "go a bush" (51) to relieve themselves. It also contains a number of unusual forms, which reflect archaic JC morphology: *grandy* appears frequently (cf. Ross 1800); *him* is used in a variety of positions; and the form *Missa* for "mistress, miss," a rare variant, parallels a similar form appearing in a letter written in 1828 by Mrs. James Mursell Phillippo, in which the missionary's wife quotes a free black who is attempting to purchase the freedom of Rosina, an old washerwoman: "Me know missa not able to buy Rosina, and him be very sorry for him to be sold away; myself will buy him for him own good, if missa will keep part of de money him give Rosina every week" (Underhill 1881: 80).

The narrator-hero also notes code switching in the language behavior of white creoles (210, 318). Unable to comment on black speech, he describes in detail the prevalence of African culture in the foods, entertainments, music, and manners of white creole society. In Text A (*Marly* 1828: 130–31) *christen* has become *kirsten* by metathesis.

A. Kirstening

One afternoon after shell-blow, a numerous body of the negroes made their appearance at the buckra-house, to whom the overseer went to enquire what they wanted. Trajan began: —"Massa, Obeah bad for him poor neger, massa—him kill poor neger, massa. All massa's negers, want massa, to hab him buckra priest, kirsten him negers, dat Obeah no more him kill, massa. Ebery one neger, massa want to be kirstened in de buckra fashion, massa." Samuels hesitated a little, and then said, "If I should do so, you will be great thieves afterwards." Trajan answered, "No, massa, him neger, after him be buckra Christian, him no tief neber more, massa;" and as an additional effort, to prove successful in his mission, he added: "Ebery one of him Babylon negers, massa; him Lilliput negers, massa; him Joppa negers, massa; all, ebery one of him negers kirstened in de buckra fashion, massa." The overseer not having the power himself to grant their request, told them so; but added, that if they would behave themselves well, he would speak to the attorney, to get it done, with which promise they went away well pleased.

B. Sermon

The extensive sermon that follows (*Marly* 1828: 134–38) shows the author's attention to JC phonological features in terms such as *belobed, Gor Amighty, grandy savey,* and *nyamn*. However, the narrative structure of this passage (biblical chronicle) would normally offer an opportunity for variation within the past tense and for the use of JC aspect markers (e.g., *da*). Instead, strong SE interference appears in past tense and passive forms ("hab lib," "it called," "drownded").

The narrator introduces Tom Paine, a slave converted to Christianity, and his attempt to preach to his fellow slaves.

Tom Paine was exceedingly sorry that his endeavours for the conversion of his companions had failed; and finding that he was unable to persuade them to abandon their resolution, he used sometimes to hold forth to them himself. Whether his exertions were crowned with success, Marly never learned; but he feared his orations tended little to improvement, for he observed no alteration in the conduct of the negroes in consequence, and from a discourse which he one day overheard, he did not augur that much good would ever arise from Tom's spiritual labours. . . .

. . . "My belobed brederen: Dere's Gor Amighty at de top, and de Debble at de bottom. Gor Amighty make all de world, and all de folks in it; him negers, and him buckras. Gor Amighty make de first man, and him called Adam. After dat, him make him Adam, him's wife, and him called Ebe; and from him Adam, and him Ebe, all, ebery one of de folks, him negers and him buckras, hab be pickeninies. Him Adam and him Ebe, hab lib upon an estate, and it called Paradise. It hab be[8] a grandy big estate, much grandy better dan Paradise to leeward; and dere was dere, ebery ting good for nyamn, and all de fruit on it, him Adam and him Ebe, could nyamn but de forbidden fruit. Now him forbidden fruit [Author: the name of a West Indian fruit] good for him neger to nyamn, and him Ebe wanted to nyamn it, but him hab be feared, till a grandy big serpent, as grandy big as de yellow serpent, opened him's mout and spoke, as if him serpent, hab be him neger or him buckra; and told him Ebe, to pull some of it and nyamn it, and it would make him Ebe much grandy savey. Him Ebe took some of him forbidden fruit, and it good for nyamn, and him Ebe gib some of it to him Adam, and de bot nyamned it. Gor Amighty hab be grandy much angry, and him turn off him Adam and him Ebe from de estate of Paradise, in de same way, as massa de attorney, sends away de buckras, when dey do much bad. After him Adam and him Ebe hab be turned off Paradise, dey went to de mountains, and him Ebe hab two pickeninies, him Cain and him Abel. Him Cain hab be a field neger, and him Abel kept de penn. Him Cain hab be grandy much angry at him's working in de field, while him Abel hab only be keeping de cows and de oxen, de horses and de mules, and de sheep and de pigs; and him Cain killed him Abel to get de penn, and be no more de field neger. Gor Amighty hab be grandy much angry at him Cain, and him Cain hab so grandy much fear, dat hims face hab become white, and him hab be de puppa of de buckras. After dat much lang time, all de folks in de world became much bad, and Gor Amighty much angry; and him hab sent a grandy big shower of rain water, for forty days and forty nights, and drownded all de folks, but him Noah, and him's wifes, and him's pickeninies, and him's beasts; and all de oder folks, and de oder beasts, hab all, ebery one, been drownded. Him Noah, hab be a sailor, and savey dat de great rain hab to come, and him made him a much grandy big boat to sail in, and to hold him, and him's wifes, and him's pickeninnies, and him's beasts; and all de oder folks, and de oder beasts, hab all, ebery one, been drownded. Dere hab be him oder man, and him called Joseph. Him's puppa hab a grandy big penn, and grandy much sheeps, and cows, and oxen, and horses. Him hab be a grandy rich man. Him Joseph hab be de youngest of all him's pickeninies, and him's puppa hab much lobe for him Joseph. Him Joseph's broders hab be much angry at dis, and him Joseph habing be on de penn, and much far away from him's puppa's house, him's broders catch him Joseph, and sell him to de buckras who hab be in de want of neger; for de house neger. Him Joseph hab after dat, be sold to de Marshall of de prison in Egypt, not de estate of Egypt to windward, but a grandy big country, as big as de neger's or de buckra's country; and him Joseph hab be one of de prison negers. After dat, him Joseph hab become free, and him hab keep a corn store, and him Joseph hab become much rich. After dat much long time, de corn on him puppa's estate hab not grown, de rain not habing come dat year, and him's puppa and him's broders, hab no corn for dem and deir wifes, and deir pickeninies to nyamn. Him's puppa den send away him

Joseph's broders to Egypt, to buy corn, and dey hab come to deir broder's store to buy. Dey hab not savey dat de store-keeper hab be deir broder Joseph, dey hab sold for de house neger; but Joseph savey dat dey hab be him's broders. After dat, him Joseph hab forgib him's broders for dem selling him for de neger, and him tell dem dat him hab much rich, and dat it hab be much better for dem, and deir puppa, and deir wifes, and deir pickeninies, to come and lib in Egypt, dan on deir penn: it hab be a much better country. Den him's puppa, and him's broders, and deir wifes, and deir pickeninies, hab come and lib in Egypt. After dat, him Joseph hab dead, and him's puppa; and de folks of Egypt, hab made him's broders, and deir wifes, and deir pickeninies, negers, and hab make dem work in de field. Dey hab be grandy big gang, and hab for deir massa him oder man, and him called Pharaoh. Him hab make de negers work all too much, and him hab not be de good massa, but him hab be much bad to him poor negers. After dat, him negers hab become grandy much angry at deir massa, and dey all, ebery one, hab run away from de estate on which dey hab be working. Him Pharaoh hab be grandy much angry at him's negers, for dem habing run away; and him, and him's folks, hunt after dem, to make dem come back and work in de field. But him negers hab get much far away, and when him Pharaoh and him's folks hab be hunting after dem, grandy big water hab come and drownded him and him's folks, all, ebery one. After dat, him negers hab become free, and dey hab be de puppas and de mummas of de folks called Jews, and hab neber more become field negers. —Dere hab be him oder man, and him called Samson. Him Samson hab be a grandy much strong man, and him hab killed of [*sic*] de folks called Fillystones, five hunderd men, wid de jaw-bone of a him Jackamarass. And after dat, when all de folks hab be dancing in de house like him buckra-house, him Samson pulled down de house, and him hab be killed, and all de folks at de ball. Him Samson grandy much strong man; de grandy much strong man of all de mans in de world. —Dere hab be him oder man, and him called Soloman. Him hab be king of de folks called Jews, de same folks as de Jews on de Bay, but not him Jew Soloman who hab de store. Him savey grandey much more dan all de oder folks, and him de grandy much savey man in de world. Him hab eight hunderd wifes and five hunderd concubines, oder dan him's wifes. Him hab be grandy rich man, more grandy rich dan de buckras. Him as rich as de Jew. — Dere hab be de oder man, and him called Jonah. Him whale, a grandy big fish, much grandy bigger dan him big shark, swallow him Jonah; and him Jonah in him whale's belly dree days and dree nights; after dat, him whale spew him Jonah, and him hab not dead. —Dere is much oder mans, ebery one, told of in de buckra book, de Bible; and de Bible tells, dat all him dat do much good, him get much good, and all him dat do much bad, him get much bad. All for de gory[9] of Gor Amighty, for eber and eber. Amen."

C. Song: The Woodpecka

A popular song in Victorian England, "The Woodpecker" is casually mentioned by Charles Dickens in *Our Mutual Friend* and *David Copperfield*. Here, it is reproduced from *Marly* (1828: 293).

In almost every word the poem reveals features characteristic of early JC phonology. Unstressed vowels are stressed (*woodpecka*), central vowels retracted (*cull'd*), fricatives shifted to homorganic and adjacent stops (*dat, abobe, ebry leap*), initial and final consonantal clusters reduced (*moke, foun, soun*). There is rare evidence of reduction of [#h-] in *umle* and *ollow*. In a variety of environments, [r] weakens (*est, gacefully*). English dialectal present participle [-in]—the normal form in JC—also occurs.

The poem also offers a record of dialect mixing between JC and English dialects. Note the Scots influence in *mit* for *might* ~ *micht*. *Ha'd* preserves [a:] < [-ar-] of sixteenth-century "sarvent," "parson," "sarvis," once polite usage but considered vulgar in the eighteenth century and ridiculed by writers such as Fielding (Wyld 1956: 212–18). The rhyme of *hee* and *nee* with *tee* suggests northern influence (see "nigh" [ni:] in *EDD*).

The spelling of *knew* as *new* does raise the suspicion that the writer changed the appearance of the word simply to make his text seem more exotic, but the fine detail and consistency of the phonetic spellings suggest that he tried to represent what he heard.

I new by de moke dat so gacefully cull'd,
Abobe de geen ems dat a cottey was nee;
And I said if dere's peace to be foun in dis wold,
A ha't dat is umle mit ope for it hee.
Ebry leap was at est, and I ha'd not a soun,
But de Woodpecka tappin de ollow beet tee.

Text 12. Michael Scott, *Tom Cringle's Log*

Michael Scott's famous novel first appeared in the September issue of *Blackwood's Magazine* in 1829. The youngest son of a Glasgow merchant, Michael Scott (1789–1835) went to Jamaica in 1806 as manager to an estate. Later (1810), he entered business in Kingston and, save for one short absence in 1818, remained on the island until 1822. Scott's close observation of creole society enables him to show code switching in the speech of white and black Jamaicans. A white planter, Peregrine Whiffle, urges his slave to "give me my stick and massu [lift] the chair," but a few pages later he asks his English friends to "give me a lift" (1.343, 367). Mesolectal creole appears in the usage of Peter Mangrove, a black pilot, when he addresses the hero; Mangrove switches to basilectal JC when speaking to Nancy, his wife (1.258–69). The hero's white creole cousins greet him with "Cousin Taam, what you bring we?" (2.355). Not once does the narrator condemn the speech of white or black Jamaicans; rather, he uses such terms as *hedication, pull foot,* and *spruce* (1.227, 219, 356) as easily as he records the following remark by a German planter (2.328): "Liverpool! Come bring de food for de fis!" Covering all walks of society from dockhands to wealthy planters, Scott records the usage of the first two decades of the nineteenth century with phonetic spellings such as *vat, willain, soch, onder, sall,* and *pershave* (1834: 1.13, 15).

The first anecdote presented here is from Scott 1834: 1.128–29; the second, from 1.158–62.

A. A Black Sailor

The monkey was hanging by the tail from the dolphin-striker, admiring what John Crow called "his own dam ogly face in the water."

"Tail like yours would be a good ting for a sailor, Jackoo; it would leave his two hands free aloft—more use, more hornament,[10] too, I'm sure, den de piece of greasy junk dat hangs from the captain's tafferel. Now I shall sing to you how dat Corromantee[11] rascal, my fader, was sell me on de Gold Coast—

"Two red nightcap, one long knife,
All him get for Quackoo.
For gun next day him sell him wife—
You tink dat good song, Jackoo."

"Chockoo, chockoo," chattered the monkey, as if in answer.

"Ah, you tink so—sensible honimal! —What is dat? shark? —Jackoo, come up, sir: don't you see dat big shovel-nosed fis looking at you? Pull your hand out of de water—Garamighty!"

The negro threw himself on the gammoning of the bowsprit to take hold of the poor ape, who, mistaking his kind intention, and ignorant of his danger, shrunk from him, lost his hold, and fell into the sea. The shark instantly sank to have a run, then dashed at his prey, raising his snout over him, and shooting his head and shoulders three or four feet out of the water, with poor Jackoo shrieking in his jaws, whilst his small bones crackled and crunched under the monster's triple row of teeth.

B. The Black Pilot

Some time after this, we once more returned to Carthagena, to be at hand should any opportunity occur for Jamaica, and were lounging about one forenoon on the fortifications, looking with sickening hearts out to seaward, when a voice struck up the following negro ditty close to us:—

"Fader was a Corramantee,
Moder was a Mingo,[12]
Black picaniny buccra wantee,
So dem sell a me Peter, by Jingo.
Jiggery, jiggery, jiggery."

"Well sung, Massa Bungo,"[13] exclaimed Mr. Splinter; "where do you hail from, my hearty?"

"Hillo! Bungo, indeed! free and easy dat, anyhow. Who you yourself, eh?"

"Why, Peter," continued the lieutenant, "don't you know me?"

"Cannot say dat I do," rejoined the negro, very gravely, without lifting his head, as he sat mending his jacket in one of the embrasures near the water-gate of the arsenal —"Have not de honour of your acquaintance, sir."

He then resumed his scream, for song it could not be called.:—

"Mammy Sally's daughter
Lose him shoe in an old canoe
Dat lay half full of water,
And den she knew not what to do.
Jiggery, jig——"

"Confound your jiggery, jiggery, sir! But I know you well enough, my man; and you can scarcely have forgotten Lieutenant Splinter, of the *Torch*, one would think?"

However, it was clear that the poor fellow really had not known us; for the name so startled him that, in his hurry to unlace his legs from under him, as he sat tailor-fashion, he fairly capsized out of his perch, and toppled down on his nose—a feature, fortunately so flattened by the hand of nature, that I question if it could have been rendered more obtuse had he fallen out of the maintop on a timber-head, or a marine officer's.

"Eh!—no—yes, him sure enough; and who is de picaniny hofficer—Oh! I see, Massa Tom Cringle? Garamighty, gentlemen, where have you drop from? —Where is de old *Torch?* Many a time hab I, Peter Mangrove, pilot to Him Britannic Majesty squadron, taken de old brig in and through amongst de keys at Port Royal!"

"Ay, and how often did you scour her copper against the coral reefs, Peter?"

His Majesty's pilot gave a knowing look, and laid his hand on his breast —"No more of dat if you love me, massa."

"Well, well, it don't signify now, my boy; she will never give you that trouble again—foundered—all hands lost, Peter, but the two you see before you."

"Werry[14] sorry, Massy Plinter, werry sorry—What! de black cook's-mate and all? —But misfortune can't be help. Stop till I put up my needle, and I will take a turn wid you." Here he drew himself up with a great deal of absurd gravity. "Proper dat British hofficer in distress should assist one anoder. —We shall consult together. How can I serve you?"

"Why, Peter, if you could help us to a passage to Port Royal, it would be serving us most essentially. When we used to be lying there a week seldom passed without one of the squadron arriving from this; but here have we been for more than a month, without a single pennant belonging to the station having looked in: our money is running short, and if we are to hold on in Carthagena for another six weeks, we shall not have a shot left in the locker—not a copper to tinkle on a tombstone."

The negro looked steadfastly at us, then carefully round. There was no one near.

"You see, Massa 'Plinter, I am desirable to serve you, for one little reason of my own; but, beside dat, it is good for me at present to make some friend wid de hofficer of de squadron, being as how dat I am absent widout leave."

"Oh, I perceive—a large R [Author's note: runaway] against your name in the master-attendant's books, eh?"

"You have hit it, sir, werry close; besides, I long mosh to return to my poor wife, Nancy Cator, dat I leave, wagabone dat I is, just about to be confine."

I could not resist putting in my oar.

"I saw Nancy just before we sailed, Peter—fine child that; not quite so black as you, though."

"Oh, massa," said Snowball, grinning and showing his white teeth, "you know I am soch a terrible black fellow— But you are a leetle out at present,—I meant, about to be confine in de workhouse, for stealing de admiral's Muscovy ducks;" and he laughed loud and long. —"However, if you will promise dat you will stand my friends, I will put you in de way of getting a shove across to de east end of Jamaica; and I will go wid you too, for company."

"Thank you," rejoined Mr. Splinter; "but how do you mean to manage this? There is no Kingston trader here at present, and you don't mean to make a start of it in an open boat, do you?"

"No, sir, I don't; but in de first place—as you are a gentleman, will you try and get me off when we get to Jamaica? Secondly, will you promise dat you will not seek to know more of de vessel you may go in, nor of her crew, than dey are willing to tell you, provided you are landed safe?"

"Why, Peter, I scarcely think you would deceive us, for you know I saved your bacon in that awkward affair, when through drunkenness you plumped the *Torch* ashore, so—"

"Forget dat, sir,—forget dat! Never shall poor black pilot forget how you saved him from being seized up when de gratings, boatswain's mates, and all, were ready at the gangway—never shall poor black rascal forget dat."

"Indeed, I do not think you would wittingly betray us into trouble, Peter; and as I guess you mean one of the forced traders, we will venture in her, rather than kick about here any longer, and pay a moderate sum for our passage."

"Den wait here five minute,"—and so saying he slipped down through the embrasure into a canoe that lay beneath, and in a trice we saw him jump on board of a long low nondescript kind of craft, that lay moored within pistol-shot of the walls.

Text 13. [Bernard Martin Senior], *Jamaica as It Was, as It Is, and as It May Be*

Written after some twenty years' residence in Jamaica, this work presents many antiblack and antiabolitionist views. The author, Bernard Martin Senior, an unsympathetic observer, may have made little attempt to standardize the speech of blacks portrayed in his memoir, anxious as he was to show them in the most unfavorable light from his point of view. He claims to give truthful accounts of the Sam Sharpe rebellion (also called the Baptist rebellion) of 1831, but the tone and drift of his descriptions differ considerably from those of contemporaries such as the Baptist missionary James Mursell Phillippo. Similarities between the JC usage of writers so opposed in viewpoint suggest that their records do indeed capture the language usage of the 1830s. The verbatim testimony of the apprentice James Williams in 1837 also lends credibility to the form of the creole set down by Senior in this episode ([Senior] 1835: 38).

Charles Campbell's comments (1828: 19), and the Jamaica Religious Tract Society (1846: 118) noted a similar rationale for theft from massa. The distinction between taking and stealing in the following anecdote is an old one and well established. Marsden (1788: 43), for one, quotes a black man, who is being flogged for theft, as saying, "Massa, me no teevee, me takee." Marsden recorded the incident during a year's stay on the island at Rhimesbury Estate, Clarendon, in 1784.

Arguing with Massa

A proprietor, who had been but a few weeks in the island, observing that much of his Indian corn had been stolen, reprimanded the watchman, and threatened to punish him if he permitted further depredation. The negro, with the greatest *non chalance*, immediately thus addressed the master: "Massa please, massa no know de way of dis country yet; when massa been longer wid me, massa will know how dem dibide de crop of corn." "How, sir! what do you mean?" said the master: "do you suppose I will allow my corn to be stolen when I go to the expence of putting a watchman in the corn piece to protect it?" "No, massa, me no mean dat," replied the plausible fellow; "but me tell massa, *for true*, how dem share de corn. Massa plant de corn wid him niggah (negro.) Massa clean it well, bumbye, corn begin to get ripe, and bird take him for share. Niggah keep always taking for him share. Den, when quite ripe, massa take what is left *for him share!*"

Text 14. James M. Phillippo, *Jamaica: Its Past and Present State*

Sent to Jamaica in 1823 as a Baptist missionary, James Mursell Phillippo became one of the leading missionaries to Jamaican blacks in the years preceding and following Emancipation. In 1821 on first encountering the working-class English of Bradford in Yorkshire, Phillippo and other students in training for the ministry found the local dialect unintelligible, and he noted that "the more polished tongue was alike unintelligible to their grimy auditors" (Underhill 1881: 22). He must have developed his linguistic skills, for his value as a recorder of Jamaican Creole can be seen both in the major early work published in 1843, from which the following samples have been chosen, and in letters and other writings included in the biography published by E. B. Underhill in 1881. The evidence Underhill presents from diaries, letters, and other writings shows that both Phillippo and his wife Hannah Selina (née Cecil) had an intimate knowledge of Jamaican society. From their records one can see that the foundations of a language continuum were firmly laid. Changes of register were realized in shifts of morphology and syntax, and JC language behavior clearly reflected social groupings. The Phillippos' records also bring to light features now lost in JC, such as the archaic "missa" ("miss, missis"), which Mrs. Phillippo notes in two verbatim dialogues, one with her old washerwoman Rosina and the other with a free black who offers to buy and free the old woman seized in payment of her owner's debts (Underhill 1881: 80–81).

From Underhill we also learn that the Phillippos ran schools as well as church missions; they worked mainly with blacks, having less contact with coloreds and hardly any with whites. On one occasion Phillippo gave great offense to the white upper-class parents of some of his pupils when, during the illness of a teacher, he combined the elementary and secondary schools so that all of the children, slave and free, black and white, sat together in school.

We have placed Phillippo's texts ahead of Madden's, because Phillippo worked in Jamaica for ten years prior to 1834. Although some of the material he presents, including the letter from John Duglass, postdates Emancipation, much of his book deals with the conditions of slavery and draws on his experiences in the 1820s and early 1830s.

Phillippo reprints many letters, some showing basilectal structures (Text B), others in formal SE with only a few JC features (Text A), and others in SE (e.g., a letter from a brown woman [234]). The letters reflect the same kind of style shifting determined by topic and audience as is found in the code switching of the Jamaican speaker.

It is in Phillippo's interest to show JC speakers as intelligently conversant with the Bible and Christian doctrine. Nevertheless, his records of "church discourse" compare usefully with Williams (1826: 105–6 and Text 10.A) and *Marly* (1828, Text 11.B), in which the speakers are viewed as ridiculous.

A. Letter from John Duglass

Phillippo states that the following application (Phillippo 1843: 299) was made to him "by a poor black man on behalf of himself and others, who had been for some time deprived of the means of Christian instruction."

3rd May, 1841.

My Dear Minister— I have now to Right, and beg you to assist us, as now we are Sheep without a Shepherd, and we will be glad to have you, my Dear Minister, to enclose us again as so much sheep that have gone astray, by having no Pastor. So by our free will we shall be much thankful to my Dear Minister if you will come amongst us, that we may carry on God's work once more again, and satisfy we hungry soul; and we request the chapple to be regester for the Baptist Missionary Society. The name of the place is Content.

Signed on behalf of the family,
John Duglass.

B. Letter from Richard Bullock

The following is a letter of thanks for the donation of a Bible and hymn books to the congregation of Spanish Town (Phillippo 1843: 325). Note the far more standardized usage in a letter from a "colored woman" (Phillippo 1843. 234). Richard Bullock was a slave whom Phillippo describes as a leader in the church.

Christian Friends, —Me desire to return you our hearty and sincere tanks for de present of de books dat we have receive, and dat we hope dat de blessing of Almighty Fader may descend uppon ebery ephod dat is use in promote dat course of de Gospel, and dat your prayers and our prayers may unite togeder in praising Almighty Fader for de gift of a preached Gospel, and in sending his ministers to proclaim mercy unto de heathens, and for de prosperity of our minister and his dear partner in life, dat dey may be spare, and dat der days may be prolong, and dat massa's ministerial duty may be attend to wid dat solemnity of heart and wid dat pure affection towards God's glory, and dat many sinner may be bless wid de gift of de spirit, dat at lass both preacher and hearers may be heirs of dat mansion which our blessed Massa Jesus had gone to prepare, and dat de blessing of Almighty Fader may be sent upon us, dat we may not be weary in well doing.

I remain your humble sarvant,
Richard Bullock.
Spanish Town, Jamaica, July 28, 1826.

C. A Deacon's Prayer

Phillippo's ability to remember and record exact JC becomes evident in the following extract (Phillippo 1843: 341–46). Here he sets down from memory a long prayer, and although one might question his accuracy in so long a text, the discourse shows a remarkable consistency of JC sound and structure.

The following is a prayer that was offered up sometime since by a deacon of the church at Spanish Town, at a missionary prayer-meeting, and is inserted to convey an idea of the fervour and pious sentiment which usually pervade the supplications of the people. It was transcribed from memory as soon as the meeting was concluded, and the author can pledge himself to its accuracy, both as to sentiment and language.

"O, dow great and blessed God, we tank and bless dy holy name dat dow give we another opportunity of meeting togeder in de place where prayer is wont to be made. We acknowledge wid shame and confusion of face we great unwordiness to approach dy sacred footstool, and much less to handle dy sacred name between we polluted lip. We have not done one ting right nor fittin in dy sight ever since we born up to dis present hour. We have sin gainst de all time wid a high hand and a tretched out arm, and if dow been strick to mark our offence, O gracious God, we bin cut down long before dis like de wortless cumberer of de ground. When we tink of dy great love to we poor dying sinner, dat dow sent dy beloved son to pill him precious blood upon de cross, an buffeted, an spit upon, an mock by cruel man, what cause heb we, O blessed Massa, to call upon we heart, an all de power of we soul, to bless and praise dy holy name! Dow do great tings indeed for we, an yet we heart so hard, we will so stubborn and rebellious, we conscience so hardened, we understanding so dark, dat instead of loving de as we ought, we do notin but sin an grieve dy Holy Spirit. Oh! left we not to weself, for if dow do we tumble pon de dark mountain, an we feet catch in de trap de enemy of soul eber laying to draw we into. O do dow broke we stubborn heart, for it is desperate wicked bove all tings, it is full of ebery cage of unclean bird. O do dow root dem out same as Massa Jesus did cast out de debils out of de man wandering mong de tombs; and may we sit down like him at de feet of Jesus, clothed and in we right mind.

"O Lord, me heart is full, but me is poo ting, no able to find word to tell de my want an desire. Me know not how to pray, nor what to pray for, but me heart is open to de like a well widout a cover, and me come dis night, hungring and thirsting, to eat de bread of life, and bring me empty pitcher, like de woman of Samaria, to draw water out of de well of salvation. O send we not empty away. Bless we, even we also, O our Fader, for dow hast promis if poo sinner call pon de, dow will hear dem, for dy ear dont heavy dat it cannot hear, neider dy arm shorten dat dow cannot save. Remember Mary Magdalene and de tief pon de cross; dow didst wash dem wid dy precious blood, and dow is able to save to de uttermost all dat come unto de by him. O Lord, save or we perish. Blot out all we sin like a tick cloud from dy book of remembrance, an grant dat we may love de more, and sarve de better, ebery hour of we life. May we hate sin, an fly from it as from de ting of de sarpent and de corpion, an continually receive fresh supply of grace from de till we keep wax tronger and tronger, and appear perfect before de in Zion. O do dow bless we dear minister, who call pon me unwordy servant for call pon him God my God. O do dow bless de metsage of salvation dat has been deliver on de past sabbath. Do dow pare him life, and able him to lift up him voice like a mighty trumpet, dat sinner may see dem danger, and now begin to fly to de. O Lord water de seed sow from Sabbath to Sabbath, dat him no labour in vain, nor pend him strength for nought, but dat he may hab many seal for him ministry, and many soul for him hire. Many come here, O gracious Master, to pend an idle hour, or to mock pon dy precious word. O do dow bring down dem high look, and soften dem hard heart, dat dey may trow down dem rebellious weapon, and fight against de no mo, for dow say, whoeber fight against de and prosper? O Lord sarch dem heart as dow did Jerusalem wid a lighted candle, an enable dem dat dem may see dem state as dow see it, an as dem self will see it, if dow cut dem off widout an intrus in dy precious blood. Turn dem from dem evil way, as dow did de city of Ninevah. Dow only can soften dem hard heart. Man cannot do it; it is dy work, dear Jesus—dy work alone to make de leper clean. Dow say Paul plant, Apollos water, but God give de increase. O, blessed Master, we plead wid de. Broke dem heart as dow did Saul of Tarsus, dat dey may not rush down to de pit of destruction, where mercy neber come: we ax de for mercy's sake. Many dem lib like dem got no soul to save, no soul to lost. Top dem in dem mad career, and turn dem like de river of water is turned, dat de may no more blasflame dy name, nor broke dy Sabbath, nor prosecute dy little one any more. O Lord, we eye is up unto de; have mercy pon dem befo dy mercy clean gone for eber. Blessed God, do dow look pon dy man-servant who train up de children in de cool; strengthen him for him difficult work; gib him patience dat him may be able to bear wid all dem preverse temper; and able him dat he may train up dem youthful mind to love and sarve dee, dat when we head lay low in de grave dey may rise up, fill we places mo better dan we, and become a generation to call de blessed. "Dow hast bid we pray for de whole world, from de king pon his throne to de meanest pleasant [*sic*] pon de dunghill, derefo do dow hear we poo broken supplication for all we poo broder and sister who is sick; for de poo prisoner shut up in de dungeon; for all de poo widow an orphan; for all dat travel by sea or by land; an fo all de poo beggar, like Lazarus, laying down at de rich man's gate, full of sore. O Lord comfort dem; bind up dem wound, like de good Samaritan did to de poo man fell mong de tieves, when de priest an Levite passed by, an may dem affliction drive dem back to be like de prodigal son return hom to him fader house.

"Heb mercy, O Lord, pon de four corners of de world, where dem washing up tocks and tones, and de workmanship of dem own hand. Neber hear of Massa Jesus' blood to wash away dem guilty stain. O Lord, make de cales fall off dem dark eye like dow did Saul of Tarsus, when him going raven to Damascus to prosecute dy people. Send blessed European to teach dem how dem may excape dy wrath, which one day will be pour out pon de world. May dey cast away dem idol, and sa [*sic*] what we heb any mo to do wid idol, for dey cannot save we soul; notin but dy blood, dear Jesus, dy blood alone. Has dow not said, dat like as de sun go tro de earth, so de light of dy Gospel shall shine tro de whole world? Has dow not said dat Jesus shall see of de trabel of him soul, and shall be satisfy? Dat like as de rain come and de snow from Heaben and cannot be gader up again by man, so dow would shower down dy blessing pon de whole world? Has dow not said in dy precious word, dat all nation, an king, an queen, shall bow down to dy authority? O do dow fill up dy gracious promise, and tur up all we heart more dat we may wrestle wid de like Jacob, dat dis time may soon come when dy son an daughter shall come from de East and de West, from de Nort and from de Sout, and sit down wid Abraham, Isaac, and Jacob, in de kingdom of God. O, we long for see dat blessed day: hasten it, blessed Jesus. Let not dy chariot-wheel tarry no longer. We ax it for Jesus' sake, to whom, wid de and de Holy Spirit, we excribe neber-ceasing praises. Amen."

Text 15. Richard Robert Madden, *A Twelvemonth Residence in the West Indies*

Sent to Jamaica in 1833 as one of the special magistrates charged with overseeing Emancipation and Apprenticeship, Dr. R. R. Madden was a highly educated, well-traveled man who had worked in Italy, Turkey, and Egypt and had some skill in foreign languages. In the passionate pursuit of his duties he became acquainted with many slaves, including Abū Bakr al-Ṣiddīq, known in Jamaica as Edward Donlan, whose letter to Robert Tuffit (a fellow slave and scholar of Arabic) was published by Madden (1835: 2.136–38). Madden's diligence in noting the language of the people of Jamaica, and his care in recording statements suggest that he has rendered a fairly accurate record of current usage in the following excerpts (Madden 1835: 2.103, 105–6).

A. The Language of Flattery

On most plantations there is a litigious negro, who regulates the quarrels of the other negroes with one another, and takes on himself the general direction of their discontent. He is generally a shrewd, plausible fellow—has a good deal of Congo saw, or, in other negro parlance, sweet mouth[15]—and, likewise, a certain portion of what the Members of the Assembly call slack-jaw—Hibernice, the gift of the gab. When he wheedles buckra, he does it like an adept in adulation—he daubs his vanity all over. "Massa much too good to neger; what for neger wish him free? him want no nyam; salt plenty; plenty bittel;[16] too much every thing. Him too much happy with him sweet Massa—nebber to want free. Him born slave—why for no, him not always slave? Him no fuss of Augus neger,[17] him for true Massa's own neger? —who care for Willyforce neger? Hi chu! who have the imperance to call him free neger?"

B. Mathew's Oration

Mathew appeared before Madden for inciting others to insubordination on a property where the special magistrate, Mr. Lloyd, had only recently been explaining the new law to the apprentices (104). On the following defense Madden concludes: "This man wanted to do mischief, and I thought deserved punishment. But even in this instance, where, by misrepresenting the exposition of the law to the negroes, a spirit of partial discontent was created, the very negroes themselves gave evidence against him, and after his punishment, acknowledged that he justly deserved it" (2.106–7). As a self-defense addressed to a white audience, the speech is naturally designed to impress—hence high-style items *uprighteous* and *imperance*.

Well, Massa, since the day me born, me always live like a good negur, and a perfect Christian, on Salisbury Plain. Me fader and moder—(he was begged not to go back to the days of his youth)—well, massa, leave fader and moder one side—when me was first Christened by Parson Camill—(intimation that the charge against him had nothing to do with his baptism)—well, massa, no matter about the Christen, soon as me grow up, and able to talk a leetel, me always yeerie good advice—(requested to pass over his childhood)—well, massa, say no more of piccanini times—new parson open schools: ebery Sunday go to school; soon know plenty—(reminded to leave his school-days for the present times)—well, my good massa, say not one word more about school, what signify for true how much poor neger larn? what for neger larn to read book? —to beat gombah all day Sunday? no! to tell oder negro nancy story all day long? to play bonjaw all day Sunday? No! to go ofter John Canoes in big holidays, or spend piccanini Christmas (Easter) dancing, and all oder vanities? no, massa! me go to school to larn uprighteous conduck, and to be a perfect Christian. Me neber do nothing bad; work for massa like a good neger; never teef massa's goods; never tell oder neger bad; never make mischief 'gainst busha. Magistrate come to me and yeerie de complaints; him tell we all de law, den me axe what crime for law punish neger so dat we regulate our conduck. Him den reckon all crime up. Fus him tell us "insubordination;" den me say what for dat mean? him say imperance to massa; den me axe what dat mean? him say, if massa tell me for to do something, and we don't yeerie very well, dat mean imperance. Den me axe if imperance mean saucy, and him say yes. But black neger constable say, what for axe all dese things? ebery body know what dese things mean. But me axe once more, 'pose me want to pray to Gar Almighty, and busha says there is something else to do, does dat mean imperance? Constable cry again, ebery body knows about dat; den me tell him, ebery constable stops neger's mouth—a false constable, and has taken oath falsely, and ebery body swears false, him belly swell, and him die, but neber said constable die so. —Neber said magistrate was a false, and unjust magistrate: him know himself too well, and ebery body know him to be perfect Christian.

Text 16. James Williams, *Narrative of the Cruel Treatment . . . of a Negro Apprentice*

The testimony of James Williams, an apprentice freed and taken to England by the philanthropist Joseph Sturge, provides an excellent example of code switching between a formal, standardized register and a creole register to which Williams shifts in moments of stress and dramatic intensity. Williams was about eighteen years old when he made this statement; the opening paragraphs of the testimony state that he was born at Penshurst in St. Ann, and had been the property of a Mr. and Miss Senior, owners of that estate. The following extract (Williams 1837: 6–8) describes the incidents of 1834, when, in Williams's words, his former owner vowed that "if [the slaves] is to be free, he will pretty well weaken [them], before the six and the four years done" (3)—that is, before the end of their period of apprenticeship.

From the circumstances of his befriending by the philanthropist Sturge and from the tenor of remarks such as "It wasn't a man make the world, and man can't command it: the one that make the world will come again to receive it, and that is Jesus Christ!" (9–10), James Williams appears to have been a Christian convert with quite an extensive grasp of the language and doctrine of the missionary movement. His quotations of the exclamations of others being put to the treadmill ("massa me no able! my 'tomach, oh! me da dead, oh!"), fitted into his own formal and mesolectal discourse, show his accuracy in reporting the language behavior of different situations. He also uses the phrase "try my best endeavour" (18), which has evolved into "my endeavour-best" in current JC, a heritage of missionary language.

An Apprentice's Testimony

Mr. Rawlinson [the magistrate] come on a Friday evening, and I was to have take next day for my day; but massa send me word that me not to take the day, as he want to bring me before the magistrate; I was frightened and didn't go next morning: then I heard that magistrate said as I take the day against orders, when him and me meet he would settle it: I was quite frightened when I hear this, and I go away to Spanish Town to see the governor; but didn't see him, as he was up in the mountain: I go back to Saint Ann's, and hide in the woods about Penshurst and Knapdale; I stop about seven weeks, and then go back to Spanish Town; I went to Mr. Ramsay, and he gave me paper to Mr.

Emery, the Captain of Police, at St. Ann's; I met him on the road; he took me and put me in dungeon at Carlton; was kept there from Wednesday till Friday morning, then policeman came and took me to Brown's Town, and put me in cage till next day; then Mr. Rawlinson had me handcuffed and sent me to Penshurst, and put me in dungeon for ten days before he try me.

On the eleventh day Mr. Rawlinson came and slept there that night; next morning he had me brought out, and asked me about the running away, and I told him I go away because I was frightened when I hear how him and massa threaten me; then he sentenced me to St. Ann's Bay workhouse, for nine days, to get fifteen lashes in going in; to dance the tread-mill morning and evening, and work in the penal gang; and after I come back from the punishment, I must lock up every night in dungeon till he visit the property again, and I have to pay fifty days out of my own time for the time I been runaway.

Then they handcuff me to a woman belonging to Little-field, to send to the workhouse; she have little child carrying on her back, and basket on her head, and when she want to give picaniny suck, she obliged to rest it on one hand to keep it to the breast, and keep walking on: police don't stop to make her suckle the child. When we get to the workhouse, that same evening they give me the fifteen lashes; the flogging was quite severe and cut my back badly; then they put collar and chain upon my neck, and chain me to another man. Next morning they put me on the tread-mill along with the others: at first, not knowing how to dance it, I cut all my shin with the steps; they did not flog me then—the driver showed me how to step, and I catch the step by next day; but them flog all the rest that could not step the mill, flogged them most dreadful. There was one old woman with grey head, belong to Mr. Wallace, of Farm, and she could not dance the mill at all, she hang by the two wrists which was strapped to the bar, and the driver kept on flogging her; —she get more than all the rest, her clothes cut off with the Cat—the shoulder strap cut with it, and her shift hanging down over that side—then they flog upon that shoulder and cut it up very bad; but all the flogging couldn't make she dance the mill, and when she came down all her back covered with blood. They keep putting her on the mill for a week, and flog her every time, but when they see she could not dance it, they stop putting her on; if they no been stop, they would have kill her.

There was about thirty people in the workhouse that time, mostly men; nearly all have to dance the tread-mill morning and evening; six or eight on the tread-mill one time, and when them done, another spell go on, till them all done; every one strap to the bar overhead, by the two wrists, quite tight; and if the people not able to catch the step, them hang by the two wrist, and the mill-steps keep on batter their legs and knees, and the driver with the Cat keep on flog them all the time till them catch the step. The woman was obliged to tie up their clothes, to keep them from tread upon them, while they dance the mill; them have to tie them up so as only to reach down to the knee, and half expose themself; and the man have to roll up their trowsers above the knee, then the driver can flog their legs with the Cat, if them don't dance good; and when they flog the legs till they all cut up, them turn to the back and flog away; but if the person not able to dance yet, them stop the mill, and make him drop his shirt from one shoulder, so as to get at his bare back with the Cat. The boatswain flog the people as hard as he can lay it on—man and woman all alike.

One day while I was in, two young women was sent in from Moneague side, to dance the mill, and put in dungeon, but not to work in penal gang; them don't know how to dance the mill, and driver flog them very bad; they didn't tie up their clothes high enough, so their foot catch upon the clothes when them tread the mill and tear them; —and then between the Cat and the mill—them flog them so severe,— they cut away most of their clothes, and left them in a manner naked; and the driver was bragging afterwards that he see all their nakedness.

Dancing tread-mill is very hard work; it knocks the people up—the sweat run all down from them—the steps all wash up with the sweat that drop from the people, just the same as if you throw water on the steps.

One boatswain have to regulate the pole of the mill, and make it go fast or slow, as him like; sometimes them make it go very fast, and then the people can't catch the step at all—then the other boatswain flogging away and cutting the people's legs and backs without mercy. The people bawl and cry so dreadful, you could hear them a mile off; the same going on every time the mill is about; driver keep the Cat always going while the people can't step.

When them come off the mill, you see all their foot cut up behind with the Cat, and all the skin bruise off the shin with the mill-steps, and them have to go down to the sea-side to wash away the blood.

After all done dance the mill, them put chain and collar on again, and chain two, three, and sometime four together, and turn we out to work penal gang—send us to different estate to work—to dig cane-hole, make fence, clean pasture, and dig up heavy roots, and sometimes to drag cart to bring big stone from mountain-side, about two or three miles from the bay; have to drag cart up steep hill. About ten o'clock they give we breakfast,—one quart of corn boiled up with a little salt; sometime they give we a shad between two or three of we.

They keep us at work till between four and five o'clock, then take us back to the workhouse—take the chains off we all, and make us go upon the mill again, same fashion as in the morning. After that them put us into the bar-room—put the chain and collar on again and our foot in the shackle-bar, to sleep so till morning. All the woman put into one room, and all the man in another; them that have any of the breakfast left from morning, eat it after them lock up; but them that eat all the allowance at breakfast, must starve till morning.

10

The Later Nineteenth Century

Text 17. Henry G. Murray, *Manners and Customs of the Country a Generation Ago*

In the preface to his memoir, Henry G. Murray admits to having "Anglicised the native idiom, for the benefit of readers, not 'to the manner born.' " His narrative is set firmly in SE, yet the dialogues incorporated in it and, most notably, the following "Nancy Story" of Mudfish (Murray 1877: 21–23), present features of JC syntax, morphology, and phonology in careful, consistent detail. Murray seems equally at home narrating in SE or JC. A brown man, and an educated one, he would have had access to and control of a wide range of usage, while his talent as a dramatic reader would have drawn from the traditions of the wake and the tea-meeting. The story offers such archaisms as *chookoo, disha-ya,* and *good-belly pigeon;* the frame of the narrative suggests that much of the detail must have been drawn from reminiscences of Murray's childhood and youth.

Mudfish and Watchman

"Once upon a time in a Chookoo dere was hard time[1] dere. Nobody couldn't get nuttin[2] to eat. Bud dem fly all bout da look for someting to eat, but dem couldn't get nuttin; so tay one day, de word come say,[3] one gentleman corn piece for y-o-n-d-e-r hab plenty corn; and de corn well an ripe. As de news come so pigeon dem[4] all da fly fe go dere. Mudfish in a water; from him wake da morning, so tay in a breakfast time, him yery bud wing da go ya—pa, pa, pa; pa, pa, pa; him say, 'poor me boy! da warra disha ya to-day? Him swim go da shore side, den when pigeon dem top da riverside fe drink water, him hax dem say, 'Bra, whi side unoo da go?' Dem say, 'Ha Bra! buckra corn piece ripe, sa! We da go dere!' Mudfish say, 'Bra unoo carry me go wid unoo, no?' Pigeon dem say, 'Cho, mudfish! tan where you day, man. What you da go do da cornpiece!' Mudfish would'nt satisfy; him tan dere da shoreside, so pigeon dem come da waterside come drink water, him beg dem, 'Bra, unoo carry me go, no!' Dem say, 'Mudfish, tan where you day, man.' Mudfish top dere, neber move, tay bam-bye good-belly pigeon come dere come drink water. Mudfish say to him, 'Bra pigeon carry me go wid you, no! Him say, 'Bra, what you da go do a cornpiece?' Mudfish say,' 'Me too love corn, Bra.' Him say, 'how you fe go!' Him say, 'Bra, you no make me lie down da you back.' Him say, 'Bra, suppose you fall down?' Him say 'Bra, me will hold on.' Him say, 'Bra Mudfish, me no want car[5] you.' Him say, 'Bra car me!' Good-belly pigeon take him so carry him. When dem catch da cornpiece, dem put Mudfish da ground; den so de pigeon dem da eat corn a top, Mudfish da da bottom da pick up wha drop, da eat. When dem all busy da eat, yery word come say 'Watchman da come;' pigeon dem begin da fly da go way—ya 'pa, pa, pa., Mudfish say, 'Good-belly pigeon take me up no?' Him say, 'Bra, we cant wait fe you. Bra me ben tell you say you must'nt come ya; da you hard ears you take so come ya.'— Mudfish say, 'poor me boy, me done for to-day.' So dem oder pigeon da fly da go, him beg dem fe take him up. Dem say, 'Cho man, who da go boder with you? Dat man bring you ya, make him take you no!' Dem all lef Mudfish go way. When Watchman come, him see Mudfish, him say, 'wha you da do ya? How you lef water so come ya? Him say, 'Bra, da pigeon bring me come ya.' Watchman take him up an put him da him kutakoo, say, 'I wi carry you to buckra make you tell him wha you da do ya.' So Watchman da walk da go 'long, so, him da sing. Mudfish talk to himself say 'Dis Watchman ya love sing.' Watchman say, 'I love sing, yes.' Mudfish say, 'Ah! Bra Watchman, ef you want fe hear man sing, da me.' Watchman say, 'a so?' Mudfish say "yes, but I cant sing widout water; put me in a one packy o' water and I wi sing fe you. Watchman do so. Mudfish shake himself, den begin fe sing—

> 'Yerry groomer corn pempeny,
> Groomer yerry;
> Pigeon bring me da groomer yerry.'

Watchman dance. Him say, 'Mudfish you sing well, sa.' —Mudfish say, 'put me in a tub o' water an I wi sing better, Bra.' Watchman put him in a big washing tub o' water. Mudfish sing again; Watchman dance so, till de sweat drop off da him face. Him say, 'Mudfish, you sing too sweet.' Mudfish say, 'Dis put m[e] riber side make I smell riber water.' Him say, 'No Mudfish, bambye you make me fool!' Mudfish say, 'No Bra, no cajon put my body, dis put my tail, make it touch de water, and I wi[ll] sing fe you make you dance like you mad.' Watchman say, '[I] will do it, but take care you make me fool.' Him say, 'No Bra Watchman, put me down.' Mudfish begin sing; Watchman begin dance. So Mudfish da sing, so him da wriggle him tail. How de sing sweet Watchman him neber look 'pon Mudfish. Mudfish wriggle and sing—Mudfish wriggle and sing, til[l] him get into de water; as him get in dere so, him raise up him head an him say, 'Bra Watchman, me gone, yerry!' —Watchman jump after him, but bufo you coulda say 'Jack,' Mudfish tail gone! A dat make you hear dem say 'neba make Mudfish tail touch water.' "

This story was duly applauded, and wound up with the usual "Jack Mandora."

Text 18. [Henry G. Murray], in "Creole Folklore from Jamaica"

The following tale and poem were reproduced by William C. Bates in an article published in *Journal of American Folklore* 9–10 (32–33) (April–June 1896): 124, 125. Bates attributes both to Henry G. Murray.

A. The Origin of Woman

A discussion arose between black Lizzie and her husband upon the origin of man. Harry laid it down for an axiom that he was made from the dust of the earth, because the minister said so. "I mek out o' dust fe' sartin." To him, according to the story, Lizzie replies: "Me no mek out o' none dirt."[6] Then Harry: "Ef you don' mek out o' dirt, wha' you mek out o'? You mek out o' dirt, yes!" "I don't mek out o' notin' o' de kin'." "Den wha' you mek out o'? You mus' mek out o' some goolin' (golden) ting or noder, den?" "I don' mek out o' no goolin' ting, an' I don' mek out o' none dirt. I mek out o' bone." "Mek out o' wha'?" "Bone!" "Bone?" "Yes, bone to be sho'." "Wha' kin' o' bone?" "Rib's bone! you na hea' minista' say so?" "Well, I don' know wha' fe' say 'bout dat; I don' like fe' say dat wha' minista' say not de trut'; but I mean fe' say, when minista' read 'bout dat rib's bone, him must mean buckra ooman, becasin so dem white, so de bone white. Ef you mek de same, you' 'kin would a ben white." "Cho," said Lizzie, "ef you been open[7] you' ears, 'tidda da sleep, you would a hea' de minsta' say de 'kin notin', but de blood, da de ting, becasin in de book say, dat white-o, brown-o, black-o,[8] all mek de same blood; you eba' see white blood an' black blood?" "Look you," said Harry, "you know how me uncle Jame use fe' to say ooman came in dis worl'?"[9] "Cho, no boda me." "Neba' min', I da go tell you. Dem mek two men; de fuss one mek berry well, but when dem mek de oder one, it kinda' 'poil. Den as dem look upon it, so it da jump about, and shake him head, and do all kin' o' 'tupid ting, like a how woman hab fe' go on. Den one o' dem hol' him, say, 'Wha' kin' o' ting you?' Den de oder say: 'Cho, him no use, him can' talk.' Ebery day him da go on like a dummy, till one day dem hol' him so, 'zaman him tongue, den dem see de tongue tie; dem tek a raza', cut it. As dem cut it so, bam! de ting mout begin da fly, dem coud n' 'top it. Dem say: 'Well, dem sorry dey eber cut de tongue.' From dat time, it mek you hear dem say: 'Ef you wan' ooman fe' good, gib him 'tump o' tongue' " (stump of tongue, a tongue-tie).[10]

B. Song: Oh! What Do My Buddy, O!

Bates states that the following love lyric was based on the story of one Sarah Miller, who lost her lover to a younger rival. He offers an explanation of the diction and imagery of the poem:

> Massnega is a fellow-servant, male or female; in this case the term is applied to the rival, also compared to a green leaf. "Ackie" (*Hibiscus esculentus*) is a beautiful fruit, with a thick rind of deep crimson which bursts as the fruit ripens, and shows three oblong sections, of milky-white color, imbedded in velvety compartments, and surmounted by oval seeds of a brilliant jet, called in the song the eyes of the fruit; these, when the fruit is ripened, fall to the ground and are worthless. The beauty of the simile will be appreciated by those familiar with the fruit.

The modern version is called "All di call me call Dinah."

Oh! What do my buddy, O!
Oh! What do my buddy, O!
All da coax, me da coax,
My buddy won' 'peak a wor';

All da beg, me da beg,
My buddy won' 'peak to me, O!

Massnega look 'pon my buddy, O!
Massnega look 'pon my buddy, O!
My buddy bex', my buddy bex',
My buddy won' 'peak a wor';
Me kiss him foot, buddy foot,
Buddy won' 'peak to me, O!

Dey ripe leaf dey 'pon tree top, O!
Dey dry leaf da tree root, O!
Young leaf green, young leaf green,
Young leaf won' green no mo';
It will drop from tree top,
Come down on groun' to me, O!

Ackee wear him green frock, O!
Ackee hab him black eye, O!

Text 19. William George Hamley, *Captain Clutterbuck's Champagne*

While any work of fiction must be viewed cautiously for its reliability in representing nonstandard speech, William George Hamley's novel (subtitled *A West Indian Reminiscence*) remains faithful to the syntax and sound systems of JC. The dialogue of his black and colored characters compares favorably with the usage depicted by the Jamaican Henry G. Murray. William G. Hamley (1815–1893) was commissioned in the Royal Engineers on his eighteenth birthday and retired at the honorary rank of major-general in 1872. Scant records of his West Indian service exist at the Museum of the Royal Engineers and in the Bermuda Archives, but it is clear that he, like Michael Scott, spent a portion of his youth and manhood in the British Caribbean colonies. His last position of importance was that of lieutenant governor and commander in chief of Bermuda, where he gave outstanding service to the community during the yellow fever epidemic of 1864.[11] By curious coincidence, the surname of his heroine, Arabin, appears on a memorial tablet in St. George's Anglican Church in Bermuda.

The author of a number of novels and a travelogue, Hamley also contributed to *Blackwood's Magazine*. He was fluent in French, Italian, and possibly German and showed some care in representing regional English (especially northern and Cockney speech). In much of his writing he uses nonstandard features: in a historical novel published in 1882, such spellings as "cowld," "pisen," "sarch," and "cheeld" appear in scenes of village life. His textual notes betray a fascination with etymologies and unusual language forms such as the pidgin spoken by donkey-renters in Ismailia or that used by a Portuguese merchant in London.

From internal references to Jamaican towns, villages, forts, and other locations, the novel shows that Hamley had a sound knowledge of the country. Few other texts maintain such consistent orthography or show such detailed observation of vowel quality and quantity in the creole speech. A few features (e.g., *werry, liard*) represent usage common to JC and other nonstandard English dialects.

The first extract (Hamley 1862: 181–86) belongs to a series of nautical tales very popular in Jamaica during the Napoleonic Wars and after, as is shown in Henry G. Murray's references to "Boney." Through the character of the quadroon nurse (a social and ethnic type well attested in nineteenth- and twentieth-century Jamaica), the second extract (230–33) represents the speech of the rising brown middle classes.

A. A Black Sailor's Yarn

"Me will tell you ob a great engagement between Nelson and Boney. You see, we bin cruisin' some time 'pon de coast of 'Pain; nebber go into harbour, becausin, you see, Nelson hab a most lubly nyoung[12] woman aboord, dem call Lady sunting or 'nother, me can't rightly tell de name. Well, after we keep de blue sea till de water stink faber jackfruit, and de bisket walk about de table, we begin to tink, 'Dis here no fun. Why de debil him no take we into port to get some fresh probishun, and hab a dance wid de gals?' De people beginnin' to get dam obstropolous, I can tell you, and it impossible to say what de dooce might hab come ob it, only one forenoon dem report a French frigate in sight. One of our frigates clear for action directly, and get under way to go out and meet her, when it seem she coming up quite friendly wid a flag ob truce. De lads forget all about de prog and de gals, and begin to wonder what make de Frenchman come dis side. Berry soon we hear what in de wind. Nelson pacing de quarterdeck, 'tamping him great foot, and raising him great voice, and cussin' faber madman. My, how dat man swear! Lad Gad, what you tink! de impedince ob dat Boney! Him send for tell Nelson him mus' hab de nyoung woman and carry him to France, and

Nelson better gib him up quietly, and no gib Boney de trouble for come and fatch him away. Ob course Nelson send him back a dam 'pirited answer, and tell him he quite ready whenever Boney liked to come, and he gib him coco for yam. But de passion dat man in, me nebber see sich a ting! him flog half de ship's company, and crack de gunner's cocoa-nut wid a rammer-head. Nobody didn't dare to go near him, and when de signal hofficer go up to do him dooty, and report de French fleet in sight, Nelson fly at him faber wild-cat, and he say, says he (terrible 'trong voice Nelson had), 'You infernal cussed . . . (*desunt asperrima verba*) . . . what de debil make you come 'peak to me dis-a-way? Eh, sar.' De leeftenant try again for do him dooty, and report de hennemy's sail, when Nelson square up to him wid both hands, and swear to Garamighty he knock him into next week if him no pull foot and be off. 'Knock away, admiral,' says de brabe nyoung hofficer, 'but I tell you de French fleet comin' for all dat?' 'Hei, what?' Nelson say; 'de debil! dat quite anoder ting. Ax for you pardon, sar; glad to see you to dinner and grog after we sink dese damnable French 'coundrels.' Den he pass de word for get all ready, and by de time Boney come, we hab someting warm waiting for him. You see for me dooty keep me down below, and me no see what go on when dem fust go into axion, only me hear de row and see de smoke. After lilly bit ebbery ting quiet, all de noise 'top, we can't tink how dem make sich dem short work ob it. So me run up to see, and anoder gentleman ob color, who likewise come up to look about him, infarm me dat Nelson bin and boarded Boney ship, an' all about it. When de boarders 'cramble on deck, he tell me Nelson sing out, 'Where dat lubber Boney, eh? Make me see him; me 'mash him bl——y brains out. Hah, boy, you dere, eh? Come on.' 'How de debil you know me?' Boney say; 'you ebber see me before, eh?' 'Know you, sar, by de cut ob your infernal jib,' says Nelson. 'No more nonsense; bear a hand, now. Make me 'mash you.' 'Two can play dat game,' Boney say; 'now den, come on, boy.' When dem see Nelson and Boney goin' fight, ebberybody 'top firing and hollering, and come to deir ship's side to see de battle same as me is doin' myself. In two minutes Nelson and Boney draw off 'pon de quarterdeck, and down heads. Ebberybody hold him breat', when dey run at one anoder. My fader! cr-r-r-r-ack. What a whop! Berry well, dem shake deirself and draw off again. Hei! 'noder crack, terrible hard! Boney 'tagger lilly bit dis time, but him no capsized yet. Him 'tand anoder knock. But, my king! it a pounder faber fifty-pound shot. Nelson's yeyes flash fire, and he grind him teet' horrid. Den he rush 'pon Boney, and fell him as de cook's mate knack down a bullock. Boney, nearly killed and no able for get up, rub him head and say, he fight again anoder day; dat he bin come out widout him breekfiss dat morning, and sich kind ob pretence. But Nelson sing out sharp, 'Belay dat jaw; me will teach you to sarve out sarce to a better man dan yourself. Now, lads, seize up dat light-libbered lubber; put he in irons and gag him, den chuck him in a rum cask and carry him home to King George.' When dem see Boney walloped, de French fleet 'trike and de English cheer. King George send Boney to pick oakum in Santeleny, and he make Nelson a prince ob de blood. What you tink ob dat, sar?"

"Very good indeed," said Christy, "and worth a dollar; here it is. I thought, though, that you were on quite familiar terms with Nelson; haven't I heard you say so?"

"Me couldn't say dat, massa, becausin it was not de fack, and massa know me always 'peak de trut'. Me hab berry little personal 'quaintance wid Nelson—berry little. De last time me see him was at de Gun at Deal wid a 'plendid nyoung lady. Dem jist bin dancin' when me come in, and Nelson's pipe gone out while him dance. 'Hillo, messmate,' sing out Nelson, 'shibber my timbers, gib us a light and be d—— to you.' So ob course I hand him a light, and him say, 'What will you drink, old ship—glass o' rum?' 'No, admiral,' me say, 'rum is a common liquor; any low nigger can drink rum: me prefers brandy.' 'Two glasses ob de bes' brandy,' sing out Nelson. 'Your healt', sar,' he say. 'Your good healt', admiral,' me say, and so we pull foot and part. 'Who is de coloured gentleman I take brandy wid?' I hear Nelson say jes' after. Dat de last time I see him, but I b'lieve him is generally lounging about the Point in de summer mont'; but in winter him shut up, becausin it cold dere, and you see him gettin' dam elderly; besides dat, him drink hard and bin a debilish sly feller."

B. A Brown Nurse

The following scene typifies the role that many "brown" women filled in the strictly defined social and racial hierarchy of the plantation era. The nurse's usage, clearly mesolectal, includes SE sentence structures (such as "what is dis") in which JC sound laws operate, as well as others ("you shall have it," "he wouldn't tell you so") that are uninterrupted SE. Her usage also includes the unmarked past tense ("he come court me before he sick"), the nonverbal predicator ("he most my first sweetheart") and the sound changes [θ] > [t] and [đ] > [d].

The doctor had insisted on the attendance of a nurse; and accordingly there sat near [Lieutenant Lorton] the grandly-developed form of Miss Malvina MacGlashin, her dark wool concealed by a cotton handkerchief, which was knotted across the nape of her neck, with two enormous mosaic drops in her ears, a triple chin, a chintz wrapper of a florid design, and reaching a little below her knees, and a pair of morocco slippers, the heels whereof were well trodden down, and the toes pointing inwards like those of a parrot. Miss Malvina was a lady of colour, somewhere about quadroon in blood, and tolerably light-brown. Her age was between forty and fifty; she was inclined decidedly to embonpoint; a fine bridge on her nose was the charter by which she claimed kinship to the MacGlashin, and a pair of lips about two inches thick conspired with hair and skin to indicate the source of her hybrid existence.

"Isn't it nearly time for the medicine, Malvina?" inquired the sufferer, who has been restless for some little while.

The brown lady rose, and with a motion which we should esteem neither light nor graceful on this side of thè Atlantic, lifted Lorton's watch and showed it to him, for the revelations of the timepiece were foolishness to Miss Malvina.

"Wants ten minutes," Lorton said, "but that doesn't signify; I can take it now."

"My chile," replied Miss Malvina, with a whining drawl, "when de dactar say a ting, it is praper to do it; so you mus' wait till de tree hour is up, and den I will give you de draff."

"I expect Mr Knox here to see me directly," pleaded the patient, "and we may as well get the medicine over before he comes."

"Very well, my chile," said Miss MacGlashin, "it is near de time now, and if you promise me not to talk too much to Meesta Knox, you shall have it. See now, only dis half of de mixture, and den dis nice piece of pink shaddock. Dere now, he really take it good; now den, pop in de shaddock, and the nassy taste will soon gone; so, so, dat is it. Now, let we make de room look leetle bit neat and tidy before de visitor come in. Where dat creature Sampson?"

Miss Malvina knew her work too well to call or knock in a sick-room for the assistance she required. She stepped into the verandah herself for the purpose of sending down a message by the first passenger; and in so doing she caught sight of Sampson rolling in the grass below, whom she forthwith summoned to the upper chamber by the title of "lazy, wort'less hangman." It was wonderful the gentleness with which they moved about and arranged the room. Plates, glasses, and bottles quickly disappeared; table-covers were smoothed, and chairs set in their places. Lorton had a clean shirt put on him, and his hair carefully and gently dressed; then he and his apartment were perfumed with eau-de-Cologne.

"Ah, that's nice!" he said; "I really think I feel a little better!"

"Yes; only keep quiet, and do as you is told, and you will soon be better, my chile. De fus' young man I ever nus, he very much in de same way as you is, and I bring him round. Nice young man! he come court me before he sick: I used to pretty den; dat is a long time ago. He most my fus' sweetheart. Chaw! how I lub him! Those times was different from now. De officers more attentive to de young ladies, and de sailor officers bring in prize-money, and make we handsome presents. My! how de doubloons fly about! never see dem now. And de beautiful horses and de kittureens! I shall never see de like again. Hei! What dat you have dere?" suddenly said she in a loud whisper to Sampson. . . . "What is dis?" repeated Miss Malvina, following him into the verandah, and seizing a black bottle from under his arm. It was three parts full of madeira.

"I did tink it turn bad," said Sampson.

"Take it back," said Miss Malvina, not deigning to notice the lame excuse. Sampson obeyed, muttering to himself as he did so, "Dis brown lady too bad, cubbich as a 'tar-apple tree. Massa nebber do so."

. . . Miss Malvina looked toward the window, and nodded in reply to a sign from Knox, who had made a quiet reconnaissance to ascertain whether the patient was awake and prepared to receive him. A flush overspread Lorton's wan face as he shook hands and answered the usual interrogatories. Even this little excitement tried him, it was clear; seeing which, Knox addressed his conversation for a while to Miss Malvina.

"A little feverish still, Malvina—pulse variable," said he; "we must still be careful to avoid excitement."

"He will do very well, sar,"[13] replied Miss Malvina, using the severity which is proper when unprofessional people attempt to talk scientifically to an adept. "Can you tell me what is de hour?"

"Just gone three. Didn't you hear the bugle, old girl?"

"I am not an old gal, Meesta Knax. You will be good enough to recolleck dat you is talking to a leady."[14]

"Of course," Knox said, "but your figure and face are so girlish that one forgets. Let's see, you must be quite a woman now; yes, of course!"

"I am afraid dat you is making fun, sar," remarked Miss MacGlashin, composedly.

"There was a gentleman of your name at mess last night, Lawyer MacGlashin. Is he any relation?"

"He is my broder, sar."

"Indeed! I was not aware of that."

"My *white* brother, dat is. He wouldn't tell you so. They is not bery proud of their coloured relations. They can't wash out the MacGlashin blood for all dat. It is here;" and Miss Malvina placed her hand on the magnificent region above her heart.

"He ought to feel flattered," said Knox, "at having so lovely and accomplished a relation."

"Ah, sar," sighed Miss Malvina, "you is not so prejudice as dese creole whites. You cannot understand deir silly pride. I often say I will go home to Scotland, where they will not be ashamed of the MacGlashin blood, whatever is the skin it run under. De heart of dat people is warm, sar!"

"But their country is devilish cold," said Knox.

"What does de cold matter to me, sar?" said Malvina, loftily; "if I have de blood I have de spirit too, and I can bear de cold like de res' of my relations."

"You'll have to wear a kilt."

"Whatever is de proper dress, sar."

"And to live upon whisky and oatmeal."

"Of course, sar."

"And talk Gaelic."

"Yes, sar."

"And play the bagpipe."

"Whatever oder leadies does, sar."

Text 20. Captain Mayne Reid, *The Maroon*

Captain Mayne Reid was first educated with a view to the Presbyterian ministry but emigrated to America, where he had a varied career. He worked as an overseer and for a longer period as a journalist, then took a commission and fought in the Mexican War (1846–1848). It was after that that he settled down to write and produced thirty-four novels. *The Maroon* purports to be a tale told to the author by an elderly Maroon who entertained him in the mountains of Trelawny. Of the following two extracts (Reid 1862: 2.190–99, 222–25), the second is noteworthy for its attempt to represent a nonstandard usage tied, like creole, to a particular ethnic situation; like many writers of his time, Reid is anti-Semitic and racist in his views.

While a number of unfamiliar phonological and grammatical features throw doubt on the authenticity of the work, others give it historical and linguistic value: note Reid's *obaseeah* and Moreton's *obisha* (1793: 143), Reid's *missa* and the same form in Mrs. Phillippo (Underhill 1881: 80). The writer obviously knows Jamaican and, specifically, Maroon food; he is familiar with local artifacts (*cutacoo,*

[261]), with practices such as the branding of slaves, and with local trees, plants, and birds. He is obviously interested in dialect and uses it for characterization in his anti-Semitic portrayal of the Jew in Text B, in contrasting social differences between the Cormantin obeah man and the domestic (Text A), and in ridiculing the "toff" ("Aw, ba Jawve" [2.94]).

A. The Myal Man and the Parlormaid

"Come in!" cried he, repeating his command in the same gruff voice. "You me sabbey[15]—what fo' you fear?"

"I'se not afraid, Chakra," replied the woman, though the trembling of her voice contradicted the assertion; "only," she added, still hesitating, "it's so dark in there."

"Well, den—you 'tay outside," said the other, relenting; "you 'tay dar wha you is; a soon 'trike a light."

A fumbling was heard, and then the chink of steel against flint, followed by fiery sparks.

A piece of punk was set a-blaze, and from this the flame was communicated to a sort of lamp, composed of the *carapace* of a turtle, filled with wild-hog's lard, and having a wick twisted out of the down of the cotton-tree.

"Now you come in, Cynthy," resumed the negro, placing the lamp upon the floor. "Wha! you 'till afeard! You de dauter ob Juno Vagh'n—you modder no fear ole Chakra. Whugh! she no fear de Debbil!"

Cynthia, thus addressed, might have thought that between the dread of these two personages there was not much to choose: for the Devil himself could hardly have appeared in more hideous guise than the human being who stood before her.

"O Chakra!" said she, as she stepped inside the door, and caught sight of the weird-looking garniture of the walls; "woman may well be 'fraid. Dis am a fearful place!"

"Not so fearful as de Jumbé Rock," was the reply of the myal-man, accompanied by a significant glance, and something between a smile and a grin.

"True!" said the mulatta, gradually recovering her self-possession; "true: you hab cause say so, Chakra."

"Das a fac', Cynthy."

"But tell me, good Chakra," continued the mulatta, giving way to a woman's feeling—curiosity, "how did you ebber 'scape from the Jumbé Rock? The folks said it was your skeleton dat was up there—chain to de palm-tree!"

"De folk 'peek da troof.[16] My 'keleton it was, jess as dey say."

The woman turned upon the speaker a glance in which astonishment was mingled with fear, the latter predominating.

"*Your* skeleton?" she muttered, interrogatively.

"Dem same old bones—de 'kull, de ribs, de jeints,[17] drumticks, an' all. Golly, gal Cynthy! dat 'ere 'pears 'stonish you. Wha fo'? Nuffin in daat. You sabbey old Chakra! You know he *myal-man?* Doan care who know *now*—so long dey b'lieve um dead. Wha for myal-man, ef he no bring de dead to life 'gain? Be shoo Chakra no die hisseff, so long he knows how bring dead body to de life. Ole Chakra know all dat. Dey no kill *him*, nebber! Neider de white folk nor de brack[18] folk. Dey may shoot 'im wid gun—dey may hang 'im by de neck—dey may cut off 'im head—he come to life 'gain, like de blue lizard and de glass[19] snake. Dey *did* try kill 'im, you know. Dey 'tarve him till he die ob hunger and thuss. De John Crow pick out him eyes, and tear de flesh from de old nigga's body—leab nuffin but de bare bones! Ha! Chakra 'lib yet—he hab new bones, new flesh! Golly! you him see [*sic*]? he 'trong—he fat as ebber he wa'! Ha! ha! ha!". . .

"You've brought de basket ob wittle, Cynthy?"

"Yes, Chakra—there."

"Golly! um's berry good—guinea-hen an plenty ob vegable fo' de pepperpot. Anything fo' drink, gal? Habent forgot daat, a hope? De drink am da mose partickla ob all."

"I have not forgotten it, Chakra. There's a bottle of rum. You'll find it in the bottom of the basket. I had a deal trouble steal it."

"Who you 'teal 'im from?"

"Why, master: who else? He have grown berry partickler of late—carries all de keys himself; and won't let us coloured folk go near de storeroom, as if we were all teevin' cats!"

"Nebba mind—nebba you mind, Cynthy—maybe Chakra watch *him* by'm-bye. Wa, now!" added he, drawing the bottle of rum out of the basket, and holding it up to the light. "De buckra preacher he say dat 'tolen water am sweet. A 'pose dat 'tolen rum folla de same excepshun. A see ef um do . . . "

". . . Whugh!" he exclaimed, with an aspirate that resembled the snort of a startled hog. "Whugh!" he repeated, stroking his abdomen with his huge paw. "De buckra preacher may talk 'bout him 'tolen water, but gib me de 'tolen rum. You good gal, Cynthy—you berry good gal, fo' fetch ole Chakra dis nice basket o' wittle—he sometime berry hungry—he need um all."

"I promise to bring more—whenebber I can get away from the Buff."

"Das right, my picaninny! An' now, gal," continued he, changing his tone, and regarding the mulatta with a look of interrogation, "wha fo' you want see me dis night? You had some puppos partickla? Dat so—eh, gal?"

The mulatta stood hesitating. There are certain secrets which woman avows with reluctance—often with repugnance. Her love is one; and of this she cares to make confession only to him who has the right to hear it. Hence Cynthia's silent and hesitating attitude.

"Wha fo' you no 'peak?" asked the grim confessor. "Shoo' you no hab fear ob ole Chakra? You no need fo' tell 'im—he know you secret a'ready—you lub Cubina, de capen ob Maroon? Dat troof, eh?"

"It is true, Chakra. I shall conceal nothing from you."

"Better not, 'cause you can't 'ceal nuffin from ole Chakra—he know ebbery ting—little bird tell um. Wa now, wha nex'? You tink Cubina no lub you?"

"Ah! I am sure of it," replied the mulatta, her bold countenance relaxing into an anguished expression. "I once thought he love me. Now I no think so."

"You tink him lub some odder gal?"

"I am sure of it—Oh, I have reason!"

"Who am dis odder?"

"Yola."

"Yola? Dat ere name sound new to me. Whar d's she 'long to?"

"She belongs to Mount Welcome—she Missa Kate's maid."

"*Lilly Quasheba, I* call dat young lady," muttered the myal-man, with a knowing grin. "But dis Yola?" he added; "whar she come from? A nebber hear de name afo'."

"Oh, true, Chakra! I did not think of tellin' you. She was bought from the Jew, and fetched home since you—that is, after you left the plantation."

"Arter I lef' de plantation to die on de Jumbé Rock; ha! ha! ha! Dat's wha you mean, Cynthy?"

"Yes—she came soon after."

"So you tink Cubina lub *her?*"

"I do."

"An' she 'ciprocate de fekshun?"

"Ah, surely! How could she help do that?"

The interrogatory betrayed the speaker's belief that the Maroon captain was irresistible.

"Wa, then—wha you want me do, gal? You want rebbenge on Cubina, 'cause he hab 'trayed you? You want me put de *death-'pell* on him?"

"Oh! no—no! not that, Chakra, for the love of Heaven!—not that!"

"Den you want de *lub-spell?*"

"Ah! if he could be make love me 'gain—he did once. That is—I thought he did. Is it possible, good Chakra, to make him love me again?"

"All ting possible to old Chakra; an' to prove dat," continued he, with a determined air, "he promise put de lub-spell on Cubina."

"Oh, thanks! thanks!" cried the woman, stretching out her hands, and speaking in a tone of fervent gratitude. "What can I do for you, Chakra? I bring you everything you ask. I steal rum—I steal wine—I come every night with something you like eat."

"Wa, Cynthy—dat berry kind ob you; but you muss do more dan all dat."

"Anything you ask me—what more?"

"You must yourseff help in de spell. It take bof you an' me to bring dat 'bout."

"Only me tell what to do; and, trust me, Chakra, I shall follow your advice." "Wa, den—lissen—I tell you all 'bout it. But sit down on da bedsed dar. It take some time."

B. The Myal Man and the Jew

"How long dosh it take your shpell to work?" inquired the penn-keeper, after an interval of silence, in which he seemed to be making some calculation.

"Dat," replied the negro, "dat depend altogedder on de saccomstance ob how long de spell am *wanted* to work. Ef 'im wanted, Chakra make 'im in tree day fotch de 'trongest indiwiddible cla o' 'im boots; or in tree hour he do same—but ob coorse dat ud be too soon fo' be safe. A spell of tree hours too 'trong. Dat not Obi work—'im look berry like pisen."

"Poison—yesh, yesh, it would."

"Tree day too short—tree week am de correct time. Den de spell work 'zackly like fever ob de typos.[20] Nobody had s'picion 'bout 'um."

"Three weeks, you shay? And no symptoms to make schandal? You're shure that ish sufficient? Remember, Shakra; the Cushtos ish a strong man—strong ash a bull."

"No mar'r 'bout dat. Ef he 'trong as de bull, in dat period ob time he grow weak as de new-drop calf—I'se be boun' he 'taggering Bob long 'fore dat. You say de word, Massr[21] Jake. Obi no like to nigga. Nigga only brack man: he no get pay fo' 'im work. Obi 'zemble buckra man. He no work 'less him pay."

"Yesh—yesh! dat ish only shust and fair. Obi should be paid; but shay, goot Shakra! how much ish his prishe for a shpell of thish kind?"

"Ef he hab no interest hisseff in de workin' ob de 'pell, he want a hunder poun'. When he hab interest, das diff'rent—den he take fifty."

"Fifty poundsh! That ish big monish, good Shakra! In thish case Obi hash an interest—more ash anybody elshe. He hash an enemy, and wants refenge. Ish that not true, good Shakra!"

"Das da troof. Chakra no go fo' deny 'im. But das jess why Obi 'sent do dat leetle *chore* fo' fifty poun'. Obi enemy big buckra—'trong as you hab jess say—berry diff'cult fo' 'pell 'im. Any odder myal-man charge de full hunder poun'. Fack, no odder able do de job—no odder but ole Chakra hab dat power."

"Shay no more about the prishe. Fifty poundsh be it. Here'sh half down." The tempter tossed a purse containing coin into the outstretched palm of the obeah-man. "All I shtipulate for ish, that in three weeks you earn the other half; and then we shall both be shquare with the Cushtos Vochan—for I hash my refenge to shatisfy ash well as you, Shakra."

"Nuff sed, Massr Jake. 'Fore tree day de 'pell sha' be put on. You back come to de Duppy Hole tree night from dis, you hear how 'im work. Whugh!"

The gourd shell was again brought into requisition: and, after a parting "kiss" at the cognac, the "heel-tap" of which remained in the hut, the precious pair emerged into the open air.

The priest of Obi having conducted his fellow-conspirator across the lagoon, returned to his temple, and set himself assiduously to finish what was left of the liquor.

"Whugh!" ejaculated he, in one of the pauses that occurred between two vigorous pulls at the bottle; "ole villum Jew wuss dan Chakra—wuss dan de Debbil hisseff! Doan' know why *he* want rebbenge. Das nuffin' to me. I want rebbenge, an', by de great *Accompong!* I'se a g'wine to hab it! Ef dis gal proob true—she *muss* proob true—in tree week de proud, fat buckra jussis dat condemn me to dat Jumbé Rock—'Cussos rodelorum,' as de call 'im—won't hab no more flesh on 'im bones dan de 'keleton he tink wa' myen. And den, when 'im die—ah! den, affer 'im die, de daughter ob dat Quasheba dat twenty year 'go 'corn de lub ob de Coromantee for dat ob de yellow Maroon—maybe her dauter, de Lilly Quasheba, sleep in de arms ob Chakra de myal-man! Whugh!"

Text 21. Thomas Russell, *The Etymology of Jamaica Grammar*

Thomas Russell's short description of JC is unique: no other writer of the period attempted to give an account of the creole and none admitted to the existence of observable, systematic rules in it: "every corruption resolves itself into certain fixed rules." But Russell's preface also claims that *The Etymology* was "prepared as a source of social amusement" for his friends. Evidence of the language attitudes characteristic of Jamaicans of all classes—and especially those of the higher classes—emerges in his exasperated and amused condescension to the forms of JC. The work consists of little more than word and phrase lists arranged according to the grammatical categories then current in English pedagogy, but Russell's grammar nevertheless offers useful insights into phonology, morphosyntax, and lexicon. Because of its singular nature, we have reproduced *The Etymology* (Russell 1868) in full.

The author is Jamaican and obviously well educated. His address in the preface is given as "Mary Hill P.O." and his remarks on accentuation in Chapter 1 suggest an intimate observation of estate life. He says that "people who live on sugar estates . . . (especially on such estates which employ Africans)" use a different, African-based intonation from that of "the settlers in the . . . mountainous parts of the island." In his African word list he preserves terms now virtually lost in twentieth-century JC, such as *asono* from Twi *e-sono,* "elephant," which *DJE* cites in 1958 as "a very large animal which used to live in Jamaica, India, Africa, and South America, . . . ate human flesh . . . [and] is now extinct."

Although Russell sets out his data in a naïve way, he lists features which reveal the closeness of nineteenth-century JC to its African sources (e.g., *toroo* < *true;* cf. modern Twi *toroo; casara* < *cassava,* instead of *cassada; nyams* for *yam*). His list of Africanisms includes some words, such as *chaklata, picknin, rashe,* that in fact enter JC from European and other sources. It is possible that he arrived at his etymologies himself, or he may reflect current assumptions among the educated classes about the nature of JC. Among the items of genuine African origin he presents are *ducknoo, foofoo* from Twi and *cuscus* from the Arabic term.

One of the features of JC that he finds most unacceptable is the noun *wa-dem-call-e,* a term that happens not only to resemble an SE phrase but to correspond in meaning and function to the Kongo noun *kingandi,* glossed by Bentley (1967) as "a thing the name of which you forget, do not know, or do not care to mention." It is possible that many of the unidentified and obscure features of JC mentioned by Russell may yield links to such languages.

Prefatory Remarks

A form of language which has now been spoken for nearly two centuries by thousands of her Majesty's most trusty and loyal subjects, and one which, notwithstanding the multiplication in this land of grammars of Allen, Cornwall, Lennie, and a host of other "Regulators" of the "British West India Tongue," threatens to withstand all attempts, both at regulation and extinction, surely deserves some further notice, save that of an occasional pilfering of its rich and expressive construction and idioms, to wring out a laugh, or to brighten social gatherings, when "dry" English fails.

The object then of this little work is to awaken an interest in the minds of those who are unacquainted with the Etymology of this stubborn, but expressive corruption of the English tongue, to the end they may make themselves master of it; the use of the knowledge of which will be acknowledged by all those who have had dealings and intercourse with the people of our dear little Jamaica, whether as ministers, teachers, planters, merchants, doctors, or lawyers. This most desirable end can, however, only be attained by five years' hard study, with the help of this little work, in this our "Paradise of the West Indies," the "Home of Plenty," and the "Abode of Health." As this is not intended to be anything like an elaborate work, justice cannot possibly be done; but the writer's aim will be fully attained if he shall in any manner whatsoever materially aid any "pupil" in mastering but the mere elements of this corruption. The difficulties to grapple with are manifold; but remember, dear pupil, the good old Latin adage: *Perseverando omnia vincit.*

Introduction

Although it is evident that this, as every other corrupted form of language, is spoken by no previously well planned system, yet, as in course of time, every corruption resolves itself into certain fixed rules, so shall we find that this has settled into certain very plain and distinct ones, which are, in not a few instances, in direct opposition to those of the pure parent language.

I will now proceed to classify the different words, making, at the same time, a few observations and remarks on the peculiarities of construction, &c., under the different parts of speech.

Grammar is the art of speaking correctly, according to certain rules sanctioned by old and proper usage.

There are nine parts of speech, or sorts of words, viz.: Article,

Noun, Adjective, Pronoun, Verb, Adverb, Preposition, Conjunction, and Interjection.

Chapter I. Articles.

An article is a word put before a noun to show the extent of its meaning; and are of two kinds: Definite and Indefinite. The definite article is *de* and the indefinite *a* and *one, an* being only used as a conjunction.

It is to be observed, that *a* and *one* are used indiscriminately, and that *one* is by no means to supply the place of the proper English article *an*.

Obs. 1st—"A." will in due course be found to be a demonstrative adjective pronoun, also a preposition in place of "*of*" and "*at*," thus; (Demonstrative.) A man 'gainst de fence was ya yes-i-day. (Prepos. in place of "*of*.") "*A*" give him fe de good "*a*" him children." Prep. in place of "*at*." De man lib "*a*" Kingston. I must not omit to mention that "*a*" is also a personal pronoun, 1st person, as in the sentence "*A* give him fe de good "*a*" him children." Obs. 2nd—One is also an indefinite adjective pronoun.

REMARKS ON ACCENTUATION. —With regard to accentuation, it must be remarked that people who live on sugar estates make a peculiar stress on nouns following the indefinite article *one;* (especially on such estates which employ Africans) thus: One *man* was ya all *a* de time da look pon we (looking upon us all of the time).

This method of euphonizing by accentuation is not to be found amongst the settlers in the more mountainous parts of the island. This difference can only be accounted for in this way, I think: The estates usually employ, besides Creoles, Africans, and these latter, even after they can manage to speak "creole," still retain the deep and harsh accentuation of their own language: the Creoles imitating them become, after a time, in some measure, "infected." This is the more evident when we consider that people in the more mountainous parts, most of whom have never seen an African young man or woman, never accent words in this manner.

The worst form of accentuation is that beginning with every first noun or pronoun in a sentence, and continued upon every third word from the last; thus, De *man* da *go* a *ma-ket* fe *mutton. You* walk *long* de *sea-side* you *fine* sun *him* bery *hat.*

Sentences with the Definite and Indefinite Article: De people dem dis side lib well fe true: *De* cow fat till him fool: *De* buckra pickne hansam fe true.

One man was ya waitin fe you. *One* man keep *a* eatin-match yesi-day. A gie you a beatin if you don't mine (mind). ("*Eating match,*" *a feast*).

Chapter II. Substantives.

Nouns are the names of persons, animals, places or things. They are of two kinds generally, Proper and Common. As our purpose would not be properly gained by following barely this division, I shall treat of them under three heads.

Before proceeding, however, I must introduce a regular grammatical monstrosity: a noun made up of one interrogative, three personal pronouns, and a verb. This is the name of anything, which is either not known, or is forgotten. The noun is: "Wa-dem-call-*e*," used thus: Gie me de "wa-dem-call-*e*" ya. It must be observed that most of things [*sic*] belonging to a more civilized state of society go by this dreadful appellation, as people here usually do not know or care to know the names of such things they do not use. Considering therefore the state of civilization generally, we will find a host of "wa-dem-call-*e*" in our vocabulary.

All verbal nouns end in *in* as sign of the present participle: thus: Him get a good beatin. De "wa-dem-call-*e*" get a good brushin; De hos mak a good gallopin; Mr. "wa-dem-call-him" make a bery bad sellin yesiday manin.

1st. Nouns in which the letters, s, d, t, or other letters are merely added or dropped.

2nd. Nouns in which there is an entire change, or half of the words only used.

3rd. Nouns not belonging to the English language, or derived from it.

I. —Nouns in which certain letters are dropped or added. With regard to this head, I shall be brief, as this falls more strictly under what is called "incorrect speaking."

Observe, however, 1st. —All words which begin with *s* and end without, the *s* from the first part of the word is transferred to the last part of it; thus; De walking *ticks*. Sometimes s is prefixed and affixed to words to which it does not belong. I could not illustrate this better than by giving a model sermon of brevity and completeness delivered to a large congregation of people by a "Professor of Theology."

Sdear Sbredrens an Sistas,

My discoses stoday will sbe from the A B C scards. I stake stree lettas, sB, Cs, sDs; only stree heads' memba, sbredas an sistas, wa onos evers hear any sman spreach from cool-childrans scards! Ono swands what *a* sgwiins to says: hopen ono ase 1st heads: *sB sb*oughts its. 2nd *C, sc*uts it. 3rd, 'sD sdigs its. Conclusion: Sdigs what? Sdigs the Hearts.

It must be observed that this ludicrous addition of the *s* is only made when the speaker is "cutting English."

2ndly. —All plural nouns in *s*, or *es* drop the indication of the plural in the noun, plurality being indicated by the pronoun *dem*, joined to its corresponding noun by the conjunction *an*. Thus, De cow an dem: De horse an dem. De chair an dem.

Nouns ending in *s*, as no sign of the plural, resist this curtailing; as, glass, brass, puss, grass.

3rdly. —The letters *t* and *k* preceded by a consonant are not used; as wris (wrist).

The letter *r* preceded by *e* is dropped, and *e* changed into *a;* as matta-matta (matter.)

4thly. —The letter *d* is never used at the end of a word, when preceded by a consonant; as san, (sand) ban (band). A list of the nouns included under this head would be superfluous.

II. —Nouns in which there is an entire change, or half of the word only used, and characteristic names compounds of English words.

This change follows no certain rule, except in this: that some nouns of one or two syllables are in using repeated; as mud-mud, matta-matta.

Observe that in changing, *b* is usually changed into *v*, and *v* to *b;* thus, Savat, (Sabbath) bittle, (victuals) manubas, (manoeuvres.)

I could not do better than give some of the nouns included under this head

List of Nouns.

Ancul, Uncle
Agas, August
Bra-ra-Breda, Brother
Balinsteer, Volunteer
Blausam, Blossom
Brial, Brier
Bagga, Beggar
Cobring, A blanket
Base, Basket
Casara, Cassava
Doe-mout, Threshold
Dutty, The earth
El-nut, Oil nut, castor oil
Guaba, Guava
Gubna, Governor
Gubnis, Governess
God-bud, humming bird
Hanen, The Ant
Hebiny, Ebony
Handkicher, Handkerchief
*Jack-ass, Breadfruit
Full mout, A large kind of beans

Hashish, Ashes
Sinte, Something
Ky, the sky
Marra, Marrow
Moos-moos, Mouse
Mada, Mother
Mash-mash, Fish broken in small bits
Mamme, Mother
Nyams, Yam
Oman-kick-am, Yellow yams
Pedita, Potato
Put-put, mud
Pangshalla, Spanish elm
Poun pan, Pudding pan
Pea, Pear
Rocka-tone, Stone
Tambran, Tamarind
Ticky-ticky, Ruinate Land
Tamba, Tambourine
Pecta, Inspector
Mackiri, Mackerel
Tety, A string
Mengo, Mangoes
Watmelin, Watermelon
Tung, Town
Peggydone, A dangerous creeping prickle
Bra-nat, Breadnut
Brok-fuss, Breakfast

---

*To pad, or saddle a jackass (culinary business) is to roast it, but to ride it and gallop it is to eat it with no bad apetite [*sic*].

III. Nouns not originally belonging to the English language. The majority of these are purely African, and a few are from the Spanish language. —The following is a list of such nouns:

Those Purely African.

Asono – The Elephant.
Aham – A creeping plant.
Muse – Cassava in form of a thick paste.
Bagabo – A caterpillar.
Bogro-sal – Coarse mine-salt.
Qua-qua – Cassava in the form of a thick paste.
Benta – A rude musical instrument.
Foofoo – Diff. vegetable food, beaten into one mass and eaten with "pepper pot," hot soup— (See "Sir Bryan Edward's History of Jamaica.")
Canta – The torch wood.
Calibean – A basket snare for birds.
Bankra – A hand-basket.
Duppe – A spirit.
Congo peggy – A large species of ants.

Banja – A rude musical instrument.
Myal – Excitement bordering on madness.
Tacooma – The Spider.
Granke – The cock-roach.
Chaklata – A light meal before work or school.
Rashe – A little hasty meal.
Pickini – A child.
Duckonoo – Corn boiled in balls, and then toasted.
Ga-ge – Rum.
Gaso – A single piece of obeah.
Funge – Corn parched and beaten.
Cuscus – Gruel of any kind whatsoever.

Proper nouns, names of persons, are 14 in number. They are given according to the day of the week on which a person is born, and are as follows, with the general signification:

	MALE.	FEMALE.
Sunday – Quashe, Quasheba	Cunning,	Slender built.
Monday – Cudjoe, Juba	Strong-headed,	Clever.
Tuesday – Cobena, Bene	Inventive,	Handsome.
Wednesday – Quaco, Cooba	Bad luck,	Stout lazy.
(1) Thursday – Quaw, Aba*	Ugly, stupid,	(2) Strong, physic.**
Friday – Cuffe, Fiba	Hot tempered,	Gentle, mild.
Saturday – Quamin, Mimba	Full of tricks,	Wild, Fury.

*Note 1—An ugly stupid looking man, with grey eyes, is called a "Qruaw" by way of derision.

**2—See metonymical adjectives the meaning of "strong physic."

Words from the Spanish Language

Subana – Savannah
Grande – An old respectable woman
Habana – The flea, called usually dog flea.
Habana – Havanna.
Subul-oringa – Seville Orange.
All names of places given by the Spaniards; thus:
Akaria (Ocho Rios);
Pote'n Tony (Port Antonio)

Chapter III. Numbers.

Notwithstanding in treating of Nouns I have spoken of numbers, I shall, partly for the sake of regularity, devote a separate page to them.

Nouns have two numbers, the singular and the plural. In forming the plural, no change takes place in the Noun: plurality is, however, indicated in three ways.

1st—By cardinal numbers used with the Nouns; as De two hamper; De four man: De tree boy.

2nd—By the Adjectives *nuff, plenty-plenty, lat;* as Nuff cow pass ya; Plenty-plenty yam dig. (See observation 2nd, under pronouns about the verb to be.) Lat a man.

3rd—By the pronoun *dem,* immediately following the noun and joined to it by the Copulative Conjunction, *an,* in most cases; thus—

De horse an dem hard fe ketch, massa: De house an dem high sa: De bud an dem fat fe toroo.

Sometimes *an* is omitted; as, De boy dem cleber: De crab dem bery sweet.

Before finishing with numbers, it must be remarked, that the singular Objective Personal Pronoun *him* is used when strong emphasis is to be marked after all singular Nouns; thus, Dis teacher him bery cross. De Bible him bery true.

Chapter IV. Case and Gender.

There are three Genders, the Masculine, the Feminine, and the Neuter. There are only two ways of distinguishing sex.

1st—By different words. This is in comparatively few cases; thus, Boy, Gal, Breda, Sista, Fada, Mada, Uncul, Anty, Horse, Mare, Cock, Hen, Man, Oman, Sa, Ma'am, Son, Daughta, King, Queen, Husban, Wife, Massa, Misses.

These are about all under this head. This will not be wondered at, when we recollect that only Nouns that are absolutely necessary, the names of things, &c. with which there is a thorough acquaintance, are used; all others going under the designation of the awful Noun "wa-dem-call-*e*."

2nd—By prefixing the word Man and Oman. —This is done to animal, as well as to vegetable *names;* thus—Man-cow, Oman-cow, Man-prementa, Oman-prementa.

A list of these Nouns is unnecessary here.

Observe that some Nouns are the same in the masculine and

feminine; thus, Old witch (Wizard-witch), Exzeckita (Executor, Executrix), Prafit (Prophet, Prophetess).

Of *Cases,* I can only remark here that in the Nouns themselves there is no distinction of the possessive from the nominative and objective cases. More shall be said of Cases under Pronouns.

Chapter V. Adjectives.

Adjectives qualify Nouns, and have three degrees of comparison—the Positive, the Comparative, and the Superlative. The Comparative is formed by adding *er* to the positive; thus, Great, greater; Bad, bader; Good, gooder.

The Superlative is formed by adding *is* to the Positive; thus, Sweet, sweetis; Good, goodis; Bad, badis. The Superlative of more is moris; thus, A hab de moris mango (of wosa wosis).

There are then three ways of comparing Adjectives.

1st.—By adding *er* comparative, and *is* Superlative.

2nd.—By adding more Comparative, and moris superlative.

3rd.—By adding wosa Comparative, and wosis superlative.—See Metonymical Adjectives.

Adjectives in the positive degree are often repeated to give them weight; thus, Bad, bad-man.

There are some Adjectives not derived from the English language; but by far the greater number are. Adjectives derived from the African language, admitting of no comparison. *Buffro-buffro,* clumsy, stout. What a buffro-buffro man!

Cra-ca [*sic*]—Careless, nervous, clumsy. Dis boy well cra-cra [*sic*].

Bogro-bogro—Coarse. Wa me fe do wid dis bogro-bogro ting.

Takro-takro—Ugly, ill-proportioned. Dat is a takro-takro man.

Chaka-chaka—Disorderly (Adv.) De boy clothes so chaka-chaka.

Makla-makla—Bad taste from too many mixtures. Dis is a makla-makla drink.

Nyaka-nyaka—filthy-looking (Adv.) De yard look so nyaka-nyaka.

Menya-menya—slender. Wat a menya-menya pickni?

Chin-chilly, Small. Gie me chinchilly bit.[22]

Wenya-wenya, Meagre not fat. Dat wenya-wenya boy trong.

Adjectives derived from the English language. Some are simple, others are compounded by repeats; thus, be-be-be-be (for bigest) [*sic*]. The Adjective big and some others are therefore compared in two ways; thus, big, biger, bigis; and big, be-be, be-be-be-be.

All Adjectives of only one syllable are compared in two ways after the above form.

Observe that some Adjectives of more than one syllable are also compared by repeats, as plenty-plenty, hansam-hansam; no superlative by repeats.

Adjectives compared by *er,* is or by repeats also:

Chupit, stupid
Craffy, Rough
Farad, Froward
Blacky, Blacky
Whity, White
Natty, Knotty
Tall, Tall
Dutty, Dirty
Peckle, Speckled
Fool-fool; thus, Dis man fool-fool fe toro [*sic*] (true)
Sicky, sickly
Plenty
Hansam, Handsome
Train, Startling
'Markavle, Remarkable
Ticky, Sticky
Maschebas, Mischievous
Tout, Stout
Tear-up, thus, You see one tear-up-tear-up-dutty fella pass ya.

There are some compound Adjectives used metonymically: as,

Pick-mout, Troublesome, teasing. Refers to one who teases another to quarrel. A pick-mout boy come again fe make quarrel.

Trong-eye—Domineering, not easily brow-beaten. If Jim no bin trong-eye him would'nt get de money.

Trong-physic—Hot tempered, bad. Creole pickni too trong-physic, sista.

Trong-mout—Boisterous, brow-beating. De lawyer gain de case by trong-mout.

Sweet-mout—Winning, persuasive. Some people tak sweet-mout lib.

Big-eye—Greedy, covetous, selfish. Big-eye people nubba is fe satisfy in dis wol.

Hard-aze—Disobedient, wilful. Hard-aze people nubba prasper.

All the above adjectives are compared thus, comparative, *wossa,* superlative, *wosis; e.g.* Hendry *wossa* sweet-mout dan William, but Fedric is the *wosis.*

Observe, however, that the superlative *wosis* is not so often used, the superlative being more often indicated in this way: John *wossa* sweet-mout dan ebry body me eber see.

Dan ebry body me eber see, or Dan ebry body me know, put with the comparative *wossa,* form the superlative degree generally.

Chapter VI. Pronouns.

A pronoun is a word used instead of a noun. Pronouns are of three kinds, Personal, Relative and Adjective.

The personal pronouns are *A* (as *a* in laugh), *me, you, him, e, we, ono, dem* (*e* always short as in eat). Sing. 1st person *A* in nominative case only.

Sing. 1st person *A* in nominative case only.		
Obj. and poss.	*me,*	Masculine or Feminine.
" " "	*ME*	in all cases Masculine or Feminine.
" 2nd. "	*You*	" " " "
" 3rd. "	*Him*	" " " "
" " "	*e*	Nom. & Obj. Poss. *him*, Neuter Gen.
Plur. 1st [and] "	*We,*	all cases Masculine or Feminine.
" 2nd [and] "	*Ono*	" " " "
" 3rd [and] "	*Dem*	" " Mas. Fem. Neuter.

A Tabular View of the Diff. Persons:—

Sing. 1st—A or me = I.	Plur. 1st—We.
2nd—You.	2nd—Ono = you, ye.
3rd—Him, e, = He, she, it.	3rd→Dem = they.

Observe 1st—The third Personal Pronouns are used in a sentence immediately after the noun with which it agrees, as a second subject to emphasize the noun with which it agrees; thus, De man him mus be mad: De boy him cleber; De house *e* pretty.

Observe 2ndly—After the Nominative [subject] Noun or Pronoun, the Verb *to be* is omitted when followed by an Adjective or Adverb; thus, Him bery larned; Dey him man good sa.

Observe 3rdly—The Verb *to be* will be found to be very seldom used as an auxiliary.

In attempting to improve the Personal Pronouns, ("cutting English") some rather awkward faults are made as the using the objective feminine and masculine for nominative, and vice versa; thus, Me good sista, me tell she, bout *e*, but him tink fe her own way better than fe we. You see she pass we gate yet.

The use of the second person plural Nom: Ono all is a pack a chupit; Poss: Ono cow look berry well;

Obj: A we tell ono de trute.

The Relative Pronouns—A Relative Pronoun relates to some Noun or Pronoun going before it, called its antecedents: They are Who, Wich, Wat, Dat. The Possessive of who, Fe who (whose) Wich and wat are used interrogatively. Wara = wat or what, is now nearly obsolete.

Observe: Who, wich, dat, when used in the past tense are followed by the past participle of the Verb *to be*, accompanied by the principal Verb corrupted into *ben;* thus, De fella dat ben tak de money sick, or who or wich *ben*, etc.

In the present tense by "is" thus, Dem fella who is ya.

In the future by the preposition "fe" preceding the verb; thus, De man dat fe go no come yet. De place dat fe sell no run out yet.

Adjective Pronouns are of four kinds Distributive, Possessive, Demonstrative, and Indefinite.

Possessive pronouns; Alla him, we, e, dem, you, ono.

Sentences—Mi cow dead. Hit foot broke. We house bun (burn). E blansam [*sic*] hansam. Dem place take way las mont. You cousin come las night. Ono place clean.

Distributive, Ebry, Ebry creole ha cunny [have cunning].

Demonstrative, Sing, Dis, da or dat, or dar*i* (*i* as in lick).

The plural of dis is 3rd person pronoun dem, with the addition of the adverb ya (here), making *dem ya* = these.

The plural of da, dat or dari, is dem, with the adverb da (there), (*a* in *da* as in lay) making *dem da* = those.

Sentences—Da man no look well. Gie me dari-da, Dem ya hat wite, but dem-da black.

Observe that "dari" is nearly obsolete, da and dat being more used.

The Indefinite Pronouns—All, noon, sich, whole, any, some, all or alla used with any number; thus alla, two, tara, (other) nada [another] nara (another).

Sentences—All a dem gwine out. You nubba gie me noon sa.

Sich boy like ono, *a* don't matta. Alla two de pick'ni dem da ya.

De tara better. Nada backra come. Nara pig dead. Tara day me see him.

With regard to the appellation backra or buckra, observe, that the name backra is not use [*sic*] exclusively in referring to the white man, a brown or black gentleman is also called so in acknowledgment of his gentility, or genteel appearance; but this little "privilege" (?) is only given him with his good morning or good evening, or when he is asked a favour, otherwise he is only "gentleman" or "smart fella." Should he however, by his education and position, or money, move much in the upper class society, then he is said to turn "pure-pure backra."

Chapter VII. Of Verbs.

A verb is a word which denotes *being, doing* or *action*. Verbs are never inflected to express either number, person or tense, except in few cases when usually the irregular verb, past tense, is inflected to express the past tense; thus, I boughted a horse for ten pounds 'talin money.

Observe 1st—The past tense is represented by the past participle of the verb to be *ben* (been); thus, Me ben tell you.

2nd—By the adjunct of time expressed; thus, Me tell you yesiday. A take *e* in a la-sha = I took it in last year.

Auxiliaries are seldom used, except *ben* [for been], also *we* for will, in the formation of the future tense; thus, Me we come nex week. A we go if you pay me.

There are but three tenses, the main present, main past, and main future.

In the present tense we have the verb merely.

In the past, the verb with the auxiliary *ben;* thus, A ben go las week.

In the future, the verb with the auxiliary *we* (for will).

Observe that WE is used only in the affirmative sense, and sha'n (*a* as in law—contraction of shall not) in the negative future; thus, A we go. "A we not go," is never used, but "I sha'n go." I must notice two exceptions with regard to the auxiliary verbs.

Exception 1st—The present participle of the verb without any auxiliary is used as a kind of present incomplete tense; thus, "*A*" list'ning to you dea [dear] breda—I am listening to you dear brother.

2nd—The present incomplete is also formed by prefixing *da* to any verb; thus "A da listen to you." —I am listening to you.

In trying to "cut English," the most elegant form of the verb is the past tense of the verb to be, and the past participle used together, or with another verb, thus, A was ben told you of it. A was ben da go wen de boy come.

Observe—The sign of the Present Participle *in* (ing) is only used in verbal Nouns; thus: A we gie you a good beatin. It is an interesting fact that here one can always judge of the state of pecuniary affairs of the "boasters," by the style and manner of their language. When they "cut" the purse is not over light, and fields (especially coffee) look promising. When they give out a long drawling jargon, things are not in an over-pleasing condition; no doubt drought or vegetable diseases telling upon the crops. With the temperament peculiar to inhabitants of the tropics, this is not much to be wondered at.

There are some rather interesting and original verbs; they are:—

Hinka, Hanging after for the purpose of getting something; thus: Don't hinka-hinka after de backra massa so.

Dilly-dally, To stand about idly; Don't dilly-dally 'bout de place.

Dilly-dally is also used as an Adjective; thus: Thomas is a dilly-dally fella.

Winka-winka, To neigh as a horse.

Halla, To cry or bawl out; thus, Wye mak you halla so dis blessed marnin.

Naym, [*sic*] To eat; thus, You mus'n naym all the mangoe.

Saca-saca, To cut as with a saw; thus, Dis knife jis da saca-saca de meat.

Bokle, To catch by surprise; thus, A bokle de chap sa.

Chapter VIII. Adverbs.

Adverbs qualify Verbs, Adjectives, or other Adverbs.

A List of Adverbs.

Adverbs of time:—Tomara, yesiday, aternoon, nuba; (never), wen, (when); demejate-ly, (immediately); sun-time, (sometimes); te-day, (today); den, (then).

The compliments of the day are in the morning, *mante* or mara; good manin, good morning.

In the evening, kobite, or good eveling.[23] Kobite means properly good night, and is only used as a parting compliment.

Hade, houdy, is more used by friends to one another on meeting.

Adverbs of place.—Low-dong (below); fur (far); ya (here); wa (where); da (there); yanda (yonder).

Yanda is used in giving a rebuff and insult; thus Ga lang yanda sa, you too manish. (Go away from me, Sir, you are too froward.)

Adverbs of quantity.—'Nuff, (enough); mo-am-mo, (more and more); Him keep on beat me mo-am-mo.

Plenty-plenty. Him beat me plenty-plenty massa. It must be observed that plenty-plenty as an Adverb is more used by Coolies and other emigrants.

'Ceedingly (exceedingly).

Bery (very).

Adverbs of quality.—Well, how sofle (softly), cra-cra, takro-takro, chaka-chaka, makla-makla, nyaka-nyaka, buffro-buffro, minya-minya, wenya-wenya. (See Adjectives). De man walk so cra-cra; You clothes put on so takro-takro; You weed de place so chaka-chaka; De ting taste so makla-maklo; [sic] William yad look so nyaka-nyaka; Dat colt look so wenya-wenya.

Observe that some Adverbs of quality or manner express the sound of the action of the Verb; thus, A lick him *ply* wid de trap; Him knock me *bap* wid him fis; I hit him wid de horse wip *swi, swi;* De gun make *bow;* A hear wen de rock stone knock *dong* 'pan de tank battam; De trap fly *bram,* an cut off de puss foot; Him tumble in de pan, *bash;* De wood fal down, *pongo-rong.*

Adverbs of affirmation; Cartintly [*sic*] (certainly) yes.

Adverbs of doubt: 'Praps (Perhaps).

In trying to "cut," it sometimes occurs that several Adverbs of time are hurdled together in one sentence; thus, Sometimes, always, now and then, 'cassionally, seldam, *a* tak a drink. On hearing this mighty sentence, you can always be pretty certain that the speaker has just passed through this awful period of time, intimated in his attempt at grandiloquence.

Chapter IX. Prepositions.

A Preposition is a word put before Nouns and pronouns to shew the relation between them.

List of Prepositions.

Bout-bout; thus, A see a man da walk bout-bout de place; Crass (across); ater (after); gins (against); lang (long); rong-an-rong (round); thus, De mule walk rong-an-rong de mill; A man run rong-an-rong the paster. For *at, a* is used; thus, go *a* Maniville you see wite soja. 'Twix (twixt, betwixt); juring (during); cep (except); fo or fe (for); tro-an-tro (through); wid (with); widin (within); widout (without); to pon (upon).

Observe, that *a* is also the Preposition equivalent to of; thus, Him take de medicine fe de good *a* him body; Me work fe de good *a* me childran.

A is therefore an Article when it precedes (immediately) the Noun subject in a sentence; thus, *A* boy ride well.

A Pronoun when it precedes a Verb; thus, *A* take *e* myself.

A Preposition before a Noun or Pronoun objective; thus, Me peak fe de good *a* him charicta.

Chapter X. Conjunctions.

A Conjunction is a word which joins words and sentences together.

List of Conjunctions.

Also, an (and); as, becausin (because); fe (for); ef (if); sense (since); dat (that); den (then); dafo (therefore); aldough (although); but, ida (either); yet, excepin (except). With regard to many of these and foregoing words, Europeans usually have to rely wholly on the context to make out the true meaning of a sentence.

Chapter XI. Interjections.

An Interjection expresses the feeling or emotions of the speaker.

As inhabitants of the tropical regions, it will be found that we are not over poor in original interjections.

Not only are single words as such, but long phrases; thus, as an exclamation of horrifying surprise: Lack, lack, me mada, woy me dead!

This is one of the most common interjectional phrases, sometimes *woy* is omitted when matters are not too bad.

This phrase when *woy* is omitted is also used as an exclamation of mere wonder.

List of Interjections. Interjectional Phrases.

Me mada me dead! Exclamation caused by wonder or fear.

Lack, lack, woy me mada me dead! Great fear, personal danger.

Me fada William! (or any other name). Wonder with vexation.

Me mada Sarah! (or any other name). Wonder, wonder with vexation.

By George sa! Pleasurable wonder.

By Johnies [*sic*] sa! Pleasurable wonder.

O luck sa! Mere pleasure.

By dickans a me! Anger and fear mixed, with no power to resent.

By gums a me! Wonder, anger, and fear mixed, with no power to resent.

Single Words, Sometimes Repeated.

La-a-a-a-a-a-a-a-a! Fright, childish admiration.

Lack-lack-lack! Distress, surprise.

Kie! Admiration, satisfaction.

Loo-loo-loo-loo! Wonder.

Poloo-poloo! Unfeelingness, derision.

Poroo-poroo! Unfeelingness, indifference.

Babwa! Wonder.

Massy! (mercy) Surprise; thus, Massy! him gone a jail.

It must be observed that the interjection *babwa* is used only on estates, and their vicinity, and is of African origin. Settlers in the mountainous parts would consider it disgraceful to be heard using such a word.

Calash or calashte! Indifference.

There is still one Interjection, an exclamation of disgust, admitting of no orthography; the sound is represented by that made by a person suffering extreme pain, say tooth ache, only it is represented quickly about a dozen times.

I believe I could in no better "wind up" Jamaica Grammar than by setting forth this orthographical problem; now let him who is so clever make out this curious interjection.

Concluding Remarks.

Having endeavoured to lead the diligent and patient pupil through the etymology of our "Jamaica jargon," I would now advise him to cultivate the acquantance [*sic*] of a few of some of our best "speakers," with whom but a few conversations would make him a tolerably good scholar. The writer is most willing to give letters of introduction to any anxious to enjoy the benefit of a living teacher.

Should any pupil, however, now feel himself so much at home in the Etymology of the "language" as to attempt Syntax, which I have neither the brain, energy, or the courage to face, I wish him with all my heart success. But remember, dear pupil, that in trying to make something out of nothing, we are usually considered dangerous to our present not very grateful community, and, much against our will, have sometimes to submit our poor selves to the care of the dear, extremely considerate and kind portion of humanity styled "Doctors." Now then, wise pupil, are you willing that these three little words should be playfully branded in very bright letters on thy noble, "Solonic" forehead for our Jamaica Syntax? —*Non compos mentis*.

FINIS.

Text 22. C[harles] Rampini, *Letters from Jamaica*

Very little information can be found regarding Charles Rampini or the circumstances surrounding his compilation of *Letters from Jamaica*. In others of his works (Rampini 1890, 1897) he shows a close interest in folklore and language, and in Rampini 1884: 52, 128, he gives a careful phonetic representation of Scots speech. *Letters from Jamaica* was first published under the title *Travel Talk* (Rampini 1873: preface), and the writer claims that his text is based on notes "made on the spot." Although he sets himself a high standard of accuracy, one should note that he records at least one incident (the trial of an obeah man) that had previously been recorded by Phillippo (1843: 247–48) who in turn derived it from Barclay (1826: 191). Barclay's version records the term *summary* > "somebody," a detail of phonology lost in the later versions. The story may of course still have been in circulation at the time of Rampini's visit, but the closeness of the versions suggests that his is based on one of the written accounts.

The writer's comments suggest that the following letters (Rampini 1873: 104–10) are to his knowledge, genuine: "They are the honest expression of the negro's inmost heart, the exponents of his most sincere sentiments." No indication is given, however, of their origin or of how they came into Rampini's possession. The format of the letters is clearly derivative: standard Victorian diction mingles with JC imagery in such phrases as "Miss Lucy toots . . . so green I is like one ear of carn, an' her eye dem is so pretty." Rampini provides bracketed glosses of the diction but seems to have left spelling and syntax intact. However, it is impossible to tell whether a feature is a spelling variant or an archaic pronunciation (e.g., "i witch to send the yam hed," where *witch* may represent [š] or [č].

Love Letters

1.

My deare love, my dearest dove, —I have taken the pleasur of righten [writing] these few lines to you, hopin when they comes to hand they may find you in a perfect state of health, as it leaves me at preasent. My deare, I have never felt the enjoyment of love as I feel with you. These few lines is to let you know that it is my intenteion of maryin you, if it agreeable to you. My Deare, my mind is so taking up with you, I cannot help from righting you. I am not able to go on at present, but in time to come I hope to be your man of business. Let her kiss me with the kisses of her mouth, for thy love is better than wine. As the apple-tree among the trees of the wood, so is my love with you. Please to say howdeas [how-d'ye-do] to all kind friends for me. —I remain, love, your most affectionate love, J. A. Wite [White]. Answer as quick as possible.

2.

Dear lov, —I is wrote you a letter to beg of you to make me your lover, but you is not wrote me again. I is dead of lov every day, wen you look so hansom. I cane [cannot] sleep, cane eat. I dun no how I feel. I beg you to accep af me as your lover. The rose is not sweet as a kiss from you, my lov. Do meet me to-night at the bottom gate, and give me your lov. Miss Lucy toots [teeth] so green I is like one ear of carn, an' her eye dem is so pretty. Lard! I wish I never been barn. Poor me, Garg! [George]. I lov Miss Lucy to distraction. —Yours truly, GARG PLUMMER. Answer me sone, lov.

3.

January 25, 1865. MY DEAR LOVE, —I have taken the pleasure of writing you in time, hopen when it reaches your hand it may find you at a perfect state of health, as it leaves me at the present time. I have seeing in your letter, my dear, that you wisch to know from me if it is true Love from my heart. Dearest love, if it is not true love from the deepest part of my heart, whold [would] I set down to write you a letter, my Dear? When hear I see thy lovely face, my heart within will burnt; when hear I absent from thy face, I long for thy return. But one thing I did like to tell you again. do not make it known to the Public before we began. The reason why I say that. I heard a certain boy was telling me all about it, and that only done by you tellin you feamale friends, whom cannot help; these one secret must be yours, for this thing is not known to a soul but I and you and your brother-and-law. Therefor the fault must be yours. Do not let me hear such thing again from any body. My dear love, I will be truly wish that I could maried to you know [now], but if my life is spared we shall tark[24] [talk] further about that. My dear, pray for me that the Lord will speared my Life to become a man, for I truly wich [wish] that I and you should be one fleach and one blood. Will you not like it, my dear love? If you don't wich that, let me know by your letter. My dear girl, you don't know my love wich I have for you. May the Lord touch your heart to know these thing wich I now put before you in this letter. But I must say that I am doing you arm[25] [harm] for taken such liberty to write you such a letter as this. If it is a liberty please to let me know by your next letter. Do not send me a note again for a letter. I can not satisfy when I see a letter wich I can not take me some time to reed. If you had not paper let me know about in your next letter, and I will send you some paper. My dear love, at preasant my love for you is so strong, that I cannot express. So I even write that you may see it. It is every man deauty [duty] to write a formil [formal] letter. My pen is bad, and my ink is pale, but my love will never fail. King Solomon say that Love is strong as death, and Jealousy is cruel than the grave. Love me little, bear me longer. hasty love is not love at all

This is the first time I sat down to write you about it. I love my Dove. Your love is black and ruby—the chefer of ten thousand. You head is much fine gold. You lock are bushy and black as a raven. Your eyes was the eyes in a river, by the rivers of warter. Your cheeks as a bead [bed] of spices as sweet flowers. Your lips is like lilies. Your hand as gold wring. Your legs as a pillar of marble set upon sockets of fine gold. Your countenance as a Lebenon. Your mouth look to be more sweet. Your sweet altogether. I have no more time to write as I am so tiard and full time to go to bead. I will now close my letter with love. I remain yours truly, —— —— To Ann Williams.

4.

My dearest dear, —It is with a perplexing heart of anxiety that I take up my pen to address you this time, having propos marriage to you. I am now anxious to know the full intention of your mind, accompany with parent. On my side, let it please you to believe me that I am desireous to oblige you in whatever thought or ways that you lik. if you cannot stop up this way, but rather to be in Santi-cross [Santa Cruz], I am very willing to do so. I feel convinced that the merits of your family are not to be estimated by an ordinary standard, and that their most ardent wish is to promote your comfort and happiness. believe me I feel highly honour of being worthy elevated in such a family. In granting me this most agreeable favour, you will, my dear girl, not only dispel the peevish gloom which I am confident will hang over me if I should be deprive of your society. My greatest happiness depends upon your immediate answer. Please speak a word of regard in your parents ears. —I remain, dear Lesia, yours truly love, —— ——. 19.1.'64.

5.

Dear love, —I have the liberty of writing these few lines, hopeing that it may found you well. i writ to hare [hear] from you wether [whether] you intend to make me a fool. If you intent to, come before it is too late. If you witch [wish] you can come up, fear [for] I is not an pewpy show [puppet-show], that if you tink you will find any better than me. My mother said that she not understand how you always come here and you not tel her any thin [thing] about me. I witch to send the yam hed [yam-heads for planting], but I do not know wether I will reap the benefit of it. love is strong as death. Jelous is as cruel as the grave. the rose in June is not so sweet. like to meet and kiss you. please to send me answer as quick as passable.

6.

Dear eliza, —I take the liberty of myself to inform you this few lines hoping you may not offend as often is. I had often seen you in my hearts. Their are myriads of loveliness in my hearts toward you. My loving intentions were realy unto another female, but now the love between I and she are very out now entirely. And now his the excepted time I find to explain to my lovely appearance [presumably "apparent love"], but whether if their be any love in your hearts or mind towards me it is hard for I to know, but his I take this liberty to inform you this kind, loving, and affectionate letter. I hope when it received into your hand you receive with peace and all good will, pleasure, and comforts, and hoping that you might answer me from this letter with a loving appearance, that in due time Boath of us might be able to join together in the holy state of matremony. I hoping that the answer which you are to send to me it may unto good intention To me from you that when I always goine to write you again I may be able to write, saying, my dear lovely Eliza. —Your affectionate lover, affraied [afraid] J. S. Dear Eliza, wether if you are willing or not, Please to sent me an ansure back. Do my dear.

The last we shall give is a genuine negro valentine:—

7.

Mrs. Agostiss R——, —I hope you know Valintine is now in seson. I will take the pleasure to write you this, my hearth is yours and you are mine; but you do not know it. I love you as the bee love the flower. The flower may fade, but true love shall never. My love for you is a love that cannot be fade. You shall be my love here an' in heaven for ever. The Rose in June is not so sweet as when two lovers kisses meet. Kiss me quick and go my honey. I still remain true lover.

Text 23. Mary Pamela Milne-Home, *Mamma's Black Nurse Stories*

These tales probably incorporate recollections from Mary Pamela Milne-Home's own childhood in that they "represent pretty well what is stated on the title page" (Milne-Home 1890: Preface), and since they describe "the small white buccra sitting by its nurse" (2). Part 2 of the work consists of Anansi stories from the Appendix to Sir George Webbe Dasent's *Popular Tales from the Norse* (1859). Milne-Home uses *ar* spellings in the locative *dar,* in the preposition *ar* (till ar marnin), as well as in *darter* and *tark* to represent JC [aa]. The following tale is from Milne-Home 1890: 35–39.

Anansi and Alligator

Once 'pon a time Anansi call 'pon big Alligator, for git him a place for sleep till ar marnin'. Alligator say, "A' right, come in ar house." Anansi say, "Brar, me no want for sleep in de house, me wan' for sleep in de kitchen." "A' right," say Alligator, "you can." Now all dis time, when Anansi and Alligator was tarking, Alligator Darter was behin' de door, so dem har ebery wud. So when dem har dat Anansi was gwine to sleep in de kitchen, dem went and ketch a lat of 'corpions, for put in ar de pot, for dem know well Anansi always sarch de pots. When Anansi go to bed, him lay down for a little; when him tink eberybody dey sleep, him put him han' into de pot, when one of de 'corpions bite him. Him halla, "Lahd!"[26] When Alligator har him, him say, "Brar Anansi, what ar matter?" Anansi say, "Brar, da fleas dey bite me." When him tink Alligator gone asleep, him put han' again in de pot; him halla, "Lahd!" Alligator halla out, say, "Brar Anansi, what matter wid you, dey mek you bawl so?" "Brar Alligator, dey fleas dey bite so; lahd! dey fleas full you kitchen. Brar, dey fleas dey are too much, me can't 'tand yar." All dis time him tief. Alligator Darter yearree [hear]. When him finis', him say, "Good-by, brar, me gwine, dey flea dey are too much." Alligator Darter yearree Anansi say, so she broke out go see if Anansi tief de eggs. When she go look, she no see one, so she go tell her fader. An' her fader get up an' run arter Anansi. But Anansi, dis time, was near de sea. As Anansi go 'pon a wharf, yearree Alligator blow shell. He say, " 'Top dar, fella Anansi!" As Anansi har so, him see de boatman not far from him, so him say, "Boatman, look yar, if you tek me 'crass de sea, I got a praperty, an' me gib you half." De boatman say, "A' right." Dem get in ar de boat, an' as dey get out ar sea, Anansi see Alligator 'pon de wharf. " 'Top," Alligator halla out, " 'top dar, fella Anansi." Den Anansi say, "Pull fast, boatman, haby rain dere 'pon sea." As Alligator see dem tek no notice, him t'row himself in de sea and swim arter dem. But de boat was took quick, an' lef' him. As de boat get 'pon oder side, Anansi jump out 'pon land an' say to de boatman, "Me go an' tell my fader dat ar 'tranger come." De boatman said, "A' right." So Anansi went in ar him fader, him tell him his 'tory, an' tell him dat if de boatman or Alligator come, must tell dem dat you dunno way [where] me dey, because me gwine go clim' a tree." As Anansi could go out, so in come de boatman and ask Anansi fader way Anansi dey. Anansi fader say him dunno.

When de boatman gane, Anansi clim' 'pon anoder tree. Just as him go up him see big Alligator dey come. As Alligator come under de tree, so Anansi say, "See me yar, Brar Alligator?" Alligator say, "If I don't see Anansi, I never live in ar house again, but live in ar water." And Alligator look and look; an' dat de reason why Alligator lib in ar water. End of 'tory.

Text 24. Cumina Chant: "Tange Lange Jeni"

The religious ceremony known as "cumina" has been studied by Joseph G. Moore, Monica Schuler (1979, 1980, 1981) and others who have attempted to trace African survivals in Jamaica. Cumina is associated with the African indentured migrants who came to Jamaica between 1845 and 1861 and who helped to revive African customs and religion wherever they settled (Schuler 1979 and 1981). Alleyne (personal communication, 1987) notes the existence of Kikongo in some cumina chants. Senior (1983: 91–92) claims a Bantu origin for the cult and finds it most prevalent in the parish of St. Thomas. However the language mixture may be older and more complex than has yet been suspected, as the comments on the following chant demonstrate.

Joseph Graessle Moore collected this chant "Tange Lange Jeni" while working in a carefully limited section of Jamaica, the area of Morant Bay in St. Thomas. His respondents described themselves to him as having "African" and "Maroon" (as distinct from creole) heritage and blood lines. In the cumina ceremonies he witnessed, Moore noted the names and designations of the possessing ancestral spirits, some of African origin, some of Maroon origin, and both distinct from the gods that may also possess an entranced participant in the ritual: "Although Maroon and African cumina people live side by side, their ceremonial drumming, as well as their gods, are different" (Moore 1983: 136).

Moore's informants use the Ewe term *zo mbi* in the original sense of a ghost, as well as a Maroon equivalent *gangfrara* (Moore 140). His dissertation provides a wealth of information on the religious terminology and belief system of the cumina ritual: the sole citation in *DJE* for *zumbie* derives from Moore, for the term is not widely used in Jamaica.

The chant was translated but not glossed by Moore. It is, he says, a "country" (African) chant, not Maroon (275) and is associated with the greatest African gods. *DJE* glosses a few items, but only in reference to the chant. Apart from the gloss offered by the Ewe-speaking Odamttens, which follows the text of the chant, one should note that Westermann (1930) lists the following Ewe terms, which occur in the text and which match the interpretations of its Ghanaian translators: *kú, kúɖiɖi* "death"; *dú ye, ye-ɖúɖu* "dance"; *kɔ́kɔ* "tall"; *tsɔsísi* "river"; *ŋdí, ŋdíme* "morning"; *yɔ, yɔyɔ́, doɣтli* "call." A careful study of Bentley (1967) yielded no Kikongo items. The Ewe interpretation that follows offers new insight into the ethnic and linguistic history of cumina. Many terms (*eva, Jeni, di, and gel*) have been reinterpreted by modern JC speakers as English lexemes: in truth these items represent a frozen Ewe lexicon.

The chant bears a peculiar fascination for the student of African survivals in that it combines three or more languages. Analyzed and interpreted by Mrs. Abena Enyonam Agbley-Odamtten, herself a fluent speaker of Ewe, Twi, and Gã, the song uses an Ewe base, into which are grafted Twi words (*nsuo*), classical Ewe of the Dahomey region (*Dza ni* > *Jeni*), and a possible Yoruba overlay. Mrs. Agbley-Odamtten and Vincent Odamtten (both Ewe speakers from different branches of the Ghanaian Ewe) discern layers and accretions of language and ritual in the chant, which suggest to them that it derives from a distant stage in JC culture, possibly well before the end of the slave trade. According to Monica Schuler, Jamaicans used the term *Nago* to denote people from Dahomey: "we know Nago but dey dead." A chant that combines Central African Ewe and Ghanaian Ewe would not be surprising as Ewe recaptives might also have assisted in the religious revival (Monica Schuler, personal communication to the authors, 1987).

Unlike the reconstructed song "Quaco Sam," the cumina chant contains no allusions or historically marked terms that could help to date its origination. The fact that most of its framework derives from Ewe at least indicates that it is unlikely to have been brought to the region by those free blacks who came to Jamaica in 1845–1860, as these were mainly Krio speakers from Sierra Leone.

The chant represents a ritual set of words deriving from a vanished language, no longer used by or comprehensible to the inheritors of the ritual. Moore's rendition of the meaning makes no claim as to literal exactness; he offers no etymologies or comments on structure and lexis. A poetic rendition made by Edward Brathwaite (1978: 224–25) reproduces only a few of Moore's lines and ignores morphological features such as "wangɛ langɛ." Moore's and Brathwaite's renditions seem to assume a Twi background, although Moore offers no glosses as such (e.g., *Gaw* in verse 4, presumably a god, remains unexplained).

Brathwaite glosses *so-so* (Twi *nso,* "water"). He gives no etymological origins for his remaining glosses (*widi,* "dead"; *ku,* "call"; *pange,* "to greet"; *konakunda,* "they who all come" [1978: 224–25n]). Here, the Odamttens' glosses follow Moore's original (Moore 1983: 174), and Vincent Odamtten's literary translation follows the glosses.

Cumina Chant

1. Tangɛ langɛ Jɛni di Gəl ɛvə
Di lɔ cumɔrti pangɛ le
Gəl Im wɔto pangɛ mama le
Di le kuwidi pángɛ le

2. Tangɛ langɛ Jɛni di gəl ɛvə
Wangɛ langɛ mama o
Di le kuwidi pangɛ le
So-so langɛ widi ɔ gəl
So-so langɛ mama o
Owɔt kuqelə zɔmbi di gəl ɔlɔk
O widi pangɛ le
Gəl ɔmɔt widi pangɛ le
Di le konakunda pangɛ langɛ e
Di lɔ wɔtɔ widinnga le
Mɔnukɔ di lɔ kuwidi pangɛ le

3. Tangɛ langɛ Jɛni di gəl ɛvə
Kangɛ langɛ mama o Jɛni langɛ mama o
Di gəl ha a so-so langɛ mama o
Gəlləgɔ di lɔ kuwidi pɛngɛ lɔ
Gəl o so-so langɛ mama o
Wɔtto wipi gəlle ɛvə tangɛ langɛ mama
Di lɔ gəl lɔ kuwidi pɔngɔ le
Di lɔ gəl lɔ kowate langɛ mama
Jɛni langɛ Jɛni di gəl ɛvə tangɛ
Langɛ mama so-so
Modungo, gə, madɛingɔ, tangɛ langɛ
Mama di lɔ kum madi pangɛl
B^{h}a Jɛni B^{h}a kangɛ langɛ mamo o.

4. Tangɛ langɛ Jɛni di gəl ɛvə
Di lɔ kuwidi pɔngɛ le

Gəl a so-so madunga ya B^ha
Lɔswiti kangɛ langɛ mama o
Di lɔ kuwpi pɔngɔl mɔ
Jɛni di gəl a kumama o
Di lɔkuwidi pangɛl mɔJɛni
Di gəl a kuovɔ kangɛ langɛ mama o
Kangɛ langɛ miɛdi mɔnuka vola
Tangɛ langɛ mama o o so-so
Wɔtɔn gəl e B^hi Jɛni di lɔ
Kumɔdi pangɛ le
Tangɛ langɛ miedi mɔnuka
Gəl a so-so mɔdIngo ya
Mɔnuka e kɔngɛ langɛ mama o.

The Odamttens' Glosses

a, sometimes *la.* *This* or *the* when one wishes to indicate that the reference has been previously made to a noun (Ewe). Verse 3, line 3; verse 4, lines 3, 6, 14, 15.

bha (?) or *ba* (?). Imperative *come* or *she comes* (Gã). Verse 3, line 13.

cumorti or *kumoti.* Literally "death-pathway-medicine" (Ewe), we translated this as "this / the place of death." *Ti* actually refers to a "medicine" that is said to be made from the ground-up remains of a burnt chameleon and various herbs. This black powder is sprinkled on the ground that is to be charmed; of course this kind of charm/medicine is primarily used for the destruction of an enemy. Another meaning of *ti* signifies "being in the company of." In Twi *ti* = hear. Verse 1, line 2.

di. Search; willingness; willingly; require or demand (Ewe). *medi be* means "I want ——." However *di* may also be a corruption of *dzi* which can be translated to signify: (1.) The upper portion, such as *the sky;* (2.) *upwards;* (3.) *on, above, over, towards;* (4.) *surface;* (5.) *to be partial, as in taking someone's side in a dispute;* (6.) *according to;* (7.) *in reference, which to.* . . . Moore's translation presents a number of problems which would have been avoided had the original informant[s] known Ewe, since the specific meaning would depend on the *tonal characteristics* of the utterances and their extra-linguistic as well as their linguistic environments. We decided to keep the first meaning of *di!* Verse 1, lines 1, 2, and 4; verse 2, lines 1, 3, 6, 9, 10 and 11; verse 4, lines 1, 2, 5, 6, 7, and 8.

eve or *eva*. *She/he comes; she/he has come*, but *she/he has come* are variously signified by tone and context (Ewe).

ge'l, possibly *ga*. grand, great, huge, noble, or money. It might be that the original was *ge**, . . . an adverb signifying *almost, nearly, neighborhood*, thus indicating a proximity in Time and/or Space (Ewe). Verse 1, lines 1 and 3; verse 2, lines 1, 4, 6, and 8; verse 3, lines 1, 3, 4, 5, 6, 7, 8, 9 and 11*; verse 4, lines 1, 3, 6, 8, 11 and 14.

ha 1. or *haa* 2. 1. Also, to tear away, to scratch out, song, pig. 2. flow, flowing, flock (Ewe).

Im (?). Probably a fragment of the infinitive of *yi*, [meaning] "to go" as it is used in the progressive tense form: *mele yiyim'*, "I am going" (Ewe). Verse 1, line 3.

Jeni. Possibly *dzani*, beauty, the beautiful one, the nice one (Ewe). Verse 1, line 1; verse 2, line 1; verse 3, lines 1, 2 and 9; verse 4, lines 1, 7 and 11.

Kange. Name of a goddess, the grandmother of *Lange* (Ewe).

konakunda. Most likely *kondokondo*, signifying a tall, lanky person or an animal with a slightly bent body (Ewe). Verse 2, line 9.

kowate. *Ko* signifies poverty or barrenness (Ewe); *wate* signifies "let us go" (G).

konge. Probably a mishearing or variant of *Kange* above. Verse 4, line 15.

kugele'. Literally "death-great" or "great-death" (Ewe). Verse 2, line 6.

kum. *Ku* means "death"; the /m/ is usually an intensifier or imperative marker (Ewe). *Ku* can also mean "to dig" (Ewe). Verse 3, line 12.

kumama. Death's grandmother (Ewe). Verse 4, line 6.

kumodi. Literally "death-manner/way-search," search in the manner of the dead (Ewe). Verse 4, line 12.

kuwidi or *ku ndi*. Death-morning or, poetically, "death-dawning" (Ewe). Verse 1, line 4; verse 2, lines 3 and 11; verse 3 lines 3 and 7; verse 4, lines 2 and 7.

kuwpi. Variant of *kuwidi* above (?). Verse 4, line 2.

Lange. Probably refers to a river goddess/god. Verse 1, line 1; verse 2, lines 1, 2, 4, 5 and 9; verse 3 lines 1, 2, 3, 5, 6, 8, 9, 10, 11 and 13; verse 4, lines 1, 4, 8, 9, 10, 13, and 15.

le. Place, way, direction, at, catch, hold (Ewe). Verse 1, line 2; verse 2, lines 3, 7, 8, 9, 10 and 11; verse 3, line 7; verse 4, lines 2 and 12.

le or *lə*. Meat (Yoruba).

lego. Mountain (Gã).
lɔ. love, devotion, or collect (Ewe). Verse 1, line 2; verse 3, lines 4, 7, 8, and 11.

madeingɔ. *Madze* "I will take"; *ngo*, future, before, front, liquid surface, I will take/seize the future (Ewe). Verse 3, line 11.
madi. I wish, I would wish or demand (Ewe). Verse 3, line 12.
madunga. *Ma* indicates a negative; *du'n* signifies 'to eat'; *ga* return, big, money, great or noble. Possibly "not eating as a noble person" (eating humbly?). Or *ma* meaning "I"; therefore "I will eat well." *Du* signifies town, stranger (Ewe). Verse 4, line 3.
mama. Grandmother (Ewe). Verse 1, line 3; verse 2, lines 2 and 5; verse 4, lines 4, 8, 10 and 15.
miedi, mie e'di . . . miedi. Literally "we/you she/he wanted" (Ewe). Verse 4, lines 9 and 13.
modungo. *Mo* (?) probably means "way, manner"; *du(n)* means "eat"; *go* "calabash"; the way of eating from a calabash (?), i.e., as a pauper (Ewe)? Verse 3, line 11.
mɔnuka. *Mɔnukɔ* (Gã): *na mɔɔkɔ*. Title, a formal prefix specifically for a woman of substance: lady/emissary of the goddess/medium (Gã). Verse 2, line 11; verse 4, lines 9, 13, 15. But also an ancestral zombi: Schuler (1980) describes Mvuka as a man, the original leader of the religion, a famed rainmaker and one whose memory lives on among the cumina cultists. Moore (1983: 245–46) states that Manuka Vola, an African, died in 1928 aged more than eighty years. He has "attained a very high status equal . . . to the earthbound gods."

o, ow. As in English, an exclamation of surprise, alarm, disapproval.
ɔmo. Rice, meal, feast (Gã). Verse 2, line 8.
owot. *Owot kugele' zombi di ge'l olok*. Re-write as *O woto kugele' zombi di ge' lolo ke* (Ewe). Literally translated this reads, "O victim/maker/doer-of-storytelling death-great walk-bent search/willingly/willingness loving/lovingly devotedly root/to drop down." Poetic translation: "O! Possessed-raconteur the great death walker, bent, searching devotedly at the root of things."

Pange. God of rebirth, reincarnation. Verse 1, lines 2, 3, and 4; verse 2, lines 3, 7, 8, 9, 10; verse 3, lines 4 and 12; verse 4, lines 2 (here it might be *pon'go*, "main road"), 7 and 12.
pongol. *Kpon'goo*. Majestic (Ewe).

so-so. Divination. Note: *So* is the Ewe god/goddess of lightning. Verse 2, lines 4, 5; verse 3, lines 3, 5, 10; verse 4, lines 3, 10, 14.

tange, ton'gbe'. On the other side of the river (Ewe).
ti. To hear (Twi): *witi* "we/you have heard" or we/ you hear.

vo. Panic or fear (Ewe).

widi or *witi*. *N'di:* Morning or dawn (Ewe).

Vincent Odamtten's Verse Translation

Odamtten's verse translation was based on the assumption that "what we see is what was" (personal communication). Finding Ewe and its dialects Anexo and Dahomean Ewe to be the basic language of the chant, the Odamttens also drew on Twi, Gã, and Yoruba "whenever Ewe failed to yield a sensible translation." They note that *Lange* is probably a specific river goddess, and that *Jeni* is "Dzani or the beautiful one, the nice one and would-be emissary of the god/goddess Lange/Pange." Alternative translations are possible for verse 2, line 10; verse 3, lines 7 and 11; verse 4, lines 3, 9, and 14.

1. On the other side of the river, the great Lange,
demands the beautiful one comes willingly
Pange, the reincarnation god, demands devotion
in this place of death
Great grandmother of Pange creates legends in
this manner
Pange demands you willingly search in this
death-dawnıng

2. On the other side of the river, the great Lange,
demands the beautiful one comes willingly
Oh, grandmother of Lange, Wange
Pange demands you willingly search in this
death-dawning
The grandmother of Lange's divination, oh!
Oh, possessed-raconteur the great death walker, bent,
searching, devotedly at the root of things.
Oh, Pange is here with the dawning!
Pange is here at the dawning with a great
feast [Ed. rice]

Willingly search there with a crooked walk
for Pange, for Lange, oh!
Willingly a victim of devotion, an emissary
in that place
Lady, willingly devoted to Pange in this
place of death

3. On the other side of the river, the great Lange
demands the beautiful one comes willingly
Kange, the grandmother of Lange oh, the beauty,
the grandmother of Lange, oh!
Search the flowing of the great divination,
the grandmother of Lange, oh!
Devotion to Pange lets you search the great
mountain in this place of death
Great divination, oh, the grandmother of
Lange, oh!
Let us go to this great place, she comes on the
other side of the river, the grandmother of
Lange
Willingness, great majestic devotion in this
place of death
Willingness, great poverty and devotion lets
us go to grandmother of Lange
Beautiful Lange, searching for great beauty, she
comes on the other side of the river
The grandmother of Lange's divination
Blackman, noble *Madeingo on the other side
of the river Lange
[I would wish for love and death, I would
wish it, Lange.]

4. On the other side of the river, the great Lange,
demands the beautiful one comes willingly
Pange demands you search with devotion in this
place of death
The great divination, Thurs-day born blackwoman
she comes
Devoted Kange, grandmother of Lange collects in
the dawn, oh!
Willingly, child of death comes majestically

The beautiful one searches for the grandmother
of death oh!
The beautiful one searches with devotion in
the death-dawn for Pange
The great search for the death-bringer, Kange,
grandmother of Lange oh!
Kange, Lange I shall eat in panic of the Lady
On the other side of the river the grandmother
of Lange's divination oh!
Nobly I shall go with devotion to the
beautiful one
With Pange's love and death in that place
On the other side of the river I shall eat, Lady
The great divination of the Thurs-day born
blackwoman
Lady, Kange the grandmother of Lange oh!

Notes

Chapter 1. The Colonial Crucible

1. See Alleyne 1980: esp. 145–49; Dalby 1970/71; Hancock 1986b; Mufwene 1986; and Rickford 1986.

2. Niles 1980 treats Barbadian English as a dialect of EModE or regional dialectal English of the early seventeenth century.

3. Curtin 1969: 17–21; Robinson 1969: 12; Knight and Crahan 1979: 6. The first Europeans to engage in the African slave trade, the Portuguese were well established by the end of the fifteenth century. Blacks were well known in the Iberian peninsula by 1500. See also Chaudenson 1977: 260–63; and Hancock 1986b, for a discussion of African pidgins and their probable relationship to Afro-American creoles. Valdman 1978: 15, mentions Baragouin—a Carib trade language attested by a French missionary, Père Jacques Bouton, in 1640. Such a language may well have been present in Jamaica in the early seventeenth century.

4. Curtin 1969: 25. The new estimate for the early seventeenth century is cited by Paul Lovejoy (1982: 479–80).

5. Dallas 1803; Patterson 1973: 267–72, on uprisings led by Cormantins in association with Maroons; LePage 1960: 76; Dalby 1971; Alleyne 1980; and Bilby 1983.

6. Davies 1970: 38–42; Patterson 1973: 114–21; Fage 1969: 73–80.

7. See LePage 1960: 70–73; Taylor 1965: 20; Patterson 1973: 18–20, 95–97; Sheridan 1974: 210–11, 217; Roberts 1979: 33–36; and Higman 1976 and 1984 for population estimates and information on the importation and reexportation of slaves.

8. For the problems of estimating Jamaica's population prior to the first reliable census in 1844, see Atkins 1736: 245; LePage 1960: 36, 80–83, 91, using Edward Long's "sober" figures for estimating the white population in 1734, and the Royal African Company import-export figures in 1702–75 and 1789–98; Patterson 1973: 36, 83, 96–97; Brathwaite 1978: 152; and Higman 1976: 55, 62–63.

9. Patterson 1973: 97 cites an increase of 1.8 percent by means of slave imports, as against a natural decrease of 2.8 percent for 1746.

10. Patterson 1973: 35; Long 1774: 1.510–11; and Wentworth 1834: 1.1, 44.

11. For an excellent study of family, fertility, and economic patterns, see Barry Higman, *Slave Population and Economy in Jamaica, 1807–1834* (Cambridge: Cambridge University Press, 1976). Unfortunately no such study has been made of the period 1660–1720, when the creole society laid its foundations.

12. Craton contends that these rebellions mark a watershed in Jamaican slavery, turning planters away from Gold Coast slaves, making them work to creolize their slaves and to diminish freedom of movement and African cultural influences (1978: 55). Patterson (1973: 276) notes that a bill to block the importation of Akan slaves was defeated in the Jamaica Assembly after the 1765 revolt and that Gold Coast slaves remained highly desirable.

13. Long 1774: 2.287; Purcell 1937: 52; Pitman 1967: 37, 54. Lady Nugent (1966) mentions in her journal the numbers of Scots on the estates and Text 2 shows how the Scots figured in the slaves' imagination.

14. For the ratio of white women to men, see Long 1774: 1.377. Patterson, Brathwaite, and Higman all discuss the problems attendant on gender imbalances.

Chapter 2. Source Materials

1. For examples of the Jamaican Creole and West African Creole recorded by Crow, see his *Memoirs* (1830: 120–21, 128–29, 137, and 159, all of which are reproduced in D'Costa and Lalla (1989). See also the headnote to Text 5.

Chapter 3. Reconstructing the Sound System

1. For a useful parallel in Hiberno-English orthography of the seventeenth century, see Bliss 1979: 188–91. He cites Weinreich's discussion of "double interference" (1966: 21), but notes that the Irish case—like that of Jamaica—involves more than this: "Some of the writers of our texts were themselves Irishmen, and may have spoken a type of English which was not identical with the Standard English of the time" (Bliss 1979: 189).

2. The deletion and addition of [#h-] in the Holderness dialect of East Yorkshire corresponds exactly to JC usage: see Ross, Stead, and Holderness 1965. The feature occurs in other midland dialects, as well as in some London dialects. It appears late in JC records.

3. Norma Niles (1980: 171) discusses in detail the relationship of Barbadian phonology to that of regional and nonstandard dialects of Early Modern English. Parallels among dialectal EModE and Barbadian English and Jamaican Creole include "loss of pre-consonantal /r/: *cuss* . . . Vowel change of /u/ to /o/: *hongry* . . . Vowel change of /a/ to /e/: *ketch* . . . [and] addition of initial /j/: *yer* (hear), *yeye*."

4. Elworthy (1879: 50) cites "tha wut chocklee, and bannee, and blazee," and "tha dasent caree" as examples of auxiliary plus infinitive in southwest English dialect.

5. Jack Berry worked with D'Costa in 1970–71 to determine the role of tone as a

phonemic marker in JC. They established that classes of personal names are distinguished by high-falling ([rúòz]) for the given name, and by low-rising or low-low for the surname (e.g. *támàs tāmās,* "Thomas Thomas." See Berry (1972) for further details.

Chapter 6. Implications of the Data

1. In the JC song (Text 5) *em* alternates with *dem,* but not in any of Crow's West African samples. In the latter we find "passey" as present tense, a form attested in other writers of JC but absent from Crow's examples. See Mannix 1962: 107. *True mouth, big rogue man, Jew-Jew man* suggest the lexical compounding of pidginization. See Glossary and compare *belly-woman* (Lewis 1834: 124) and *grandee massa* (Carmichael 1833: 1.306–7). Note also Crow 1830:141–42 for features such as *mans, it be, for you gran Palaver house, all same, too much* (many). In conversation with King Holiday, another chief in Bonny, Crow records features such as "it be we country fash," "big rogue man," "we no havy head for make ship," "we father must kill dem own child" (1830: 137). Crow claims to have reproduced the speech "as nearly as [he] can remember."

Chapter 8. The Eighteenth Century

1. *Cudjoe* is an Akan dayname for a male born on a Monday. Cf. Fante *Kodwo* and Twi *Kwadwo*. See DeCamp 1967 and *DJE*.
2. Rising intonation alone distinguishes the question from the declarative sentence in JC. No rearrangement of lexical items takes place.

Chapter 9. The Early Nineteenth Century

1. *Quaco*. (< Twi *Kwàkú*). African day name for a male child born on a Wednesday, "a male belonging to *Wukú*, personal Genius, because he was born on *Wukúda*, the fourth day" (*DJE*).
2. *Obusheer.* Cf. *obisha* (Moreton 1793: 154). Both are intermediate forms of the derivation *overseer* > *busha*. Williams (1826: 202) notes these stages: "Overseer, first corrupted to Oberseer, is now Bersheer or Busha."
3. *DJE* notes Cubba as the "day name of a woman born on Wednesday" (cf. Twi *A'kúwá*. Sometimes heard as the second element in the derogatory phrase "Quashie Kubba" (St. James, St. Catherine).
4. The term *dandy* first appears in Border Scots at the end of the eighteenth century, and it was part of fashionable London English in the Regency period (1813–19) as a term denoting the "swell" or "exquisite" of the time (*OED*). Either source may have contributed it to JC. Rampini (1873: 122) states: "John Crow tink himself a dandy man."
5. Berry Hill is located in Manchester (Sibley 1978).

6. *Pan* varies with *fan* in other versions. Cf. Text 11.C, *leap* for *leaf*, and discussion of JC phonology in Chapter 3.

7. We have used the spelling Jacobs employs in his unpublished notes. He varies this form with *cotchreel* (according to a version published in the *Welfare Reporter* [January 1947] by a Mr. James T. H. Chandler, a clergyman) and *cod reel*, which occurs in Richard Hughes's novel *A High Wind in Jamaica*. Both *cotchreel* and *catchreel* may be derived from "Scotch Reel" by applying regular JC sound laws, but all three forms are as easily derived from "quadrille." Usually thought to have become popular in London society circa 1814, the quadrille was apparently known in the New World in the latter eighteenth century: a print from the Bettman archive (reproduced in the 15th edition of *The Encyclopaedia Brittannica, Micropaedia*, 8.335) shows the "quadrille being danced at an American colonial ball"; *OED* cites *The Private Letters of Lord Malmesbury* (1773: 1.269): "a few evenings ago some company were rehearsing quadrilles at Mrs Hobart's in St James' Square." The balls mentioned by Lady Nugent (1966: 14, 133, 185) suggest that white society imported whatever amusements were fashionable in Europe, and these thus became available to blacks. From all internal and external evidence one must assume an early nineteenth-century dating for the song.

8. *Hab be* appears to indicate continuity within the past and is used consistently within this text, but not in others.

9. *Gory* is also unusual but may be genuine. The lateral is often elided after a stop in JC, as in *lilly*, "little."

10. Arbitrary preposing of [h] is not common in early texts. Note Rampini (1873: 172): "I will hab to get hot hashes an' put you into dem."

11. The common term used to label people from the Akan group of West Africa.

12. An elaborately dressed person (*DJE*).

13. Term of contempt—possibly a tribal name in origin. Cf. Hausa *bungu*, "a nincompoop, country bumpkin" (*DJE*).

14. H. C. Wyld (1956: 192) describes [v] > [w] as a former "London vulgarism . . . now apparently extinct in the Cockney dialect." Cockneyisms were never common in JC, but note also *wicious* (Hamley 1862: 120); *Weenus* (Scott 1834: 1.195), and Baron-Wilson (1839: 2.214, 225): "ab talk vid im friend" and *vy*, *ven* for "why" and "when." Note that *EDD* lists the form *vagabone* under Irish, Scots, northern, and southwestern usage.

15. *Sweet mouth* also occurs in Phillippo (1843: 330), "Sweet mouth and pretty words dont always show dat de heart change."

16. In modern JC [bikl], this term has preserved the early [v] > [b] JC sound shift.

17. August 1, 1834, was Emancipation Day; therefore, a "fuss of Augus neger" is an undutiful slave.

Chapter 10. The Later Nineteenth Century

1. *Hard time* is famine, time of hardship, want, season of drought. The term occurs in many Annancy tales both as a descriptive term and as a specific gloss for

"drought, dry season." (I have observed this usage in St. James—Jean D'Costa). Several compounds occur in this tale, e.g., *water-side, shore side,* and *good-belly,* recalling the derivational process of pidginization.

2. The double negative was acceptable in EModE up to the early eighteenth century.

3. Literally "came that." Twi *sé* is a noun phrase complementizer comparable to SE *that.*

4. JC pluralizes by postposing the SE third-person pronoun (plural, oblique) *them.*

5. For *car,* "carry," see similar contracted form in Milne-Home 1890: 40; also note contemporary JC *car-go-bring-come,* "a meddler and busybody."

6. Hypercorrect *none dirt* may be an instance of the archaic use of *none* as an adjective, after Old English practice and used in the sixteenth century before vowels and /#h-/.

7. The morphosyntax of *you ben open* is conservative.

8. The forms *white-o, brown-o, black-o,* with the intrusive final vowels of West African phonotaxis, are archaic and unusual.

9. There is clear SE interference in this sentence, but note EModE and English dialectal *for to* influence on *fe' to.*

10. Literally "a stump of a tongue"; short, shortened, stumpy. Cf. *tumpa-foot.* The sentence means "if you want a woman to be good, give her a short tongue."

11. See Hamley 1871: 117, 124, 150, 187; 1878: 23, 141; 1882; Shand 1895: 9, 48; Roase 1965: 5.557, entry under William George Hamley; as well as Porter (1889: 2.137–38). A personal communication, dated November 19, 1984, from Helen Rowe, archivist of the Bermuda Archives, states that "in the section for 1864 W. G. Hamley, Lieutenant Governor and Commander in Chief . . . signed a number of the despatches to London regarding the [yellow fever] epidemic." Records in the Library and the Museum of the Royal Engineers (Chatham, Kent) show that Hamley served in Bermuda during the yellow fever epidemic of 1864 but make no reference to his postings as a junior officer.

12. JC [ɲ], familiar in words of West African origin such as *nyam,* sometimes replaces SE [j] in basilectal usage. Note that the brown nurse in Text 19.B uses *young.* Text A uses other early JC forms, such as *Garamighty, sarce, becausin,* and the regular [b] < [v] sound shift.

13. This common JC term, often heard in the exclamation "Yes sar!" preserves archaic English [ar] (later [er]). Whether with [r] or not (JC uses both [sa] and [sar]), the vowel in JC is open and not centered. Note also *saccomstance,* which in contemporary English was becoming centered as [ʌ].

14. The spelling *leady* is an example of Hamley's detailed attention to vowel quality (JC [ie] ~ SE [e:]) in establishing register and social variation in the usage of his characters. The mesolectal speaker uses SE *ladies* elsewhere.

15. Inverted word order is unusual in creole. This text—more than others—shows several highly questionable syntactic usages, of which this sentence is one. Cf. "you him see." At the same time, lexis and phonotaxis appear authentic (*'peek, pisen, berry*).

16. This spelling of SE *truth* is unattested elsewhere, but [θ] ~ [f] is a credible

variant of [θ] ~ [t] and is a feature of nonstandard British dialects such as Cockney. Wyld (1956: 291) doubts that the feature is regional.

17. Note SE [ɔi] > [ai] (sixteenth-century usage). Wyld (1956: 250–51) states that "the final adoption of [ai, i] was a slow process, and by some arbitrary standard in some words the . . . pronunciation was fixed while others were excluded." He quotes a remark dating back to William Kenrick (1773) "that it is an affectation to pronounce *boil, join* otherwise than as *bile, jine* and yet it is 'a vicious custom' . . . to use this sound [ai] in *oil, toil.*"

18. Unattested elsewhere in the data, such forms as *brack* are credible in light of JC [r] ~ [l] variation and are supported by Bilby's *braka* (1983: 72).

19. F. G. Cassidy (personal communication) notes that "glass snake" occurs in North American usage. The "glass snake" is believed to break easily, like glass. Or this could be evidence of [r] ~ [l] variation.

20. Typhus fever. Note the spelling change *p* < *ph*, suggesting a shift from SE [f] to JC [p], which could well support the suggestion that an [f] > [p] change in early JC parallels the well-documented [v] > [b] of *very* > *bery*. The main distinguishing feature setting the speech of the Jew apart from SE is the [s] > [š] change. To this variation are added the English dialect variant [w] ~ [v], the [θ] > [t] and [đ] > [d] of JC and some EModE and modern English dialects, and a smattering of French phrases.

21. The variant *massr* occurs nowhere else in the texts, but it is common in representations of American slave speech.

22. This phrase should be analyzed "chinchi-li'-bit," a tiny little bit.

23. *Kobite.* Derives from "goo'bye'-to-ye," and *mante* from a contraction of "marnin-to-ye."

24. In JC *-ar* appears as a spelling for /a:/ (e.g., Text 23: *arter, darter*).

25. Intrusive initial [h] is found early, though sporadically; dropping of the [h] is surprisingly rare in nineteenth-century documents, considering present JC usage. Note that this was once clearly distinguishable as a regional feature in Jamaica, speakers from Westmoreland and western St. Elizabeth claiming never to have heard it until they moved eastward (Eglon Whittingham, personal communication).

26. The spelling *ah* represents /aa/ in stressed syllables and /a/ in weakly stressed syllables as *fellah.* Note *ar* in *tarking, in ar,* and *ar sea;* and *a* + final *e* in *gane.* The writer makes no distinction between [a] and [aa] (cf. Rampini *lard, Garg,* Text 22), but the distinction is phonemic.

Glossary

a 1. prep. (probably < SE *at,* reinforced by Igbo *na* and Twi *da;* see *DJE* entries A[1], DA[5]; and Alleyne [1980: 111]) on, at, in, of place, time, motion. "Massa mus tap lilly bit for bait a Panish Town" (Text 3). Cf. *da* as a place marker: "Dey dry leaf da tree root!" (Text 18), but note preposition of time *da* in "him wake da morning" (Text 17), preposition of motion *a* in "You go in a Africa" (Scott 1834:1.205); also note *da* in "him come da Great Riber come see you" (Text 17).

a 2. (< of) "worn-down proclitic" (*DJE*). See "new pair a shoes" (Text 9).

a 3. "an intrusive sound . . . freq after *like, must,* etc.; prob due to phonetic analogy with W. African languages (e.g. Twi). (In written dialect it may be attached to the preceding or following word.)" (*DJE*). Note "Me nebba see a man lak-a Quaco Sam" (Text 9); "Hipsaw, my deaa! You no do like a-me!" (Text 4).

backra sb. vars. BUCKRA, BUCKERA. White man or woman. *DJE* lists nine variant spellings. Derives from Ibo, Efik *mbakára,* white man, he who surrounds or governs. Note *DJE* 2: "As a term of polite address, equiv. to sir, master, or boss." The vars. *buckera, buckra* may be pseudo-refined, anglicized forms.

bait vb. to take refreshment, to snack. "to Bait, bate. To stop at any place for refreshment" (Walker 1803). *OED:* "To cause a creature to bite for its own sake; to feed . . . 6. (*refl.* and *intr.*) Said of horses or other beasts: To take food . . . esp. at a stage of a journey. 7. *intr.* Of travellers: To stop at an inn orig. to feed the horses, but later also to rest and refresh themselves. 8. To feed, take nourishment." NB: Dickens, *Bleak House* (1853) "His brother . . . [will] ride with him . . . to the place where he will bait for the night" (Bantam ed. [1983], 794). Term has lost currency in both JC and SE. See Text 2.A.

belly woman sb. phrase. pregnant woman. See *DJE* and Lewis 1834: 254.

bery adv. < SE *very* deriv by /b/ < /v/ sound shift characteristic of early JC. Note forms such as *libba, ebery* for *liver, every.*

big-rogue-man sb. dangerous criminal(s). Pidgin term from the coast of Bonny (Crow 1830: 137).

bittle sb. < SE *victuals.*

bitty sb. poss var. of *bit,* a small Jamaican and Spanish West Indian coin valued at seven pence half-penny (*DJE* and Walker 1803). Note Murray (1877: 12) "pistereen bits." Collymore (1957: 15) glosses Barbadian "bitt" as "eight equal segments of a silver dollar" used in the British colonies.

blasfame or **b'a'pheme** vb. < SE *blaspheme.*

bline vb. < SE *blind.*

blue maugre adj. phrase. in a state of great distress or starvation (*DJE,* citing Williams 1826: 205). In Text 3.B, note sense of thin, wasted flesh: "Him no hab egg, him blue maugre to hell, me no *wantee man crab,* me wantee *woman crab.*"

bra sb. var. *brar.* < SE *brother.*

breren sb. < SE *brethren* (Text 10.A).

buckera, buckra see BACKRA.

busha sb. vars. OBISHA, OBUSHEER. < SE *overseer.*

buss sb. a kiss, a smack (SE). *OED* describes BUSS 2 as archaic and dialectal. See plural form in Moreton (1793: 154–55).

buss vb. 1. to kiss (SE). Note *OED* 1 archaic and dialectal. See entry above. Note possible pun in Moreton (1793: 154) "buss my rassa" for "kiss my ass," common vulgarism. 2. to punch, strike, kick; to burst, break open. Poss < *burst* (SE). In expression "buss yuh rass" (vulgarism) signifying "kick your arse." Note Farmer 1889 (for sb. and vb.): "a rough kiss (Gaelic *bus,* a mouth) it also has in the west the meaning of 'to punch,' a popular threat being 'I'll buss you head.' " Note JC expressions "buss open de door," "buss im mout."

b'ute sb. brute; familiar expression of defiant contempt (SE). Note use of the term to inferiors, opponents. Omission of [r] results from palatalization in early JC and in Text 6 marks the characteristic phonetic oddness of Anancy's speech.

bwai sb. < *boy.* Note *bay* circa 1300 (*OED*).

cajon sb. < SE *occasion.* 1. Occasion: "What cajon fe dem tings?" (Murray 1877: 12). 2. Need, necessity: "No, Bra, no cajon put my body, dis put my tail" (Text 17).

car vb. < SE *carry.*

catchreel sb. vars. < SE CODREEL, COTCH REEL (Text 9). < SE *quadrille* or *scotch reel.*

chakalata sb. vars. CHAKLATA, CHAAKLIT. chocolate. < Spanish *chocolate,* derived from Mexican *chocolatl* (*OED*). Usually refers to drink of hot chocolate taken before daybreak at the start of the working day.

cho exclamation. vars. CHAW CHA. signifies disgust, irritation, disbelief.

cho-cho sb. < Brazilian *chuchu.* The vine and edible fruit *Sechium edule,* eaten as a vegetable (*DJE*). Note var. CHOTA (reported by Jean D'Costa in St. Catherine, archaic) < American Spanish *chayote.*

chookoo sb. "Chookoo is the African name for a faraway place" (Murray 1877: 20; and *DJE*). NB: *chooka-chooka,* vb., "to do carelessly," "to half-wash" (*DJE*).

conconsa sb. < Twi *ŋkoŋkonsá,* falsehood, deceit. *DJE* notes three meanings: "1. Deceit, flattery. 2. A deceitful person . . . 3. Trouble or falling out between people . . . " var. *congo-saw,* a trick, a Congo mischief (folk etymology).

corochies sb. var. CAROSIS, CAROCHIES. < American Spanish *corotos,* "playthings, tools of trade, chattels, trumpery, trash" (*DJE*).

cottey sb. < American English *cot.* A small house, a hut (Walker 1811). The *-ey* ending fits JC syllabic sound laws.

craps sb. < SE *scrap;* may be sing. or plu.

crawl sb. an enclosure, pen, or building for keeping hogs or turtles (in the West Indies) (*OED*). Crow 1830: 137. See full entry in *DJE*. Note "turtle crawl" in Text 5.

cruddle vb. to curdle (by metathesis). Note *EDD:* from Scotland, Ireland, northern, and northeastern dialects, "to curdle, congeal." Also "of cloth: to 'crackle,' crinkle."

cudjoe sb. heavy stick, club. *DJE* notes "sb. and vb. dial; prob < *cudgel,* infl in form by CUDJOE 1." See Text 9: "Driba Harry . . . tek him cudjo a him han, knock him whip a Busha do."

cutting english sb. phrase. exaggerated, rhetorical use of learned language for show or for satire.

da 1. prep. in, at, on (see also A 1). Note "prinkle de fowl da me grave" (Murray 1877: 15).

da 2. pron. vb. is it, is that; that is, it is: "How you can say da fe you money?" (Murray 1877: 15); "Da for me bible book" (Williams 1826: 195); and "Ef da me eat Mammy Luna's pease-O / Drowny me water" (Lewis 1834: 254).

da 3. vb., continuative and progressive aspect marker. Note "we no want fe come back ya; come da wander all bout worl . . . da turn rolling calf" (Murray 1877: 15). Also habitual aspect marker: "he da cross de sea" (Text 10.B).

da 4. def. article or dem. adj. the; that. "You look ebery day wid crooked tick for find da pass" (Crow 1830: 129).

dat rel. pron. < SE *that.* "Me get somebody dat can read" (Williams 1826: 194).

de 1. adv. there; var. DAY. See *DJE* for adv. and prep. Note "me drop in dé" (Text 6).

de 2. locative copula; copula. is, are there; var. DAY. See *DJE* and Alleyne (1980: 80–85, 87). Note "Tavern no de a country place" (Text 7), lit. "Taverns are not there (not to be found) in the country parts"; "dem no gib you water—no one drop day" (Text 10.A).

dirty sb. earth, ground, terra firma; < Twi *dɔ̀té* (*DJE*). var. DUTTY. "De man a dirty dé a go nyam you" (Text 6), lit. "the man down there on the ground is going to devour you." Note "O Tom . . . tan da dutty!" (Murray 1877: 16). Pronounced [doti] in JC and homophonic with adj. derived from SE *dirty,* as in the phrase *dutty clothes* /doti kluoz/.

dish-ya. pron. emphatic. Usu. DIS-YA or DISA-YA. Lit. "this here" < SE *this* and *ya* meaning "here."

do sb. < SE *door* (Text 10).

eerie adj. smart, fashionable; excellent, well, in good state of body or mind. Glossed by Lewis (Text 8) as "buckish" (i.e., stylish, dandified) and "hearty" (happy, prosperous). This term raises major problems of phonological and semantic reconstruction. Note *DJE Supplement:* "1976, [H. P. Jacobs], This is *irie,* which sprang into prominence in 1974 as a word for 'grand' or 'lovely.' I have never heard it spontaneously pronounced by anybody, and Hibbert . . . did not seem certain of its pronunciation. I think it is Monk Lewis's word *eerie.*" The pronunciation [airi] is widely known today, and no other var. occurs in Rastafarian or general usage. The term is used consciously as a Rastafarian term for "excellent," "very pleasant," "propitious," "very fortunate" (of states or circumstances), "handsome," "pleasing" (as in "everyting irie," everything's fine). Note response to greeting: "How you do?" "Irie, bredda, irie."

ephod sb. SE. a priestly garment; fig. a sign of piety. See Young (1980); Exod. 25:7: "stones to be set in the ephod"; I Sam. 2:18: "Samuel . . . a child, girded with a linen ephod"; I Sam. 14:3: "the Lord in Siloh, wearing an ephod."

fe, fee See FOR.

Feesus < SE *Ephesus.*

Fillistones < SE *Philistines.*

for possessive marker. var. FA, FE, FI. Usual JC form is /fi/, "for" being regarded as hypercorrected. *DJE* notes under FI: "2. possessive particle dial; . . . < *for,* preceding a pronoun, or . . . a person's name or idenifying phr . . . Belonging to (thus /fi-mi/ belonging to me, my mine . . .)."

for purposive connective or, in the sense "for to," infinitive marker. *DJE* notes "1. To (as introducing an infinitive verb). 2. In modal expressions (obligation, compulsion, etc.) . . . where Ja dial omits the verb *to be,* and some of the modal force is shifted to *fi* making it quasi-auxiliary."

fum vb. 1. to beat or flog. 2. to pound in a mortar. See *DJE* which comments "prob onomatopoeic, but poss also infl by an African word. (The iterated form is usually a noun, FUM-FUM)." See Text 7: "he will fum me."

fum-fum sb. a flogging, beating. See Text 5: "And never gae dem boys fum-fum." This appears to have been the common term for a beating in eighteenth- and nineteenth-century JC.

Garamighty sb. vars. incl. GAR A'MIGHTY, GOD A'MIGHTY. God almighty. The lambdacized form seems to have been the common JC term in the eighteenth and early nineteenth centuries. See Dallas 1803: 1.112–13.

gemman sb. < SE *gentleman.*

gib vb. < SE *give.* Proverbial expression "gib him coco for yam" (Text 19), i.e., tit for tat.

gin'am sb. < SE *gingham.*

gombah sb. vars. GOOMBAH, GUMBAY. name applied to various types of drum, "but all seem to be played with the fingers rather than with sticks" (*DJE*); probable connection with Kongo *ŋgoma*, *ŋkumbi*, "a drum."

good-belly adj. pidgin compound of SE items: kind, kind-hearted, generous, good-natured.

grandy adj. 1. < SE grand; great, excessive, big: "grandy tanks" (Ross 1800: 4) and "grandy strength" (*Marly* 1828: 213). 2. Intensifer. See Text 11: "Pharaoh hab be grandy much angry" and "grandy rich man."

grandy sb. < SE *grandmother*, *grandam*. Title of respect for an old woman, "Grandie, you mus hab my breakfas' ready" (Rampini 1873: 125); also a grandmother (*DJE*).

groomer sb. poss. a hooked stick for picking fruit. Text 18: "Yerry groomer corn pempeny, / Groomer yerry; / pigeon bring me da groomer yerry" could be rendered "Listen, hooked stick, corn is plentiful; / Hooked stick, listen: / Pigeon, bring me there (?), that (?); hooked stick, listen." Poss. < Eng. dial. *groom*, *crome*, *cromb*, as sb. meaning a hooked stick used to pull down the branches of trees, or vb to pull or hook down something (*EDD*). *OED* has "a hook, a crook; *esp.* 'a stick with a hook at the end of it, to pull down the boughs of a tree, to draw weeds out of ditches', etc.," which exactly describes the long stick with a wire hook at one end, much in use in Jamaica for picking fruit.

guzu sb. vars. GUZUM, GASO. *DJE* 2. "an act of obeah, or witchcraft." Note Kimbundu *nguzu*, strength, power, force (*DJE*).

gwine vb. < SE *going*. *EDD* lists vars. GWAIN, GWAININ, GWANE.

hab vb. Vars. include HABBY, HABBEE, HAVY. < SE *have*. These are found mainly in the oldest texts (see Texts 3, 5).

hard ears adj. phr. < SE elements. Stubborn, resisting advice or persuasion, self-willed.

hipsaw vb. and sb. To dance, to shake. A hip-shaking dance. Apparently derived from *hip* + Twi *saw*, to dance (*DJE*). "Hipsaw! my deaa! You no do like a-me! / You no jig like a-me! / You no twist like a-me!" (Text 4).

hot vb. < SE *hurt*. To hurt, injure, cause to suffer.

hot adj. 1. < SE *hurt* as in *hurtful*. Painful, stingingly hurtful. 2. < SE *hot*. Note semantic overlapping between the vb and adj.

Jack Mandora etymology unknown. *DJE* states that it is the "first part of a formula traditionally used to end an ANANCY STORY." Often combined with "me no choose none," the formula carries an ironic, dismissive tone, absolving the narrator of responsibility for the tale.

jeints sb. plu. < SE *joints*. *EDD* notes var. *jeints* in northern usage.

jook vb. To prick, to drive a sharp point into something; (intr) to be pricked (as by thorns). See under JUK in *DJE:* "Fulani *jukka*, spur, poke, knock down; . . . Cameroons pidgin *čuk*, injection; *čuk-am* pierce, prick."

junka pan sb. phrase. Meaning obsc. Poss a pan for storing and carrying food (Text 9). Note *DJE* JUNK 2: "A large piece or lump, esp of meat."

junka pipe sb. phrase. A tobacco pipe with a very short stem (*DJE*). Note *junky pipe* in Rampini 1873: 117.

kackaw sb. Excrement, filth (Moreton 1793: 131). *DJE* states: "origin uncertain, prob multiple—cf Sp and Fr *caca*, excrement, Mende *ka*, waste matter . . . , Twi *kãŋ-kãŋ*, stinking."

ketch vb. < SE *catch*. *DJE* notes that pronunciation /keč/ is "common in Eng. dial and colloq speech generally."

kittureen, kittareen sb. "a kind of covered vehicle and, in the West Indies, a kind of horse-drawn buggy" (*OED*) commonly used in the eighteenth and nineteenth centuries.

knaum vb. See NYAM.

learn vb. to teach, instruct. *OED* notes "to impart knowledge, now vulgar," and refers to usages occurring between 1200 and 1899.

lilly adj. var. YITTY. < SE *little;* in mod JC usu /likl/. *EDD* lists *lail, lal, li:l, lil.* Reduplication in JC may also account for the form [li-li].

loblolly sb. SE. A thick gruel or spoon-meat (*DJE*); a sloppy stew served to slaves and laborers; *fig* meaning silly, pudding-hearted. Note "wibble wabble loblolly" (Text 10.A), an expression of contempt and derision. Ligon (1657: 43) notes that the diet of the Barbadian planters consisted of "potatoes, loblolly, and Bonavist" and that while the white laborers and servants ate loblolly willingly, African slaves disliked it. *DJE* adds that it was also "a rustic or nautical dish or simple remedy. Taken as a type of something soft, 'without firmness or character.' " Note also T. H. White, *The Age of Scandal* (London, 1950), 82–83: "The Loblolly Men . . . made a platform with the [seamen's] chests, on which the surgeons laid out their saws and chisels. When the action began, and the eighty pound shot began to thump against the wooden walls, and to splinter them, and to enter, the Loblolly Men seized the casualties and hauled them screaming to the platform, where the surgeons sawed off any shattered limb as quickly as possible." White is here describing the British navy in the eighteenth century.

macky greeting. Good morning. Cf. Maroon term *ja-ma-kie*, "good morning" from Dalby 1971: 42, in the context of Twi elements in use among Maroons. *DJE* notes Twi *makyé!* "good morning," cites JC term as accompanying a curtsey.

macky adj. or MUCKY MASSA, "pretending to be a superior person" (*DJE*).

machete sb. < Spanish *machete* (*DJE*). *OED* cites usages with first-syllable stress 1598–1887 (*DJE*).

massa tenky sb. phrase. a gift, probably a trinket betokening master's favor: "Swalla-henkychi tie me head, Massa tenky tie me troat" (Text 9). In this instance probably a scarf or ribbon (the persona is a woman). *DJE* has simply "a gift"; term is not specifically male or female in reference.

massoo vb. < Twi *mású* To raise, lift up (*DJE*).

maugre adj. var. MAAGA. < SE *meagre.* In phrase "blue maugre to hell" (Text 3.B), thin, wasted. Cf. *blue devils, blue language, blue day* (day of misfortune) (*EDD*) and JC *blue-lights,* obscenities.

metody sb.< SE *Methodist. EDD* lists *Methody, Mettody,* from Irish, Scottish, and northern usage.

mingo sb. an elaborately dressed person, probably < Sp. *Mingo* (*DJE*).

myal sb. see **myal, myal dance, myalism, myalist, myal man** (*DJE*). Refers to a form of spell-casting very similar to obeah but usu. claimed to be "good" magic used to take away the harmful spells set by obeah men.

na completive particle in sentence-final position. Modern JC var. /nʌ/, indicating emphasis of preceding verb phrase; e.g., "Tell me, no?" meaning "Please do tell me."

nan interjection, query. < English dialect *nan,* aphetic form of *anan, anon.* A polite inquiry signifying the speaker's failure to understand what has been addressed to him/her (Text 7). *OED* cites Sussex and Shropshire dialect, archaic by the nineteenth century. See *OED* for common usage in EModE and also in Barbadian (Niles 1980: 130).

nebba < SE *never.*

no adv. particle. See *DJE:* "introducing an exclamation, interrogative in form but requiring no answer: 'Isn't it (that), Don't you?' "

no mo adv. phrase. < SE *no more.* Mere, only, alone (*DJE*).

no mo so connective phrase. no more than that. See Text 6: "Bro'er Deat' say me fe go make up fire, but no mo so me no yerry."

no so adv. phrase. obscure, possibly only; nothing but. See *DJE.* Usages parallel mod JC *no so-so,* lit. "is there not only, nothing but." See Text 10.A: "we die yesterday, no so tomorrow"; "no so boiling brimstone, nutten else for drink, tay de flame come trough you nose."

nyam vb. vars. KNAUM, N'YAM, NYAMN, YAM-YAMME. to eat; to eat greedily; to devour. *DJE* derives from words denoting *food* and *eat* in several W. African languages. Cf. Wolof *ɲam, ɲam-ɲam,* to eat; Fula *ɲamu, ɲamgo* to eat; Hausa *na:ma,* flesh, meat; Twi *ɛnãm,* flesh, meat of any kind.

nyam sb. food, provender, eating (in the sense of that which is eaten). See *Marly* 1828: 52: "She exclaimed, 'Dey good nyamn for him neger, massa!' "

nyoung adj. < SE *young.*

obeah sb. 1. witchcraft. 2. an object used in casting spells. 3. the invocation and worship of spirits, including ancestral spirits. *DJE* cites Efik *ubio,* "a thing or mixture of things, put in the ground, as a charm to cause sickness or death." Obeah spells may cause a rival or enemy to fall ill or die; or they may cause someone to fall in love. Among the main materials are earth from a graveyard, knotted string securing the obeah object, candles, and a range of herbal decoctions.

obisha see BUSHA.

obusheer see BUSHA.

packy sb. < Twi *apákyi.* A vessel made by scooping out and drying the hard, gourdlike fruit of the calabash tree.

palaver sb. talk; conversation; a discussion between traders, leaders (Text 5). *DJE* has also sense of "noisy abuse." < *palavra* (Portuguese), word, speech, talk. *OED* notes *palavra,* "used by Portuguese traders on the coast of Africa for a talk with the natives," cites 1735 (". . . a Palaaver being called, Peter recovered two Ounces of Gold . . . ") and 1771 ("No doubt they're all barbarians. . . . I'll try to make palaver with them though").

pempeny adj. plentiful, plenty. See PEM-PEM and PEMPENY in *DJE.* < Twi *a-pém,* a thousand, *mpempem* thousands. *DJE* notes that Murray (Text 17) "may illustrate a different word" but makes some sense in context.

perrit sb. < SE *spirit.*

pickninny sb. < Portuguese *pequenino* child. Mod. JC form is *pickney.* See *DJE.*

pills sb. pun in song (Text 5), where "pills" refers to cannonballs used in battle (Crow's footnote).

prog sb. *OED* 1: a cant term for food, provisions, and *EDD,* noting the term to be in general use in Scotland and America, adds that it is "especially food to be consumed out of doors or away from home."

puckerie sb. or adj. Obscure. Cf. mod JC *pokro,* etymology unknown (*DJE*), glossed as "extremely poor," possibly worthless, trashy (note mod JC "Me no want dem ole pokro clothes," St. Andrew, Jean D'Costa, 1973). Usage in Text 10.A suggests sense of "that which cheats, deceives": "'De bible say dem painted puckerie—dem cheat you yeyes—dem all rotten.' Here a voice cried out, 'Sneezer you lie—you puckerie yourself—you wibble wabble loblolly' " (may be biblical "sepulcher" in this context). Term also seems to imply something concrete: consider Yorkshire *pokey,* in *EDD:* "a slang term for goods paid for on the 'truck' system; . . . it was no uncommon thing for part of the wages to be taken out in 'pokey' . . . ; Goods brought home in the '*piece-poker* in which (weavers) carried pieces. Many of the old manufacturers employing hand-loom weavers kept a shop with groceries and drapery, etc., and forced the weavers to take part-payment in goods or 'truck,' i.e. 'pokey.' "

pull foot vb. phrase. *DJE* reads "1. To run away . . . 2. To move rapidly." In these texts the usual sense is of slaves running away.

putta-putta sb. mud. Cf. Twi *pɔ̀tɔ-pɔtɔ* (*DJE*)

rassa sb. < SE *arse.* By metathesis and addition of vowel according to JC sound laws. Note Krio *ras* "1. buttocks. 2. term of abuse" (Fyle and Jones 1980), and also JC *rass,* obscene term for anus, backside.

ratoon sb. < Spanish *retono* a fresh shoot or sprout (*DJE*). The second growth of sugarcane, which sprouts after the first cutting of the canes.

Regan gown sb. regency gown.

sabby vb. to know. *DJE* lists *sabi-so* < *savvy.*

sangaree sb. < Spanish *sangria*, a spicy beverage of wine and orange juice or other flavorings, a favorite drink among West Indian planters. See *OED*.

sarmint sb. < SE *sermon*. *EDD* notes *sarmon* (Lancashire) and *zarmon* (Berkshire).

say See *se*.

se connective particle with sense of *that* after verbs of hearing, learning, listening, understanding, etc. See main entry in *DJE*. < Twi *sé*, "after a previous verb . . . introducing the words spoken." Note Text 9: "Me yerry se de dance a Berry Hill." Vars. SEH, SAY.

shay-shay sb. a vigorous, lively dance. *DJE* suggests < French *chassé*.

shay-shay vb. to dance in a provocative fashion: "Shay-shay decent, gal!" (old woman overheard scolding girl at dance, 1948—Jean D'Costa).

shell-blow sb. the time marked by the blowing of a conch shell to summon slaves to work, to the midday meal, etc. var. CAUCHIE (< conch-shell)—"Cauchie blow yet?"—recorded in Trelawny 1945–51 (Jean D'Costa).

shivel adj. < SE *civil*.

somebody sb. var. SUMMARY (Barclay 1826: 191). < SE *somebody*, in mod JC *smadi*. 1. someone, somebody. 2. anyone. 3. a person. Note sense (2) in "me no kill somebody" and sense (3) in "You wicked somebody," (Williams 1826: 196).

sinicky adj. < SE *sneaky*.

so-so adj. 1. of a thing: alone, by itself; 2. mere, ordinary (*DJE*, which cites Portuguese *so*, "alone, sole," and Yoruba *sho-sho*, "only"). Has sense of "nothing but."

stamp-an-go sb. < SE, from an order given in the British navy to sailors for the performance of certain duties (*DJE* and *OED*). A fritter made from dried codfish. Also called "stamps."

sunting sb. < SE *something*. 1. a thing. 2. something. Note mod JC *sinting*.

swalla-henkychi sb. phrase. vars. incl. SWARRA, SWALLOW. An elaborate headdress or head tie; a head kerchief tied with high-flying points, swallowtail fashion. See Text 9.

sweet vb. In *DJE* "1. To please greatly. 2. Also const *up:* to try to please, be sweet to." Note sexual overtones in Text 4.

sweet-mout adj. Glib, persuasive.

tafferel sb. *OED* 2: "The upper part of the flat portion of a ship's stern."

tajo vb. etymology unknown. Sense obscure, probably sexual. See Moreton 1793: 157: "Tajo, tajo, tajo . . . O laud, O! / Tajo, tajo, tajo! / You work him, mackey massa! / You sweet me, mackey massa! / A little more, my mackey massa!" Possibly Portuguese source or Eng. dialect "Ta, Joe," meaning "Thanks, Joe."

tan vb. < SE *stand*.

tate sb. < SE *estate*.

tatta sb. father; grandfather; also respectful term of address to elderly man. See *DJE:* TAATA, term for "father" occurs in a number of W. African languages, e.g., Ewe *tatá*.

tay prep. until, till. Note var. TE.

tenky sb. < SE *thanks, thank you.* 1. thank you. 2. a gift (*DJE*).

uno pron. Vars. ONOO, UNOO, UNNU (*DJE*). you (plur.) < Ibo *unu,* "you" (plur.).

unno exclamation of negative emphasis. Var. INO. Murray 1877: 16: "Unno! Tom ded, mek him go."

wagabone sb. < SE *vagabond. EDD* notes *vagabone* in Scots, Irish, and northern usage.

warm sb. < SE *war.* unusual form occurring in W. African discourses in Crow 1830: 141–42; possibly African pidgin rather than JC.

warra interrogative pronoun. vars. WURRAH, WHARRA. why, for what; what. See *DJE*. Text 9: "Da warra mo we wanty?"

Weenus prop. name. < SE *Venus.*

wibble wabble adj. unsteady, wobbly. *OED* notes as colloq. form, earliest citation 1847.

wily prop. name. < SE *Violet.*

wind vb. *DJE:* "To twist and turn the hips, esp provocatively, in dancing or walking."

wittal See VITTEL, BITTLE. Note *EDD wittal* in Midland and Suffolk usage. < SE *victuals.*

woio exclamation. expression signifying distress. See Williams 1826: 189: "make de buckra man cry *woio.*" Note *DJE* WAAY-WAAY, a cry of distress.

wo wo adj. obscure, but poss. feeble, useless. See phrase "wo wo palaver" in Crow 1830: 142. Note Christaller 1881: 560–61: *wo* "13. *mmŏrsã a woawo no kakra,* weak, diluted brandy or spirit; *nsã yi, woawo no,* this wine is mixed with water. 14. *yede áwò anó,* we (have) had a dispute with each other."

yam-yamme See NYAM.

yerry vb. vars. YE-HEARY, YEARY, HEAREE. to hear, often imperative, "hear! listen!" Note Williams 1826: 190: "Ye heary, my Brar." This form could be a reinterpretation by Williams.

yeye < SE *eye.* Note *EDD yees* in Devonshire 1790. For the [i:] sound, note *EDD* [i:] as a dialectal variant and [ni:] for *nigh* in Lancashire and northwest Devonshire.

Bibliography

In the references that follow, citations of Kingston as place of publication refer to Kingston, Jamaica, West Indies, without exception.

Abbott, E. A. 1966. *A Shakespearean Grammar: An Attempt to Illustrate . . . Differences between Elizabethan and Modern English*. New York: Dover. Originally published in 1870.

Akers, Glen Alan. 1981. *Phonological Variation in the Jamaican Continuum*. Ann Arbor: Karoma.

Allen, Grant. 1893. *Ivan Greet's Masterpiece*. London: Chatto and Windus.

Alleyne, Mervyn C. 1971. Acculturation and the Cultural Matrix of Creolization. In *Pidginization and Creolization of Languages*. Ed. Dell Hymes. Cambridge: Cambridge University Press.

______. 1980. *Comparative Afro-American*. Ann Arbor: Karoma.

Allsopp, Richard. 1972. Some Suprasegmental Features of Caribbean English. In *Conference on Creole Languages and Educational Development*. Ed. Dennis Craig. St. Augustine, Trinidad: UNESCO and University of the West Indies.

America—South-of-U.S. Feb. 1926 and March 1926. Catalogue of books, pamphlets, maps, and prints relating principally to Jamaica. In the National Library of Jamaica, Kingston.

Andrews, J. B. 1880. Anansi Stories. *Folklore Record* 3 (1): 53–55.

Atkins, John. 1736. *A Voyage to Guinea, Brasil, and the West Indies*. London: Cesar Ward and Richard Chandler.

Bailey, Beryl Loftman. 1962. *A Language Guide to Jamaica*. New York: Research Institute for the Study of Man.

______. 1966. *Jamaican Creole Syntax: A Transformational Approach*. Cambridge: Cambridge University Press.

Bailey, Richard W., and Manfred Görlach, eds. 1982. *English as a World Language*. Ann Arbor: University of Michigan Press.

Banbury, Rev. Thomas. 1894. *Jamaica Superstitions; or, The Obeah Book*. Kingston: Mortimer De Souza.

Baptist Mission. 1833. *A Narrative of Recent Events Connected with the Baptist Mission in This Island*. Kingston: Jordan and Osborn at the *Jamaica Watchman*.

Baptist Tracts. 1823. *Services at the designation of Mr. James Phillippo as a Missionary to the Island of Jamaica.* Rhodes House Library, Oxford.

Barclay, Alexander. 1826. *A Practical View of the Present State of Slavery in the West Indies.* London: Smith.

Baron-Wilson, Margaret. 1839. *The Life and Correspondence of M. G. Lewis.* London: Colborn.

Bates, William C. 1896. Creole Folklore from Jamaica. *Journal of American Folklore* 9 (32): 38–42, 10 (33): 121–28.

Baudet, Martha M. 1981. Identifying the African Grammatical Base of the Caribbean Creoles: A Typological Approach. In *Historicity and Variation in Creole Studies.* Ed. Arnold Highfield and Albert Valdman. Ann Arbor: Karoma.

Beckford, William. 1788. *Remarks upon the Situation of Negroes in Jamaica.* London: Egerton.

———. 1790. *A Descriptive Account of the Island of Jamaica.* 2 vols. London: Egerton.

Beckwith, Martha Warren. 1969. *Black Roadways: a Study of Jamaican Folk Life.* New York: Negro Universities Press. Originally published in 1929.

Belisario, Isaac M. 1837. *Sketches of Character in Illustration of the Habits, Occupations and Costume of the Negro Population in the Island of Jamaica.* Kingston: the artist.

Bell, H. J. 1893. *Obeah.* 2d ed. London: Low, Marston.

Bennett, J. Harry. 1964. Cary Helyar, Merchant and Planter of Seventeenth-Century Jamaica. *William and Mary Quarterly* 3d series, 21 (1): 53–76.

Bentley, Rev. W. Holman. 1967. *Dictionary and Grammar of the Kongo Language.* Farnborough, Hants.: Gregg Press. Originally published in 1887.

Berry, Jack. 1972. Some Observations on Residual Tone in WI English. *Conference on Creole Languages and Educational Development.* Ed. Dennis Craig. St. Augustine, Trinidad: UNESCO and University of the West Indies.

Bickell, Rev. R. 1825. *The West Indies as They Are; or, A Real Picture of Slavery but More Particularly as It Exists in the Island of Jamaica.* London: Hatchard and Son.

Bickerton, Derek. 1973. On the Nature of a Creole Continuum. *Language* 40: 640–69.

———. 1975. *The Dynamics of a Creole System.* Cambridge: Cambridge University Press.

———. 1977. Pidginization and Creolization: Language Acquisition and Language Universals. In *Pidgin and Creole Linguistics.* Ed. A. Valdman. Bloomington: Indiana University Press.

———. 1979. Beginnings. In *The Genesis of Language.* Ed. Kenneth Hill. Ann Arbor: Karoma.

———. 1981. *Roots of Language.* Ann Arbor: Karoma.

———. 1984a. Language Bioprogram, Hypothesis. *Behavioral and Brain Sciences* 7 (2): 173–88.

———. 1984b. The Role of Demographics in the Formation of Creoles. Paper presented at the 13th Annual Colloquium on New Ways of Analyzing Variation, held at the University of Pennsylvania, Philadelphia.

———. 1984c. The Language Bioprogram Hypothesis and Second Language Acquisition. In *Language Universals and Second Language Acquisition*. Ed. William Rutherford. Amsterdam: John Benjamins.

Bigelow, John. 1851. *Jamaica in 1850; or, The Effects of Sixteen Years of Freedom on a Slave Colony*. New York: Putnam.

Bilby, Kenneth. 1983. How the "Older Heads" Talk: A Jamaican Maroon Spirit Possession Language and Its Relationship to the Creole of Surinam and Sierra Leone. *New West Indian Guide* 57: 37–88.

Black Man's. ca. 1833. *The Black Man's Lub Song*. Caricature and verse sketched and written by a native Artist. London: Lew. Dicro. Filed in the National Library of Jamaica, Kingston.

Blassingame, John W. 1977. *Slave Testimony: Two Centuries of Letters, Speeches, Interviews, and Autobiographies*. Baton Rouge: Louisiana State University Press.

Bliss, Alan. 1979. *Spoken English in Ireland, 1650–1740*. Dublin: Dolmen Press.

Blome, Richard. 1678. *Description of the Island of Jamaica*. London: Newman.

Bonner, Tony. 1974. Blue Mountain Expedition Exploratory Excavations at Nanny Town by the Scientific Exploration Society. *Jamaica Journal* 8 (2, 3): 46–51.

Brathwaite, Edward. 1977. *Our Ancestral Heritage: A Bibliography of the Roots of Culture in the English-Speaking Caribbean*. Kingston: Savacou.

______. 1978. *The Development of Creole Society in Jamaica 1770–1830*. Oxford: Basil Blackwell. Originally published in 1971.

Bridges, Rev. George William. 1814. *The Annals of Jamaica*. London: Murray.

Browne, Patrick. 1756. *The Civil and Natural History of Jamaica*. London: Osborn and Shipton.

Bryan, Patrick. 1973. Emigres, Conflict, and Reconciliation: The French Emigres in Nineteenth-Century Jamaica. *Jamaica Journal* 7 (3): 13–19.

Burchell, William Fitzer. 1849. *Memoir of Thomas Burchell, Twenty-two Years a Missionary in Jamaica*. London: Green.

Burrowes, Audrey, and Richard Allsopp. 1983. Barbadian Creole: A Note on Its Social History and Structure. In *Studies in Caribbean Language*. Ed. L. Carrington. St. Augustine, Trinidad: Society for Caribbean Linguistics, School of Education, University of the West Indies.

Campbell, Charles. 1828. *Memoirs*. Glasgow: Duncan.

Campo-bell, John Talbott. 1736. *The Speech of Mr. John Talbott Campo-bell, a Free Christian Negro, to His Countrymen in the Mountains of Jamaica, to Which Is Subjoined the Speech of Moses Bon Saam, Another Free Negro*. London: n.p.

Candler, John. 1840. *Extracts from the Journal while Travelling in Jamaica*. London: Harvey and Darton.

Carmichael, Mrs. A. C. 1833. *Domestic Manners and Social Condition of the White, Coloured, and Negro Population of the West Indies*. 2d ed. 2 vols. London: Whittaker and Treacher.

Carnegie, James. 1971. The 19th Century Optimist of the Chapel: The Friendly Witness of James M. Phillippo, Author of *Jamaica: Its Past and Present State*. *Jamaica Journal* 5 (1): 11–15.

Carr, William. 1828. *The Dialect of Craven in the West-Riding . . . of York*. London: W. Crohts.

Carrington, Lawrence D. 1971. *Notes on a Common Phonetic Transcription System for Use by Creole Scholars*. St. Augustine, Trinidad: University of the West Indies, School of Education. Photocopy.

———. 1982a. Review of *The Genesis of Language*. Ed. K. C. Hill. *Caribbean Journal of Education* 9 (1): 55–65.

———. 1982b. Re-assessing the Issues Related to Creole Genesis. Paper presented at the Fourth Biennial Conference of the Society for Caribbean Linguistics, Paramaribo, Surinam.

———. 1987. The Substance of Creole Studies—a Re-appraisal. In *Papers in Honor of John Reinecke*. Ed. Glenn Gilbert. Honolulu: University of Hawaii Press.

Cassidy, Frederic G. 1961. *Jamaica Talk: Three Hundred Years of the English Language in Jamaica*. London: Macmillan.

———. 1966. Multiple Etymologies in Jamaican Creole. *American Speech* 41: 211–15.

Cassidy, Frederic G., and Robert LePage. 1961. Lexicographical Problems of *The Dictionary of Jamaican English*. In *Creole Language Studies* 2. Ed. R. B. LePage and David DeCamp. London: Macmillan.

———. 1980. *Dictionary of Jamaican English*. 2d ed. Cambridge: Cambridge University Press.

Cercignani, Fausto. 1981. *Shakespeare's Works and Elizabethan Pronunciation*. New York: Oxford University Press.

Chambre, Major Alan. 1858. *Recollections of West-End Life*. 2 vols. London: Hurst and Blackett.

Chaudenson, Robert. 1977. Toward the Reconstruction of the Social Matrix of Creole Language. In *Pidgin and Creole Linguistics*. ed. Albert Valdman. Bloomington: Indiana University Press.

Christaller, Johann Gottlieb. 1933. *A Dictionary of the Asante and Fante Language Called Tshi*. 2d ed. Basel: German Evangelical Missionary Society. First published in 1881.

———. 1964. *A Grammar of the Asante and Fante Language Called Tshi*. Farnborough: Gregg Press. Originally published in 1875.

Clark, John, Walter Dendy, and James M. Phillippo. 1865. *The Voice of Jubilee: A Narrative of the Baptist Mission, Jamaica*. London: Snow.

Clarkson, Thomas. 1822. *The Cries of Africa to the Inhabitants of Europe*. London: n.p.

Claypole, William, and John Robotham. 1980. *Caribbean Story*. London: Longman.

Coleridge, Henry Nelson. 1826. *Six Months in the West Indies*. London: Murray.

Collins, Dr. 1811. *The Present Ruinous Situation of the West India Islands Submitted to the People of the British Empire*. By a native of Jamaica. London: n.p. British Library.

Collymore, Frank. 1957. *Notes for a Glossary of Words and Phrases of Barbadian Dialect*. Bridgetown: Advocate. Originally published in 1955.

Comitas, Lambros. 1968. *Caribbeana, 1900–1965: A Topical Bibliography*. Seattle: University of Washington Press, Research Institute for the Study of Man.

______. 1977. *The Complete Caribbean, 1900–1975: A Bibliographic Guide to the Scholarly Literature.* 3 vols. Millwood, N.Y.: KTO Press, Research Institute for the Study of Man.

Coomber, Melvin. 1969. A Description of Krio Phonology. M.A. thesis. Georgetown University, Washington, D.C.

Cooper, Thomas. 1824. *Facts Illustrative of the Condition of the Negro Slaves in Jamaica.* London: Hatchard and Son.

Cotter, Charles Sylvester. 1946. The Aborigines of Jamaica. *Jamaican Historical Review* 1 (2): 137–41.

Coulthard, Gabriel. 1968. Jewish Tombstones. *Jamaica Journal* 2 (1): 8–10.

Cox, Edward Godfrey. 1938. *A Reference Guide to the Literature of Travel,* vol. 2: *The New World.* Seattle: University of Washington Publications in Language and Literature.

Crahan, Margaret, and Franklin Knight, eds. 1979. *Africa and the Caribbean: The Legacies of a Link.* Baltimore: Johns Hopkins University Press.

Craig, Dennis R., ed. 1972. *Conference on Creole Languages and Educational Development.* St. Augustine, Trinidad: UNESCO and University of the West Indies.

Craigie, Sir William. 1937. *Northern Words in Modern English.* Oxford: Clarendon Press.

Craton, Michael. 1978. *Searching for the Invisible Man: Slaves and Plantation Life in Jamaica.* Cambridge, Mass.: Harvard University Press.

______. 1979. *Roots and Branches: Current Directions in Slave Societies.* Vol. 6, no. 1 of *Historical Reflections.* Ed. Michael Craton. Waterloo, Ont.: Waterloo University.

Crow, Captain Hugh. 1830. *Memoirs.* London: Longman, Rees, Orme, Brown, and Green.

Cundall, Frank. 1934. *The Aborigines of Jamaica.* Kingston: Institute of Jamaica.

______. 1939. *Place-Names of Jamaica.* Revised by Philip M. Sherlock. Kingston: Institute of Jamaica.

Curtin, Philip E., ed. 1967. *Africa Remembered: Narratives by West Africans from the Era of the Slave Trade.* Madison: University of Wisconsin Press.

Curtin, Philip E. 1969. *The Atlantic Slave Trade.* Madison: University of Wisconsin Press.

Dalby, David. 1970/71. The Place of Africa and Afro-America in the History of the English Language. *African Language Review.* 9: 280–98.

______. 1971. Ashanti in the Language of the Maroons. *African Language Studies* 12: 31–51.

Dallas, R. C. 1803. *History of the Maroons.* 2 vols. London: Longman and Rees.

Davies, K. G. 1970. *The Royal African Company.* New York: Atheneum. Reprinted from London: Longman, 1957.

Davis, Alison. 1984. Behind the For-to Filter: For-to Infinitives in Belfast English and the Theory of Government. *Sheffield Working Papers in Linguistics* 1: 56–71.

D'Costa, Jean. 1968. Language and Dialect in Jamaica. *Jamaica Journal* 2 (1): 71–74.

______. 1978. *Jamaican Patois: Vocabulary and Phraseology.* Kingston: U.S. Peace Corps.

———. 1984. Louise Bennett's Dialect Poetry: Problems of Variation along a Creole Continuum in a Literary Text. In *Studies in Language Ecology*. Ed. Werner Enninger and Lilith Haynes. Wiesbaden: Franz Steiner.

D'Costa, Jean, and Barbara Lalla, eds. 1989. *Voices in Exile: Jamaican Texts of the 18th and 19th Centuries*. Tuscaloosa: University of Alabama Press.

DeCamp, David. 1967. African Day-Names in Jamaica. *Language* 43: 139–49.

DeCamp, David, and Ian Hancock, eds. 1974. *Pidgins and Creoles: Current Trends and Prospects*. Washington, D.C.: Georgetown University Press.

De la Beche, H. T. 1825. *Notes on the Present Condition of the Negroes in Jamaica*. London: Cadell.

De Montagnac, Mrs. 1884. A Jamaican Melody of the Seventeenth Century. *Journal of the Institute of Jamaica* 2: 632–35.

Dillard, J. L. 1963. Towards a Bibliography of Works Dealing with the Creole Languages of the Caribbean Area, Louisiana, and the Guianas. *Caribbean Studies* 3 (1): 84–95.

Dobson, E. J. 1968. *English Pronunciation, 1500–1700*. 2 vols. 2d ed. Oxford: Clarendon Press.

Drascher, Dr. Wahrhold. 1932. Deutsche Siedlungen auf Jamaika. English translation with letter by Frank Cundall, *Daily Gleaner*, Dec. 17.

Dreadful Account. ca. 1834. *A Dreadful Account of a Negro Who for Killing the Overseer of a Plantation in Jamaica Was Placed in an Iron Cage Where He Was Left to Expire*. London: Evans.

Dubois, Felix. 1897. *Timbuctoo the Mysterious*. Translated from the French by Diana White. London: Heinemann.

Echteld, J. J. M. 1962. *The English Words in Sranan*. Groningen: J. B. Wolters.

Edwards, Bryan. 1794. *The History, Civil and Commercial, of the British Colonies in the West Indies*. 2 vols. 2d ed. London: Stockdale.

———. 1796. *The Proceedings of the Governor and Assembly of Jamaica in regard to the Maroon Negroes*. London: Stockdale.

Elworthy, Frederic Thomas. 1877. *Outline of the Dialect of West Somerset*. London: Trübner.

———. 1879. *Specimens of English Dialects: Devonshire. "The Exmoor Scolding."* English Dialect Society no. 25. London: Trübner.

Emerick, Abraham J. 1915 and 1916. *Obeah and Duppyism in Jamaica* and *Jamaica Mialism*. Bound together. Woodstock, Mi.: n.p.

Fage, J. D. 1969. *A History of West Africa*. Cambridge: Cambridge University Press.

———. 1980. Slaves and Society in West Africa. *Journal of West African History* 21 (3): 289–310.

Farmer, John S. 1889. *Americanisms Old and New: A Dictionary of Words, Phrases, and Colloquialisms*. London: Poulter.

Forde, Cyril Daryll, ed. 1968. *Efik Traders of Old Calabar; Containing the Diary of Antera Duke, an Efik Slave-Trading Chief of the Eighteenth Century*. London: Dawsons for the International Africa Institute.

Foulks, Theodore. 1833. *Eighteen Months in Jamaica*. London: Whittaker, Treacher, and Arnott.

Franck, Harry Alverson. 1920. *Roaming through the West Indies*. New York: Century.

Fries, Charles C., and Kenneth Pike. 1949. Coexistent Phonemic Systems. *Language* 25: 29–50.

Fyle, Clifford, and Eldred D. Jones. 1980. *A Krio-English Dictionary*. New York: Oxford University Press.

Gardner, W. J. 1971. *A History of Jamaica*. London: Cass. Originally published in 1873.

Gilbert, Glenn, ed. 1987. *Pidgin and Creole Languages: Essays in Memory of John E. Reinecke*. Honolulu: University of Hawaii Press.

Gill, Alexander, 1971. *Logonomia Anglica*. Trans. and ed. Dorothy Dixon. Ph.D. diss., University of Southern California, Los Angeles. Microfilm. Originally published in 1619.

Gilman, Charles. 1978. A Comparison of Jamaican Creole and Cameroon Pidgin English. *English Studies* 59: 57–65.

______. 1979. Proto-Creole /r/. In *Readings in Creole Studies*. Ed. Ian F. Hancock. Ghent: E. Story-Scientia P.B.V.A.

Goldie, Hugh. 1964. *Dictionary of the Efik Language*. Ridgewood, N.J.: Gregg Press.

Gosse, Philip. 1851. *A Naturalist's Sojourn in Jamaica*. London: Longman.

Goveia, Elsa. 1956. *A Study of the Historiography of the British West Indies to the End of the Nineteenth Century*. Mexico: Instituto Panamericano de Geografia e Historia.

Grant, William. 1913. *The Pronunciation of English in Scotland*. Cambridge: Cambridge University Press.

Hall, Douglas. 1969. *Free Jamaica, 1838–1865: An Economic History*. London: Caribbean Universities Press.

Hall, Robert A., Jr. 1958. Creolized Languages and Genetic Relationship. *Word* 14: 367–73.

______. 1966. *Pidgin and Creole Languages*. Ithaca: Cornell University Press.

______. 1977. Pidgins, Language Learning, and Culture Contact. *Journal of Creole Studies* 1 (1): 29–32.

Hamel. 1827. *Hamel the Obeah Man*. 2 vols. London: Hunt and Clarke.

Hamley, Col. William G. 1862. *Captain Clutterbuck's Champagne: A West Indian Reminiscence*. Edinburgh: Blackwood. Originally published in *Blackwood's Magazine*.

______. 1871. *A New Sea and an Old Land*. Edinburgh: Blackwood.

______. 1878. *Guilty or Not Guilty? A Tale*. Edinburgh: Blackwood.

______. 1882. *Traseaden Hall*. 3 vols. Edinburgh: Blackwood.

Hancock, Ian F. 1969. A Provisional Comparison of English-Based Atlantic Creoles. *African Language Review* 8: 7–72.

______. 1971. A Survey of the Pidgins and Creoles of the World. In *Pidginization and Creolization of Languages*. Ed. Dell Hymes. Cambridge: Cambridge University Press.

______. 1976. Nautical Sources of Krio Vocabulary. *International Journal of the Sociology of Language* (The Hague) 173: 23–36.

______. 1977. Pidgin/Creole Origins: Historical vs. Documentary Evidence. In *Pidgin and Creole Linguistics*. Ed. Albert Valdman. Bloomington: Indiana University Press.

______, ed. 1979. *Readings in Creole Studies*. Ghent: E. Story-Scientia P.V.B.A.

———. 1986a. Componentiality and the Creole Matrix: South West English Contribution. Paper presented at the Sociolinguistics Symposium no. 6, Newcastle-upon-Tyne, April 1986. Forthcoming in *English in Black and White*. Ed. Michael Montgomery. Columbia: University of South Carolina Press.

———. 1986b. The Domestic Hypothesis, Diffusion, and Componentiality: An Account of Atlantic Creole Origins. In *Substrata versus Universals in Creole Languages: Papers from the Amsterdam Creole Workshop, April 1985*. Ed. Pieter Muysken and Norval Smith. Amsterdam: John Benjamins.

———. 1987. A Preliminary Classification of the Anglophone Atlantic Creoles with Syntactic Data from Thirty-three Representative Dialects. MS. Shortened version appearing in *Pidgin and Creole Languages: Essays in Memory of John E. Reinecke*. Ed. Glenn Gilbert. Honolulu: University of Hawaii Press.

Handler, Jerome S., and Frederick W. Lange, with the assistance of Robert V. Riordan. 1978. *Plantation Slavery in Barbados: An Archaeological and Historical Investigation*. Cambridge, Mass.: Harvard University Press.

Hendrix, Melvin K. 1982. *An International Bibliography of African Lexicons*. Metuchen, N.J.: Scarecrow Press.

Hesseling, Dirk Christiaan. 1979. *On the Origin and Formation of Creoles: A Miscellany of Articles*. Linguistica Extranea Studia 4. Ed. and trans. T. L. Markey and Paul Roberge. Ann Arbor: Karoma.

Highfield, Arnold, and Albert Valdman, eds. 1981. *Historicity and Variation in Creole Studies*. Ann Arbor: Karoma.

Higman, B. W. 1976. *Slave Population and Economy in Jamaica, 1807–1834*. London: Cambridge University Press.

———. 1984. *Slave Population of the British Caribbean, 1807–1834*. Baltimore: Johns Hopkins University Press.

Hoetink, Harry. 1979. The Cultural Links. In *Africa and the Caribbean: The Legacies of a Link*. Ed. Margaret Crahan and Franklin Knight. Baltimore: Johns Hopkins University Press.

Holm, John. 1980. The Creole "Copula" that Highlighted the World. In *Perspectives on American English*. Ed. J. L. Dillard. The Hague: Mouton.

———. 1984. Variability of the Copula in Black English and Its Creole Kin. *American Speech* 59 (4): 291–309.

———. 1986. The Spread of English in the Caribbean Area. In *Varieties of English around the World: Focus on the Caribbean*. Ed. Manfred Görlach and John Holm. General series vol. 8. Amsterdam: John Benjamins.

Holm, John, and Alison Schilling. 1982. *Dictionary of Bahamian English*. Cold Spring. N.Y.: Lexik.

Horrors. 1805. *The Horrors of the Negro Slavery Existing in Our West Indian Islands*. In *Tracts on Slavery*, vol. 14. London: Hatchard.

Hughes, Richard. 1949. *A High Wind in Jamaica*. Harmondsworth, Eng.: Penguin.

Huttar, George. 1981. Some Kwa-like Features of Djuka Syntax. *Studies in African Linguistics* 12 (3): 291–323.

Hymes, Dell H., ed. 1971. *Pidginization and Creolization of Languages*. Proceedings of a Conference Held at the University of the West Indies, Mona, Jamaica, April 1968. Cambridge: Cambridge University Press.

Importance. 1740. *The Importance of Jamaica to Great Britain Consider'd in a Letter to a Gentleman*. London: Dodd.

Jacobs, H. P. 1945. The Untapped Sources of Jamaican History. *Jamaican Historical Review* 1 (1): 92–98.

______. 1957. The Spanish Period of Jamaican History: An Assessment of the Present State of Knowledge. *Jamaica Historical Review* 3: 79–93.

______. 1972. Old Bedward of Spring Garden. *Jamaica Journal* 6 (2): 9–13.

______. n.d. Unpublished Notes from the Personal Collection of H. P. Jacobs, H. P. Jacobs Estate, Kingston.

Jamaica Baptist Missionaries. 1832. *Facts and Documents connected with the Late Insurrection in Jamaica and the violations of Civil and Religious Liberty arising out of it*. London: Holdsworth and Ball.

Jamaica Government Archives. 1789. St. Thomas-in-the-Vale Vestry Minutes. Government Archive Office, Spanish Town, Jamaica.

______. 1822. Hanover: Slave Court, Lucea, 1822–1823. Government Archive Office, Spanish Town, Jamaica.

Jamaica Religious Tract Society. 1846. *Jamaica Enslaved and Free*. London: Religious Tract Society.

Jamieson, John. 1885. *Dictionary of the Scottish Language*. Abridged by John Johnstone. New ed. revised by John Longmuir. London: W. P. Nimmo.

Jefferson, A. 1971. Towards a Bibliography of Materials of Interest to Linguists Working in the Caribbean Area: Materials at the Library, UWI, Mona. Mona, Kingston, University of the West Indies. Mimeographed.

Jekyll, Walter, ed., 1907. *Jamaican Song and Story*. London: David Nutt.

Joyce, P. W. 1910. *English as We Speak It in Ireland*. London: Longman, Greene.

Kay, Paul, and Gillian Sankoff. 1974. A Language Universals Approach to Pidgins and Creoles. In *Pidgins and Creoles: Current Trends and Prospects*. Ed. David De-Camp and Ian Hancock. Washington, D.C.: Georgetown University Press.

Kelly, James. 1838. *Voyages to Jamaica and Seventeen Years' Residence in that Island*. 2d ed. Belfast: Wilson.

Kirk, John Foster. 1892. *A Supplement to Allibone's Critical Dictionary of English Literature and British and American Authors*. Philadelphia: Lippincott.

Kloe, Donald R., ed. 1974. "Buddy Quow," *Southern Folklore Quarterly* 38 (2): 81–90.

Knight, Franklin, and Margaret E. Crahan. 1979. The African Migration and the Origins of an Afro-American Society and Culture. In *Africa and the Caribbean: The Legacies of a Link*. Ed. Margaret Crahan and Franklin Knight. Baltimore: Johns Hopkins University Press.

Kopytoff, Barbara Klamon. 1978. Early Political Development of Jamaican Maroon Societies. *William and Mary Quarterly*, 3d series, 35 (2): 287–307.

Koromantyn Slaves. 1823. *Koromantyn Slaves; or, West India Sketches*. London: Hatchard and Sons.

Kup, A. P. 1975. *Sierra Leone: A Concise History*. New York: St. Martin's Press.

Labat, Jean Baptiste. 1931. *The Memoirs of Père Labat, 1693–1705*. Trans. and abr. Phillip Gosse. London: Constable. Originally published in 1693.

Ladefoged, Peter. 1968. *A Phonetic Study of West African Languages: An Auditory-*

Instrumental Survey. West African Language Monographs 1. Cambridge: Cambridge University Press.

Lalla, Barbara. 1979. Sources for a History of Jamaican Creole. *Carib* 1: 50–66.

———, ed. 1981. Quaco Sam: A Relic of Archaic Jamaican Speech. *Jamaica Journal* 45: 20–29.

———. 1983. The Consonant System of Early Jamaican Creole. *Carib* 3: 37–51.

———. 1986a. Tracing Elusive Phonological Features of Early Jamaican Creole. In *Varieties of English World-wide: Focus on the Caribbean*. Ed. Manfred Görlach and John Holm. Amsterdam: John Benjamins.

———. 1986b. Documenting Morphosyntactic Change in Jamaican Creole. Paper presented at the Sixth Biennial Conference of the Society for Caribbean Linguistics, University of the West Indies, St. Augustine, Trinidad.

Lawton, David. 1963. Suprasegmental Phenomenon in Jamaican Creole. Ph.D. diss. Michigan State University, Ann Arbor. University Microfilms.

———. 1968. The Implications of Tone for Jamaican Creole. *Anthropological Linguistics* 10 (6): 22–26.

LePage, Robert B. 1957–58. General Outline of Creole English Dialects in the British Caribbean. *Orbis* 6: 373–91, 7: 54–64.

———. 1960. An Historical Introduction to Jamaican Creole. In *Jamaican Creole: Creole Language Studies* 1. Ed. R. B. LePage and David DeCamp. London: Macmillan.

———, ed. 1961. *Creole Language Studies* 2. London: Macmillan.

LePage, Robert, and David DeCamp, eds. 1960. *Jamaican Creole: Creole Language Studies* 1. London: Macmillan.

LePage, Robert, and Frederic G. Cassidy. 1961. Lexicographical Problems of *The Dictionary of Jamaican English*. In *Creole Language Studies* 2. London: Macmillan.

LePage, Robert, and Andrée Tabouret-Keller. 1985. *Acts of Identity*. London: Cambridge University Press.

Leslie, Charles. 1741. *A New History of Jamaica*. Dublin: Nelson.

Lewis, Matthew G. 1834. *Journal of a West India Proprietor*. London: Murray.

Lewis, Maureen Warner. 1979. The African Impact on Language and Literature in the English-Speaking Caribbean. In *Africa and the Caribbean: The Legacies of a Link*. Ed. Margaret Crahan and Franklin Knight. Baltimore: Johns Hopkins University Press.

Ligon, Richard. 1657. *True and Exact History of Barbados*. London: Moseley.

Littleton, Edward. 1689. *The Groans of the Plantations*. London: n.p.

Livingstone, William Pringle. 1899. *Black Jamaica: A Study in Evolution*. London: Sampson, Marston.

Long, Edward. 1774. *History of Jamaica*. 3 vols. London: Lowndes.

Lovejoy, Paul E. 1982. The Volume of the Atlantic Slave Trade: A Synthesis. *Journal of African History* 28 (4): 473–502.

Madden, Richard Robert. 1835. *A Twelvemonth Residence in the West Indies*. 2 vols. London: James Cochrane.

———. 1843. *The Slave Trade and Slavery*. London: James Madden.

______. 1891. *The Memoirs from 1798–1886*. Ed. by his son, Thomas M. Madden. London: Ward and Downey.

Mannix, Daniel. 1962. *Black Cargoes: A History of the Atlantic Slave Trade, 1518–1865*. New York: Viking Press.

Marly. 1828. *Marly; or, A Planter's Life in Jamaica*. Glasgow: Griffin. London: Hunt and Clarke.

Marsden, Peter. 1788. *An Account of the Island of Jamaica*. Newcastle: Hodgson.

Mathews, Samuel Augustus. 1822. *The Willshire Squeeze, to Which Are Added Specimens of the Negro Familiar Dialect and Proverbial Sayings with Songs*. Demerara: Printed for the Author at the Guiana *Chronicle* office.

Matthews, William. 1935a. Sailors' Pronunciation in the Second Half of the Seventeenth Century. *Anglia* 59: 193–251.

______. ca. 1935b. South West Dialect in the Early Modern English Period. *Neophilologus* 24: 193–209.

Milne-Home, Mary Pamela. 1890. *Mamma's Black Nurse Stories: West Indian Folklore*. Edinburgh: Blackwood and Sons.

Mintz, Sidney W. 1971. The Socio-Historical Background to Pidginization and Creolization. In *Pidginization and Creolization of Languages*. Ed. Dell Hymes. Cambridge: Cambridge University Press.

Mittelsdorf, Sibylle. 1978. *African Retentions in Jamaican Creole: A Reassessment*. Ph.D. diss. Northwestern University, Evanston, Ill. Ann Arbor: University Microfilms International.

Montgomery. 1812. *Montgomery; or, The West Indian Adventure*. A novel by a gentleman resident in the West Indies, Jamaica. 3 vols. Printed at the office of the Kingston *Chronicle*.

Moore, Joseph Graessle. 1983. Religion of Jamaican Negroes: A Study of Afro-Jamaican Acculturation. Ph.D. diss. Northwestern University, Evanston, Ill. 1953. Ann Arbor: University Microfilms International.

Moreton, J. B. 1793. *West India Customs and Manners*. 2d ed. London: Parsons. Originally published in 1790.

Mufwene, Salikoko S. 1986. The Universalist and Substrate Hypotheses Complement One Another. In *Substrata versus Universals in Creole Languages*. Ed. Pieter Muysken and Norval Smith. Amsterdam: John Benjamins.

Mühlhäusler, P. 1974. *Pidginization and Simplification of Language*. Pacific Linguistics Series B, no. 26. Canberra: Australian National University.

Müller, Elizabeth. 1981. Some Remnants of German Heritage in Jamaican Speech. *Jamaica Journal* 45: 30–31.

Murray, Henry Garland. 1877. *Manners and Customs of the Country a Generation Ago: Tom Kittle's Wake*. Kingston: Jordan.

[______]. Reproduced in William C. Bates. 1896. Creole Folklore from Jamaica. *Journal of American Folklore* 9 (32): 124, 10 (33): 125. Bates identifies Murray as his source for the material presented in Text 18.

Murray, James A. H. 1873. *The Dialect of the Southern Counties of Scotland*. Transactions of the Philological Society, 1870–72. London: Asher.

Murray, W. C. 1891. *A Day with Joe Lennon: The Rosewell Duppy Doctor.* Kingston: Vendryes.

Musgrave, W. 1880. Anancy Stories. *Folklore Record* 3 (1): 53–55.

Mutschmann, Heinrich. 1909. *A Phonology of the North-eastern Scotch Dialect on an Historical Basis.* Bonn: P. Hamstein.

Muysken, Pieter, ed. 1981. *Generative Studies on Creole Languages.* Dordrecht, Holland: Cinnaminson, Foris.

Nicol, Joseph. 1967. *Lexique français-mandingue, mandingue-français.* Washington, D.C.: Peace Corps.

Niles, Norma. 1980. Provincial English Dialects and Barbadian English. Ph.D. diss. University of Michigan. Ann Arbor: University Microfilms.

Nodal, Roberto. 1972. A Bibliography . . . on the Creole Languages of the Caribbean, Including a Special Supplement on Gullah. *Afro-American Studies Report* 2. Department of Afro-American Studies, University of Wisconsin at Milwaukee.

Nugent, Lady Maria. 1966. *Lady Nugent's Journal of Her Residence in Jamaica from 1801 to 1805.* Rev. ed. Philip Wright. Kingston: Institute of Jamaica. Originally published in 1839.

Patterson, Orlando. 1973. *The Sociology of Slavery.* London: McGibbon and Kee, 1967. Rpr. Kingston: Sangsters.

Peck, Louis G. 1961. *A Life of Matthew G. Lewis.* Cambridge, Mass.: Harvard University Press.

Phillippo, James M. 1843. *Jamaica: Its Past and Present State.* London: Snow.

Pieterz, J. L. 1945. Translations from Some Spanish Documents Relating to Jamaica: Articles of Capitulation at the Conquest of Jamaica, 1655. *Jamaica Historical Review* 1 (1): 100–115.

Pinckard, George. 1806. *Notes on the West Indies . . . and the Coast of Guyana.* 3 vols. London: Longman, Hurst, Rees, and Orme.

Pitman, Frank Wesley. 1967. *The Development of the British West Indies, 1700–1763.* London: Cass.

Polomé, Edgar. 1981. Historicity and Variation in Creolization and Diachronic Linguistics. In *Historicity and Variation in Creole Studies.* Ed. Arnold Highfield and Albert Valdman. Ann Arbor: Karoma.

Porter, Whitworth. 1889. *History of the Corps of the Royal Engineers.* 2 vols. London: Longman, Green.

Primus, Wilma J. 1972. Creole and Pidgin Languages in the Caribbean: A Select Bibliography. In *Conference on Creole Languages and Educational Development.* Ed. Dennis Craig. St. Augustine, Trinidad: UNESCO and University of the West Indies.

Purcell, Richard J. 1937. Irish Colonists in the British West Indies. *Journal of the American Irish Historical Society* 31: 47–54.

Ragatz, Lowell Joseph. 1928. *The Fall of the Planter Class.* New York: Century.

Rampini, Charles. 1873. *Letters from Jamaica.* Edinburgh: Edmonston and Douglas.

———. 1890. *Tales of Old Scotland.* Edinburgh: MacNinen and Wallace.

———. 1894. *Shetland and the Shetlanders: Two Lectures Delivered before the Philosoph-*

ical Institution, Edinburgh, on the 5th and 8th February, 1894. Edinburgh: John Menzies.

______. 1897. *A History of Moray and Nairn*. Edinburgh: Blackwood.

Ramsey, E. B. 1861. *Reminiscences of Scottish Life and Character*. Boston: Ticknor.

Randel, William. 1960. Survival of Pre-English Place Names in Jamaica. *Names* 8 (1): 24–29.

Randolph, Howard R. 1969. The Archaeology of Jamaica and Its Position in Relation to Circum-Caribbean Culture. Ph.D. diss. Yale University, 1950. Ann Arbor: University Microfilms International.

Rawley, James A. 1981. *The Transatlantic Slave Trade*. New York: Norton.

Redden, J. E., et al. 1963. *Twi Basic Course*. Washington, D.C.: Foreign Service Institute, Department of State.

Reid, Captain Mayne. 1862. *The Maroon*. 2 vols. London: Hurst and Blackett.

Reinecke, John E. 1938. Trade Jargons and Creole Dialects as Marginal Languages. *Social Forces* 17: 107–18.

Reinecke, John E., et al. 1975. *A Bibliography of Pidgin and Creole Languages*. Oceanic Linguistics Special Publication 14. Honolulu: University of Hawaii Press.

Renny, Robert. 1807. *An History of Jamaica*. London: Cawthorn.

Renourd, G. C. 1836. Routes in North Africa by Abu Bekr es siddike. *Journal of the Royal Geographical Society* 6: 100–113.

Rice, Frank, ed. 1962. *A Study of the Role of Second Languages in Africa, Asia, and Latin America*. Washington, D.C.: Center for Applied Linguistics.

Rickford, John. 1981. Variation in a Creole Continuum: Quantitative and Implicational Approaches. Ph.D. diss. University of Pennsylvania, 1979. Ann Arbor: University Microfilms International.

______. 1984. The Historical and Sociolinguistic Significance of Early Guyanese Texts. Paper presented at the 5th Biennial Conference of the Society for Caribbean Linguistics, University of the West Indies, Mona, Jamaica, August 28–September 1, 1984.

______. 1986. Social Contact and Language Diffusion. *Language* 62 (2): 245–90.

______. 1987. *Dimensions of a Creole Continuum: History, Texts, and Linguistic Analysis of the Guyanese Creole*. Stanford: Stanford University Press.

Roase, Frederick. 1965. *Modern English Biography*. London: Nelson.

Roberts, George W. 1979. *The Population of Jamaica*. Millwood, N.Y.: Kraus. Originally published in 1957.

Robinson, Carey. 1969. *The Fighting Maroons of Jamaica*. Kingston: Sangster.

Ross, Frederick, Richard Stead, and Thomas Holderness. 1965. *A Glossary of Words Used in Holderness in the East Riding of Yorkshire*. English Dialect Society series C, no. 16. Vaduz: Kraus Reprint. Originally published in 1877.

Ross, George. 1800. Diary. MS in Fourah Bay College Library. Freetown, Sierra Leone.

Rubin, Joan. 1963. A Bibliography of Caribbean Creole Languages. *Caribbean Studies* 2 (4): 51–61.

Russell, Thomas. 1868. *The Etymology of Jamaica Grammar*. Kingston: DeCordova, MacDougall.

Salazar, Carmen V. 1974. A Comparison of the Papiamento and Jamaican Creole Verbal Systems. M.A. thesis. McGill University, Montreal.

Sankoff, Gillian. 1979a. The Genesis of Language. In *The Genesis of Language*. Ed. Kenneth Hill. Ann Arbor: Karoma.

———. 1979b. Linguistic Variation in Pidgin and Creole Studies. Paper presented at the Conference on Theoretical Orientations in Creole Studies. St. Thomas, U.S. Virgin Islands.

Schlesinger, Benjamin. 1967. The Jews of Jamaica: A Historical View. *Caribbean Quarterly* 13 (1): 46–53.

Schuchardt, Hugo. 1979. *The Ethnography of Variation: Selected Writings on Pidgins and Creoles*. Linguistics Extranea Studia 3. Ed. T. L. Markey. Ann Arbor: Karoma.

———. 1980. *Pidgin and Creole Languages: Selected Essays by Hugo Schuhardt*. Ed. and trans. Glenn Gilbert. London: Cambridge University Press.

Schuler, Monica. 1979. Myalism and the African Religious Tradition in Jamaica. In *Africa and the Caribbean: The Legacies of a Link*. Ed. Margaret Crahan and Franklin Knight. Baltimore: Johns Hopkins University Press.

———. 1980. *"Alas, Alas, Kongo": A Social History of Indentured African Immigration into Jamaica, 1841–1865*. Baltimore: Johns Hopkins University Press.

———. 1981. Afro-American Culture. In *Roots and Branches: Current Directions in Slave Societies*. Vol. 6, no. 1, of *Historical Reflections*. Ed. Michael Craton. Waterloo, Ont.: Waterloo University.

Scott, Michael. 1834. *Tom Cringle's Log*. 2 vols. Edinburgh: Blackwood. Originally published in *Blackwood's Magazine* in September 1829. First published under its own cover in 1833.

[Senior, Bernard Martin]. 1835. *Jamaica as it was, as it is, and as it may be*. By a retired military officer. London: T. Hurst.

Senior, Olive. 1983. *A–Z of Jamaican Heritage*. Kingston: Heinemann Educational Books and the Gleaner.

Shakespeare, William. 1953. *Macbeth*. Ed. Kenneth Muir. Arden series. London: Methuen.

———. 1958. *The Tempest*. Ed. Frank Kermode. Arden series. London: Methuen.

———. 1959. *King Lear*. Ed. Kenneth Muir. Arden series. London: Methuen.

———. 1967. *II Henry IV*. Ed. A. R. Humphreys. Arden series. London: Methuen.

Shand, Alexander Innes. 1895. *Life of General Sir E. B. Hamley*. 2 vols. Edinburgh: Blackwood.

Sheridan, Richard. 1974. *Sugar and Slavery: An Economic History of the British West Indies, 1623–1775*. Baltimore: Johns Hopkins University Press. Originally published in 1973.

Short Journey. 1790. *A Short Journey in the West Indies*. 2 vols. London: Murray and Forbes.

Sibley, Inez Knibb. 1978. *Dictionary of Place-Names in Jamaica*. Kingston: Institute of Jamaica.

Sloane, Sir Hans. 1707–25. *A Voyage . . . to the Islands Madera, Barbados, . . . and Jamaica*. 2 vols. London: The British Museum for the Author.

Smith, Abbott E. 1947. *Colonists in Bondage: White Servitude and Convict Labor in America, 1607–1776*. Chapel Hill: University of North Carolina Press.

Smith, Pamela Coleman. 1905. *Chim-Chim: Folk Stories from Jamaica*. London: n.p.

Smith, William. 1744. *A New Voyage to Guinea*. London: John Nourse.

Some Modern Observations. 1727. *Some Modern Observations upon Jamaica by an English Merchant*. London: n.p.

Spencer, John. 1971. *The English Language in West Africa*. London: Longman.

Statement of Facts. 1837. *A Statement of Facts Illustrating the Administration of the Abolition Law and the Sufferings of the Negro Apprentices in the Island of Jamaica*. London.

Stephen, Sir Leslie, and Sir Sidney Lee, eds. 1960. *Dictionary of National Biography*. London: Oxford University Press.

Stewart, James. 1808. *An Account of Jamaica and Its Inhabitants by a Gentleman Long Resident in the West Indies*. London: Longman.

______. 1823. *A View of the Past and Present State of the Island of Jamaica*. London: Oliver and Boyd.

Stewart, William. 1962. Creole Languages in the Carribbean. In *Study of the Role of Second Languages in Africa, Asia, and Latin America*. Ed. Frank Rice. Washington, D.C.: Center for Applied Linguistics.

Strong, Leonard. 1850. *Gospel Reminiscences in the West Indies*. Bath: Binny and Goodwin.

Taylor, Douglas. 1961. New Languages for Old in the West Indies. *Comparative Studies in Society and History* 3: 277–88.

______. 1963. The Origin of West Indian Creole Languages: Evidence from Grammatical Categories. *American Anthropologist* 64 (4): 800–814.

______. 1977. *Languages of the West Indies*. Baltimore: Johns Hopkins University Press.

Taylor, S. A. G. 1965. *The Western Design: An Account of Cromwell's Expedition to the Caribbean*. Kingston: Institute of Jamaica.

Thomas, Mary E. 1974. *Jamaica and Voluntary Laborers from Africa, 1840–1865*. Kingston: Institute of Jamaica.

Thompson, R. W. 1962. A Caribbean Sister for Krio. Review of *Jamaica Talk* by Frederic G. Cassidy. (Freetown) *Sierra Leone Studies* (16): 227–32.

Tinelli, Henry. 1981. *Creole Phonology*. The Hague: Mouton.

Trapham, Thomas. 1679. *A Discourse of the State of Health in the Island of Jamaica*. London: Boulter.

Trevaylor, Nicky [pseud. of Thomas Newall]. 1935. *Echoes from Carn, Cove, and Cromlech*. St. Ives, Cornwall: James Winham for the Federation of Old Cornwall Society.

Trinidad Sentinel. Tuesday, April 8, 1858. Foo Massa Headhitter Sentiwel.

Trollope, Anthony. 1860. *The West Indies and the Spanish Main*. 2d ed. London: Chapman and Hall.

______. 1907. *Phineas Finn*. New York: Dodd, Mead.

Trowbridge, Ada Wilson. 1896. Negro Customs and Folk Stories of Jamaica. *Journal of American Folklore* 9: 279–287.

Turner, Lorenzo Dow. 1949. *Africanisms in the Gullah Dialect*. Chicago: University of Chicago Press.

Udal, J. A. 1827. Obeah in the West Indies. *Folklore* 26: 253–95.

Underhill, Edward Bean. 1881. *Life of James Mursell Phillippo*. London: Yates and Alexander; Marlborough.

Valdman, Albert, ed. 1977. *Pidgin and Creole Linguistics*. Bloomington: Indiana University Press.

———. 1978. *Le creole: Structure, statut, et origine*. Paris: Klincksieck.

Voorhoeve, Jan. 1959. An Orthography for Saramaccan. *Word* 15: 436–45.

———. 1973. Historical and Linguistic Evidence of a Re-lexification Theory in the Formation of Creoles. *Language in Society* 2: 133–45.

Waddell, Hope Masterton. 1863. *Twenty-nine Years in the West Indies and Central Africa*. London: Nelson.

Walker, John. 1803. *A Critical Pronouncing Dictionary . . . of the English Language*. Philadelphia: H. and P. Rice et al.

———. 1811. *A Critical Pronouncing Dictionary and Expository Rules to Be Observed by the Natives of Scotland, Ireland, and London*. Philadelphia: Kite.

Warrack, Alexander. 1911. *Scots Dialect Dictionary*. London: Chambers.

Weinreich, Uriel. 1958. On the Compatibility of Genetic Relationship and Convergent Development. *Word* 15: 374–79.

———. 1966. *Languages in Contact*. The Hague: Mouton.

Wentworth, Trelawny. 1834. *The West India Sketch Book*. 2 vols. London: Whittacker.

Westermann, Dietrich. 1930. *Gbesela yeye; or, English-Ewe Dictionary*. Berlin: Georg Reimer.

Westermann, Dietrich, and Ida Ward. 1933. *Practical Phonetics for Students of African Languages*. New York: Oxford University Press.

Whinnom, Keith. 1965. The Origin of European-Based Creoles and Pidgins. *Orbis* 14: 509–27.

———. 1971. Linguistic Hybridization and the "Special Case" of Pidgins and Creoles. In *Pidginization and Creolization of Languages*. Ed. Dell Hymes. London: Cambridge University Press.

———. 1977. Lingua Franca: Historical Problems. In *Pidgin and Creole Linguistics*. Ed. Valdman. Bloomington: Indiana University Press.

Whiteley, Henry. 1833. *Excessive Cruelty to Slaves: Three Months in Jamaica in 1832*. London: Hatchard.

Williams, Cynric R. 1826. *A Tour through the Island of Jamaica in the Year 1823*. London: Hunt and Clarke.

Williams, James. 1837. *Narrative of the Cruel Treatment of James Williams, a Negro Apprentice in Jamaica from 1st August, 1834, till the Purchase of His Freedom in 1837, by Joseph Sturge, Esq., of Birmingham, by Whom He Was Brought to England*. Glasgow: n.p. Copy in National Library of Jamaica, Kingston.

Williams, Joseph J. 1932a. *Voodoos and Obeahs: Phases of West Indian Witchcraft*. New York: MacVeagh.

———. 1932b. *Whence the "Black Irish" of Jamaica?* New York: Lincoln MacVeagh, Dial.

______. 1934. *Psychic Phenomena of Jamaica*. New York: Dial.

______. 1938. The Maroons of Jamaica. *Anthropological Series of the Boston Graduate School* 3 (4): 379–480.

Williamson, Kay. 1972. *Igbo-English Dictionary*. Rev. C. N. Madunagu. Benin City: Ethiope.

Wilson, Sir James. 1927. *Old Scotch Songs, Phonetically Spelt and Translated*. London: Oxford University Press.

Winford, Donald. 1985. The Syntax of Fi Complements in Caribbean English Creole. *Language* 61 (3): 588–624.

Winford, James. 1974. Some Similarities between Jamaican Creole and the Dialect of Tobago. Caribbean Studies thesis, University of the West Indies, St. Augustine, Trinidad.

Woods, Joseph. 1784. *Thoughts on the Slavery of the Negroes*. London: Phillips.

Work, Monroe N. 1928. *A Bibliography of the Negro in Africa and America*. New York: Wilson.

Wright, Joseph. 1898–1905. *The English Dialect Dictionary*. 6 vols. New York: Putnam.

______. 1968. *The English Dialect Grammar*. New York: Oxford University Press.

Wright, Mary Elizabeth. 1913. *Rustic Speech and Folklore*. London: Milford.

Wright, Philip. See Nugent, Lady Maria.

Wright, Richardson. 1937. *Revels in Jamaica, 1682–1838*. New York: Dodd, Mead.

Wyld, Henry Cecil. 1956. *A History of Modern Colloquial English*. Oxford: Basil Blackwell. Originally published in 1920.

Young, Robert. 1980. *Young's Analytical Concordance to the Bible*. Ed. William B. Stevenson and David Wambish. Nashville: T. Nelson.

Index